JUSTICE SOCIETY OF AMERICA

THE NEXT AGE

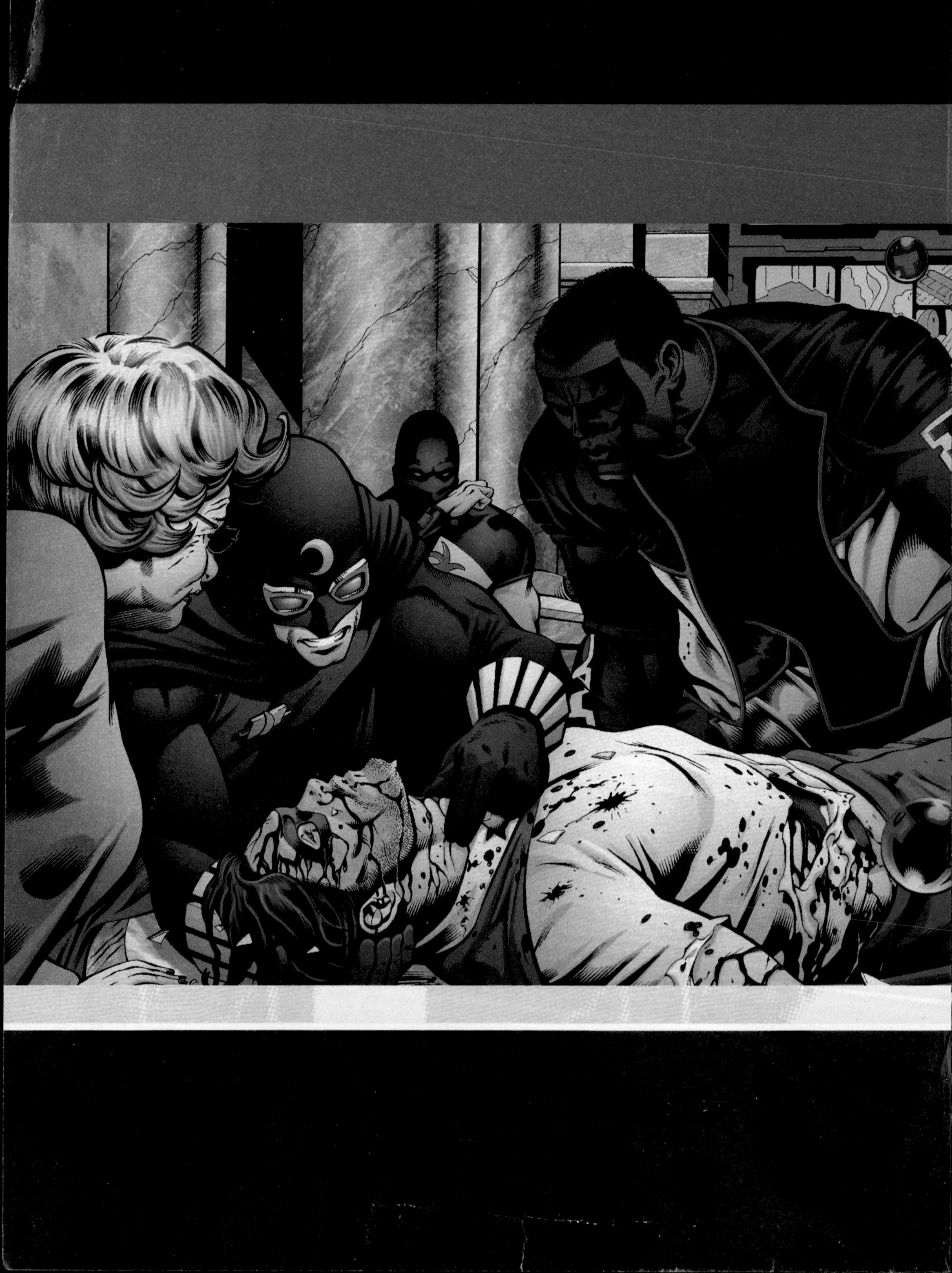

JUSTICE SOCIETY of AMERICA

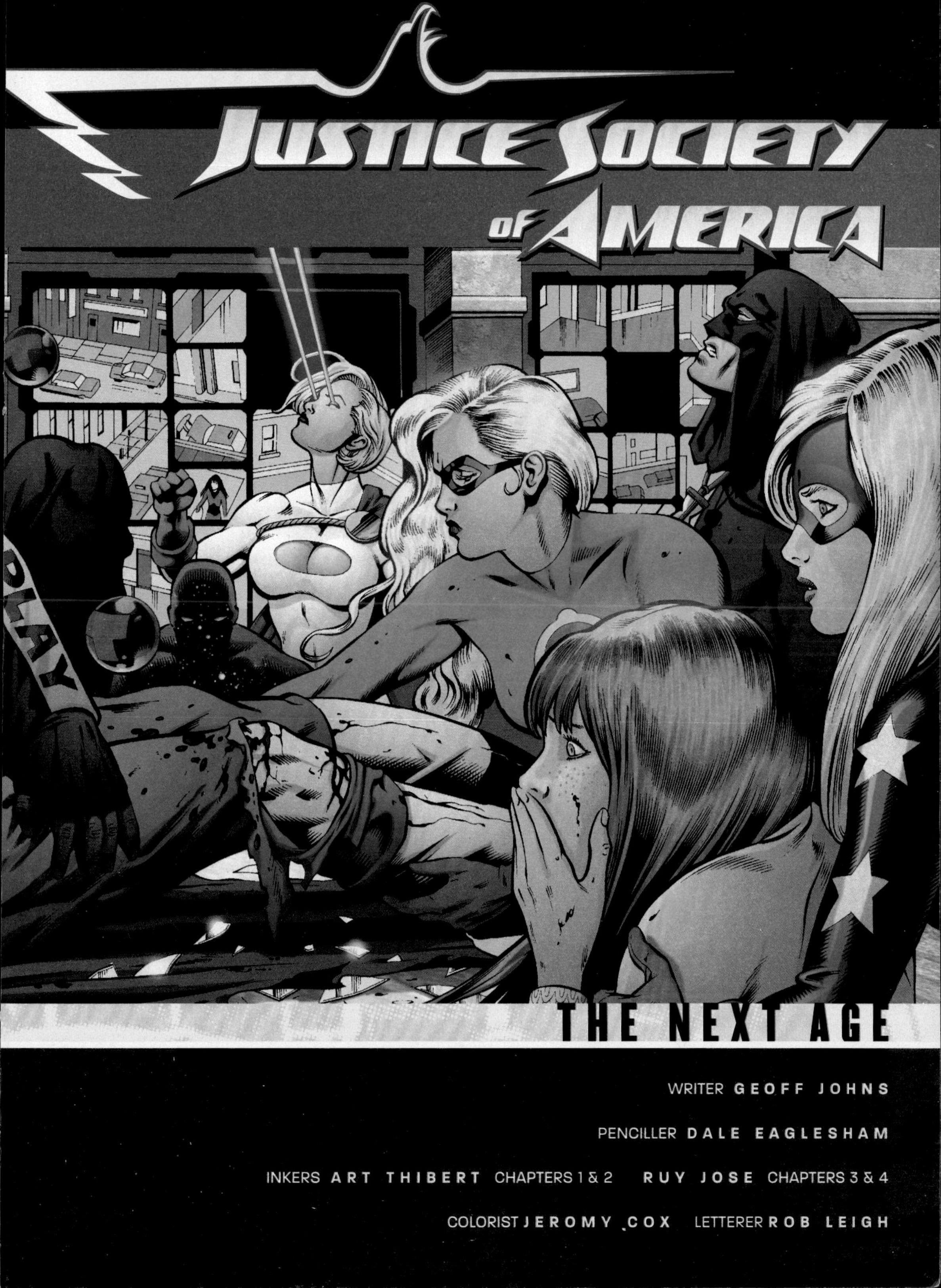
PLAY

THE NEXT AGE

WRITER **GEOFF JOHNS**

PENCILLER **DALE EAGLESHAM**

INKERS **ART THIBERT** CHAPTERS 1 & 2 **RUY JOSE** CHAPTERS 3 & 4

COLORIST **JEROMY COX** LETTERER **ROB LEIGH**

BOB WAYNE VP-SALES

JUSTICE SOCIETY OF AMERICA
THE NEXT AGE

Cover and interior KINGDOM COME background by Alex Ross
Publication design by Robbie Biederman

Published by DC Comics. Cover and compilation copyright © 2007 DC Comics. All Rights Reserved.

Originally published in single magazine form in JUSTICE SOCIETY OF AMERICA #1-4. Copyright © 2007 DC Comics. All Rights Reserved. All characters, their distinctive likenesses and related elements featured in this publication are trademarks of DC Comics. The stories, characters and incidents featured in this publication are entirely fictional. DC Comics does not read or accept unsolicited submissions of ideas, stories or artwork.

DC Comics, 1700 Broadway, New York, NY 10019
A Warner Bros. Entertainment Company
Printed in Canada. First Printing.
HC ISBN: 1-4012-1444-4 ISBN 13: 978-1-4012-1444-9
SC ISBN: 1-4012-1585-8 ISBN 13: 978-1-4012-1585-9

BY PETER J. TOMASI

It was the best of times, it was the best of times.

Not much drama inherent in that opening line, huh?

Well, I figured I'd let Geoff Johns, Dale Eaglesham and Alex Ross supply the drama within the pages of this beautiful hard-cover volume you now hold in your hands instead of little ol' me.

What I'm here to do is simply say a few words about a particular super-group consisting of three letters that I know and love rather intimately. No, not the Who (they are my favorite musical group, though), I'm talking about the JSA — the Justice Society of America, you chuckleheads!

Why do I love the JSA, you ask? Well, it all boils down to the fact that when I was about seven years old I went back to Salinas, California, where my dad is originally from, and watched him sort through all his old stuff that was packed up in the garage of his boyhood home. What he came across was a damp and dirty box of dog-eared comics, and inside was ALL-STAR COMICS #50. There was something about the costumes and characters within those pages that really struck a chord, and on the train ride back across the country (yep, that's right, I said a train — my parents wanted me to see this big, glorious country for the first time from the ground instead of the air), you better believe I memorized each and every word as I watched the Midwest pass by my window.

So, hit the fast forward. It's the winter of 1997, I'm a DC Comics editor with one mission on my mind, and much to my surprise and joy, Paul Levitz, Mike Carlin, Archie Goodwin and Denny O'Neil go for my pitch to bring back the JSA in a monthly book that would be kick-started by a big event called JSA Returns and thereby place a group of heroes I strongly felt needed to be published on a regular basis within the DCU now and hopefully forever.

Well, it's 2007 and I seriously cannot believe almost ten years have come and gone since the book's launch, and it's not only hotter than ever on the sales chart, but it's also the best written, most involving, character driven super-team on the rack, bar none.

And there're two words to explain that fact:

Geoff Johns.

And you know why Geoff Johns was born to write this book?

Four words: Nazis at a picnic.

That says it all, but so does:

Hawkman + Mace = Shattered Nazi Face.

But really, this book wears its heart on its sleeve, and there's no better scene to illustrate that point than the picnic sequence in JSA #3 where the Heywood family's having their annual reunion and Nate Heywood wades into the mix to try to save his family from the Fourth Reich. Geoff has spent two issues beautifully fleshing out the character of Nate Heywood, who we find is missing a leg in the second issue, and we're completely invested in him as he tries his best to live up to what he believes is the heroic legacy code that runs through his family lineage even though he's at a cross-roads in his life.

Now, truth be told, I hate introductions that simply rehash the story you're about to read, so I'll try to liven this one up so it gives you a peek behind the curtain, because those are always the best type of intros to read.

The little tidbit that really sticks out for me about this great series by Geoff, Dale, and Alex is this: It's 2006 and I'm still a senior editor and working with Geoff on another damn fine book we worked on together by the name of Green Lantern. Now, I'd handed the reins of the JSA monthly book over to Stephen Wacker after 80 issues because I had just been named the new Batman editor, so I needed more hours in the day to juggle all the books that now were under my purview and after 80 issues of the monthly, plus JSA RETURNS and JSA ALL-STARS, I felt it was the right time to hand the book off to a fellow editor and maintain my sanity.

Anyway, Geoff calls me and tells me he's finished the new first issue script for the relaunch of JSA, and would I like to give it a read and hear more of the cool ideas and plans he's got cooking for the series. As much as I want to, I tell him that it would be nice to simply wait for the published book to hit my desk and read it like a fan, without knowing what's coming down the pike.

So, being the cruel bastard that he is, Geoff still emails it to me and there it sits in my inbox, taunting me, chipping away at my reserves, knowing full well that my self-control has its limits. Two whole days pass and I click on the damn script because my willpower is crushed by the waves of power that travel 3,000 miles from Geoff Johns' bungalow base of villainy!

I read it. Then I read it again. Now, let me tell you, writing a first issue script is tough. It needs to accomplish a great many things, because these days you don't have much time to build a book; you gotta blast it outta the gate as fast and furious as you can and try to keep the pedal pressed to the floor as long as you can without sacrificing character and story for bells and whistles.

And in JSA #1, Geoff hits a walk-off grand-slam home run!

But...

I pick up the phone and tell him — ah hell, who am I kidding...I beg him, I scream, I plead — "Please don't do it, please Geoff, say it ain't so. Don't bring in this new character that you make me love, that you make me wanna see a monthly book dedicated to — only to kill him on the last page. You can't be that heartless. You can't be that cruel. You're gonna pull something outta the hat, right?"

"You like him that much, huh?" Geoff answers. "Yes. Yes, I do," I reply. "Hmm, maybe you're right, maybe I won't kill him." Geoff says. Whew. Relief. The sun breaks through the clouds and all is right with the world — for a day.

"Nope. He's gotta die," Geoff says the next morning. "Sorry, Pete. But wait till you hear what I've got in store for —" "Shaddap! Not another word — I'm reading the next few issues as a fan, and I want surprise, I want magic, I want to be left hanging with bated breath for the next issue! You've got me on the hook, awright — ya happy, Geoff ol' buddy?!?"

And what a hook this book is!

Look at the art by Dale Eaglesham. Power and majesty on one page, great human moments of glee and suppressed joy on another. Don't believe me? Check out that page when Maxine, Ma Hunkel's granddaughter, gets an invite to be part of the JSA from Mister Terrific and Power Girl. Look at the body language and her expressive face. Then check out that page of the hero I didn't want to have die lying on a table. Your heart breaks and your breath is taken away because you don't see it coming, and Dale really captures the power of that moment by the sheer delicate linework of the body at rest. Impressive work.

Now, there's no way I can end this without mentioning the bold, stark, always heroic covers that Alex Ross has been producing for this series. They not only jump off the rack, they jump off the page. This book is a class act all the way.

How can I wrap up this long-winded intro? Well, I've spoken to Geoff, I know what he's got planned, what he's got up his sleeve for the JSA in the coming year, and I can honestly say you ain't seen nothing yet! This is the proverbial tip of the iceberg; your eyes are gonna bleed, and your fingers are gonna blister.

Next month can't come fast enough.

— Peter J. Tomasi
July, 2007

Peter J. Tomasi, after working at DC Comics for 15 years, recently left his position as a senior editor for the company and now writes comic books and movies. His recent work includes the critically acclaimed graphic novel LIGHT BRIGADE, and the miniseries BLACK ADAM, along with other upcoming titles NIGHTWING and GREEN LANTERN CORPS.

GREEN LANTERN Engineer Alan Scott found a lantern carved from a meteorite known as the Starheart. Fulfilling the lamp's prophecy to grant astonishing power, Scott tapped into the emerald energy and fought injustice as the Green Lantern. His ring can generate a variety of effects and energy constructs, sustained purely by his will.

THE FLASH The first in a long line of super-speedsters, Jay Garrick is capable of running at velocities near the speed of light. A scientist, Garrick has also served as mentor to other speedsters, and to many heroes over several generations.

WILDCAT A former heavyweight boxing champ, Ted Grant, a.k.a. Wildcat, prowls the mean streets defending the helpless. One of the world's foremost hand-to-hand combatants, he has trained many of today's best fighters — including Black Canary, Catwoman, and the Batman himself.

HAWKMAN Originally Prince Khufu of ancient Egypt, the hero who would become known as Hawkman discovered an alien spacecraft from the planet Thanagar, powered by a mysterious antigravity element called Nth metal. The unearthly energies of the metal transformed his soul, and he and his love Princess Chay-Ara were reincarnated over and over for centuries. Currently he is Carter Hall, archaeologist and adventurer.

POWER GIRL Once confused about her origins, Karen Starr now knows she is the cousin of an alternate-Earth Superman — who gave his life in the Infinite Crisis. Her enhanced strength and powers of flight and invulnerability are matched only by her self-confidence in action, which sometimes borders on arrogance.

MR. TERRIFIC Haunted by the death of his wife, Olympic gold medal-winning decathlete Michael Holt was ready to take his own life. Instead, inspired by the Spectre's story of the original Mr. Terrific, he rededicated himself to ensuring fair play among the street youth using his wealth and technical skills to become the living embodiment of those ideals. He now divides his time between the JSA and the government agency known as Checkmate.

HOURMAN Rick Tyler struggled for a while before accepting his role as the son of the original Hourman. It hasn't been an easy road — he's endured addiction to the Miraclo drug that increases his strength and endurance, and nearly died from a strange disease. Now, after mastering the drug, he uses a special hourglass that enables him to see one hour into the future.

LIBERTY BELLE Jesse Chambers is the daughter of the Golden Age Johnny Quick and Liberty Belle. Originally adopting her father's speed formula, Jesse became the super-hero known as Jesse Quick. After a brief period without powers, Jesse has returned — now taking over her mother's role. As the new Liberty Belle, Jesse is an All-American Powerhouse.

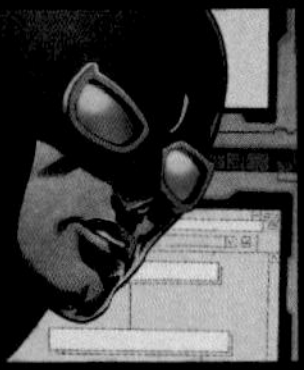

DR. MID-NITE A medical prodigy, Pieter Anton Cross refused to work within the limits of the system. Treating people on his own, he came into contact with a dangerous drug that altered his body chemistry, enabling him to see light in the infrared spectrum. Although he lost his normal sight in a murder attempt disguised as a car accident, his uncanny night vision allows him to protect the weak under the assumed identity of Dr. Mid-Nite.

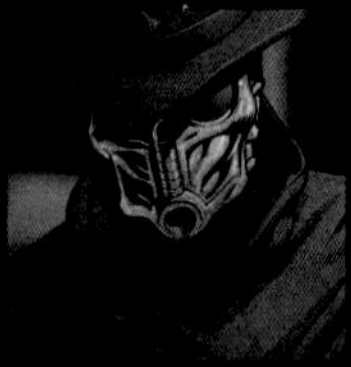

SANDMAN Sandy Hawkins was the ward of the original Sandman Wesley Dodds, and he is the nephew of Dodds's lifelong partner, Dian Belmont. After a bizarre accident, Hawkins was able to transform himself into a pure silicon or sand-form. Recently, he has been experiencing prophetic dreams. He also carries a gas mask, gas guns and other equipment.

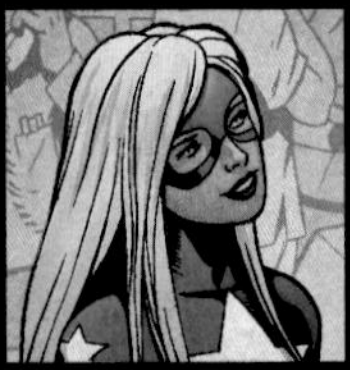

STARGIRL When Courtney Whitmore discovered the cosmic converter belt that had been worn by the JSA's original Star-Spangled Kid (her stepfather, Pat Dugan, was the Kid's sidekick Stripesy), she saw it as an opportunity to cut class and kick some butt. Now called Stargirl, she divides her time between her adventures with the JSA, and bickering/teaming up with Pat — who sometimes monitors Courtney from his S.T.R.I.P.E. robot.

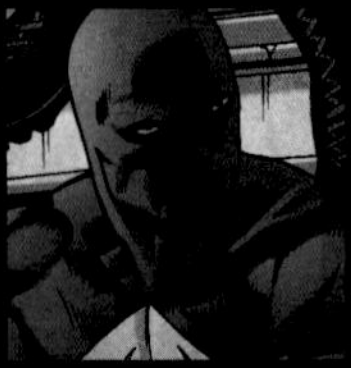

DAMAGE Grant Emerson has had a difficult life. Growing up, he was the victim of an abusive foster father. Then later, after discovering his explosive powers, he accidentally blew up half of downtown Atlanta. Last year, he was almost beaten to death by the super-speed villain known as Zoom. Grant has worn a full-face mask as Damage ever since.

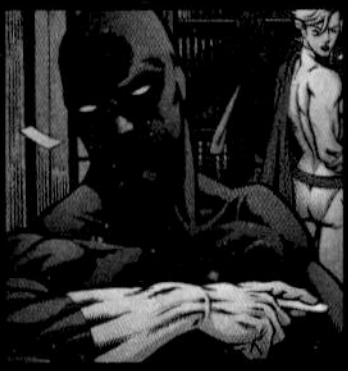

STARMAN A mysterious new Starman recently appeared in Opal City, saving its citizens numerous times. He apparently suffers from some form of schizophrenia, and hears voices in his head. Voluntarily residing in the Sunshine Sanitarium, Starman will occasionally leave and use his gravity-altering powers to fight crime.

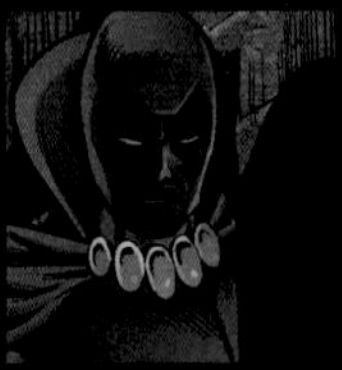

OBSIDIAN Todd Rice is the son of Alan Scott and the Golden Age villain Thorn. Since the death of his twin sister Jennie-Lynn (Jade) in the Infinite Crisis, his once dormant shadow powers have returned...

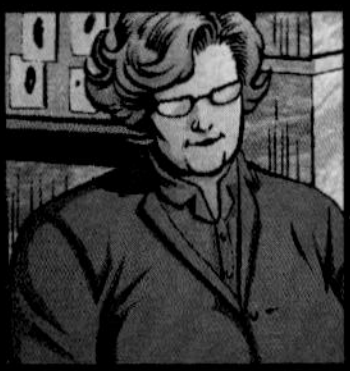

MA HUNKEL Abigail Mathilda "Ma" Hunkel was one of the first female super-heroes of the Golden Age. Wearing colorful longjohns and a cooking pot with eye-holes on her head, she was known as the original Red Tornado — fighting local criminals in her New York neighborhood. Now in her eighties, Ma is the current custodian of the Justice Society Museum.

cover by **DALE EAGLESHAM & ART THIBERT** with **TANYA & RICHARD HORIE**

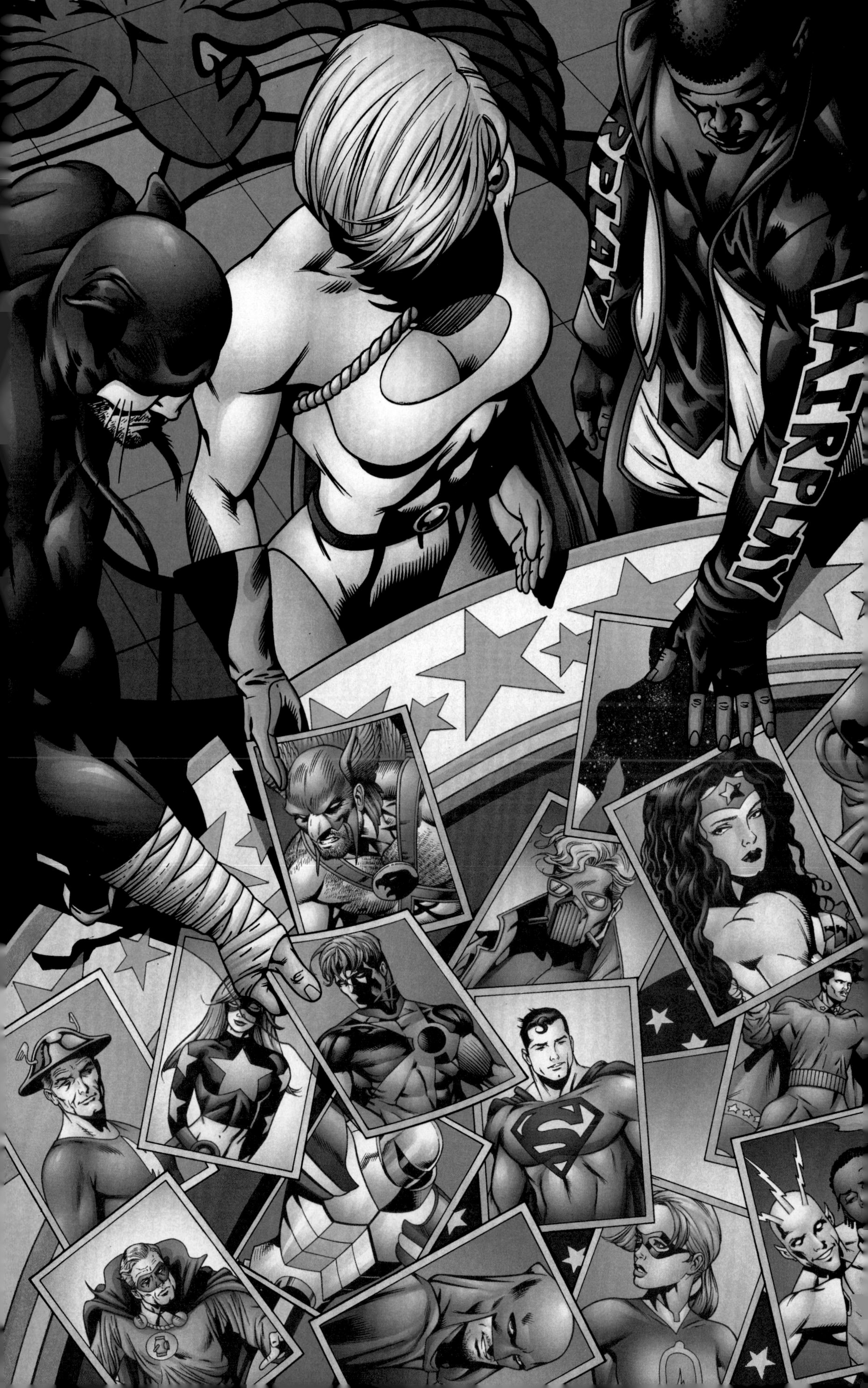
FAIRPLAY

THE NEXT AGE

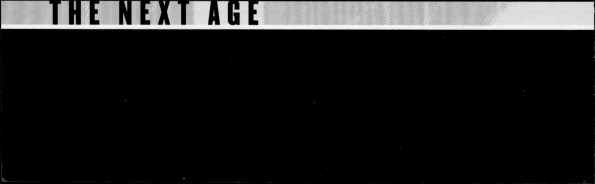

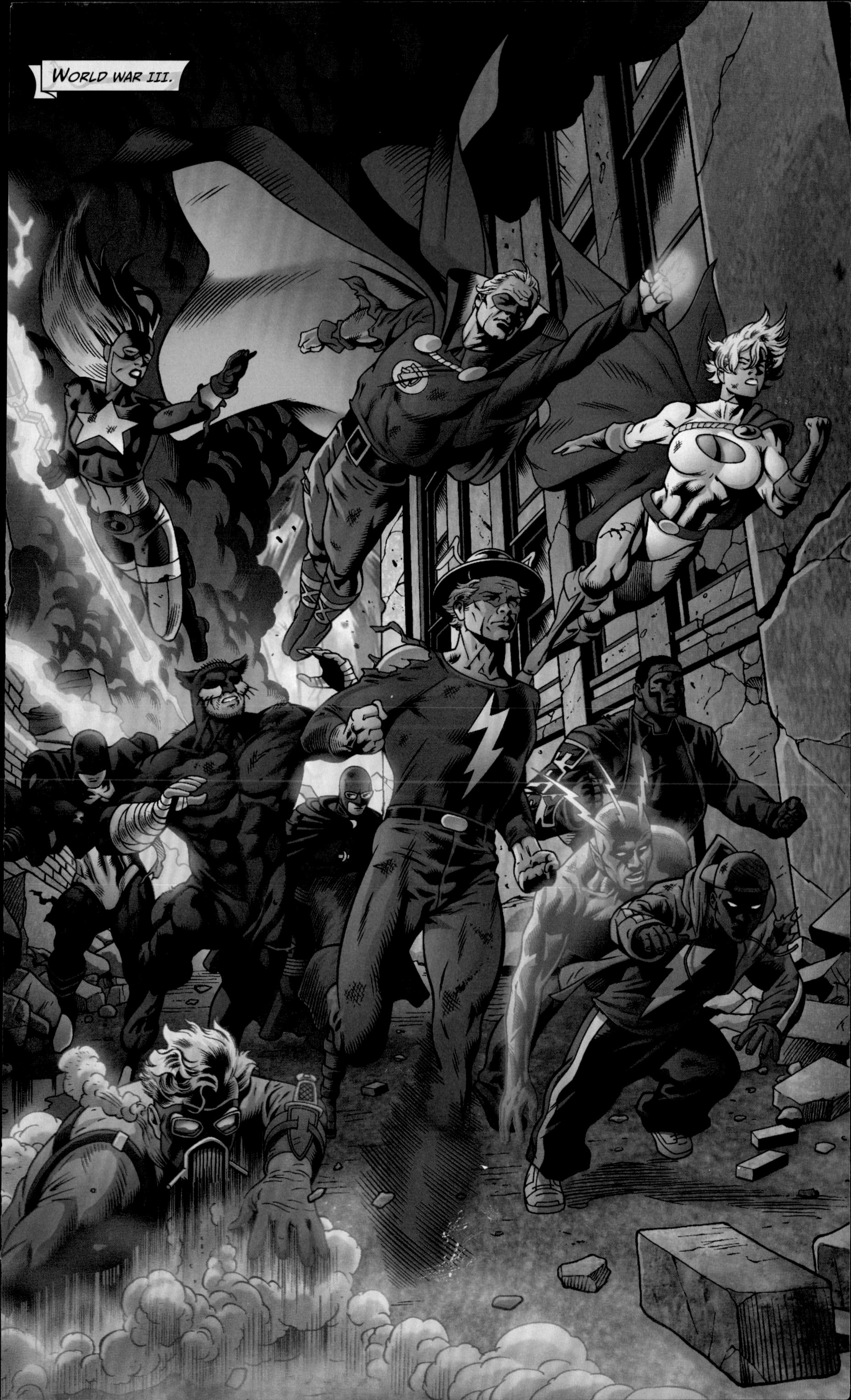
WORLD WAR III.

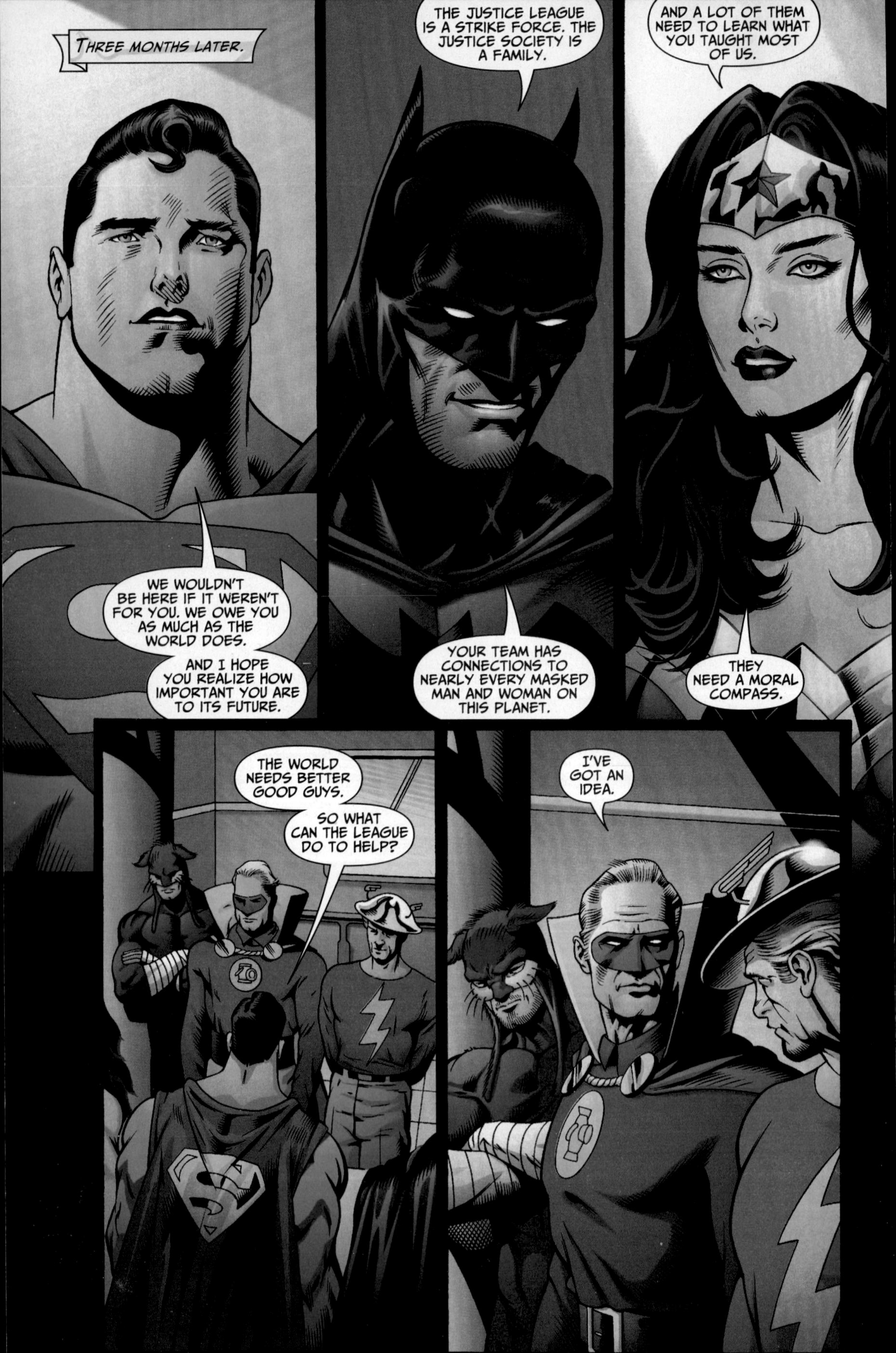
THREE MONTHS LATER.
WE WOULDN'T BE HERE IF IT WEREN'T FOR YOU. WE OWE YOU AS MUCH AS THE WORLD DOES.
AND I HOPE YOU REALIZE HOW IMPORTANT YOU ARE TO ITS FUTURE.
THE JUSTICE LEAGUE IS A STRIKE FORCE. THE JUSTICE SOCIETY IS A FAMILY.
YOUR TEAM HAS CONNECTIONS TO NEARLY EVERY MASKED MAN AND WOMAN ON THIS PLANET.
AND A LOT OF THEM NEED TO LEARN WHAT YOU TAUGHT MOST OF US.
THEY NEED A MORAL COMPASS.
THE WORLD NEEDS BETTER GOOD GUYS.
SO WHAT CAN THE LEAGUE DO TO HELP?
I'VE GOT AN IDEA.

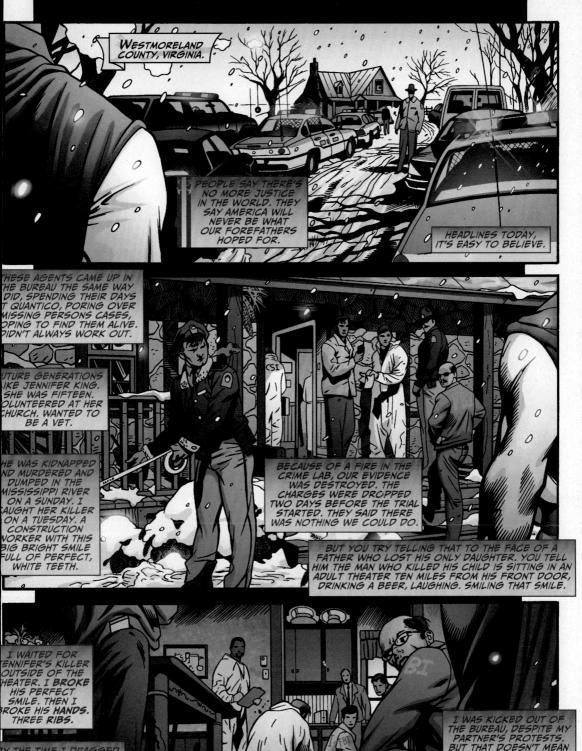

WESTMORELAND COUNTY, VIRGINIA.

PEOPLE SAY THERE'S NO MORE JUSTICE IN THE WORLD. THEY SAY AMERICA WILL NEVER BE WHAT OUR FOREFATHERS HOPED FOR.

HEADLINES TODAY, IT'S EASY TO BELIEVE.

THESE AGENTS CAME UP IN THE BUREAU THE SAME WAY I DID, SPENDING THEIR DAYS AT QUANTICO, PORING OVER MISSING PERSONS CASES, HOPING TO FIND THEM ALIVE. DIDN'T ALWAYS WORK OUT.

FUTURE GENERATIONS LIKE JENNIFER KING. SHE WAS FIFTEEN. VOLUNTEERED AT HER CHURCH. WANTED TO BE A VET.

SHE WAS KIDNAPPED AND MURDERED AND DUMPED IN THE MISSISSIPPI RIVER ON A SUNDAY. I CAUGHT HER KILLER ON A TUESDAY. A CONSTRUCTION WORKER WITH THIS BIG BRIGHT SMILE FULL OF PERFECT, WHITE TEETH.

BECAUSE OF A FIRE IN THE CRIME LAB, OUR EVIDENCE WAS DESTROYED. THE CHARGES WERE DROPPED TWO DAYS BEFORE THE TRIAL STARTED. THEY SAID THERE WAS NOTHING WE COULD DO.

BUT YOU TRY TELLING THAT TO THE FACE OF A FATHER WHO LOST HIS ONLY DAUGHTER. YOU TELL HIM THE MAN WHO KILLED HIS CHILD IS SITTING IN AN ADULT THEATER TEN MILES FROM HIS FRONT DOOR, DRINKING A BEER, LAUGHING. SMILING THAT SMILE.

I WAITED FOR JENNIFER'S KILLER OUTSIDE OF THE THEATER. I BROKE HIS PERFECT SMILE. THEN I BROKE HIS HANDS. THREE RIBS.

BY THE TIME I DRAGGED HIM BACK TO THE LOCAL OFFICE HE COULDN'T WAIT TO CONFESS. WENT TO PRISON FOR LIFE. STILL THERE TOO.

I WAS KICKED OUT OF THE BUREAU, DESPITE MY PARTNER'S PROTESTS. BUT THAT DOESN'T MEAN I STOPPED HELPING PEOPLE. DOESN'T MEAN I STOPPED BELIEVING IN JUSTICE.

WHEN THERE'S A CRIME SCENE THE F.B.I. CAN'T CRACK, I'M STILL THE ONE THEY CALL. I USED TO BE KNOWN AS SPECIAL AGENT TREY THOMPSON.

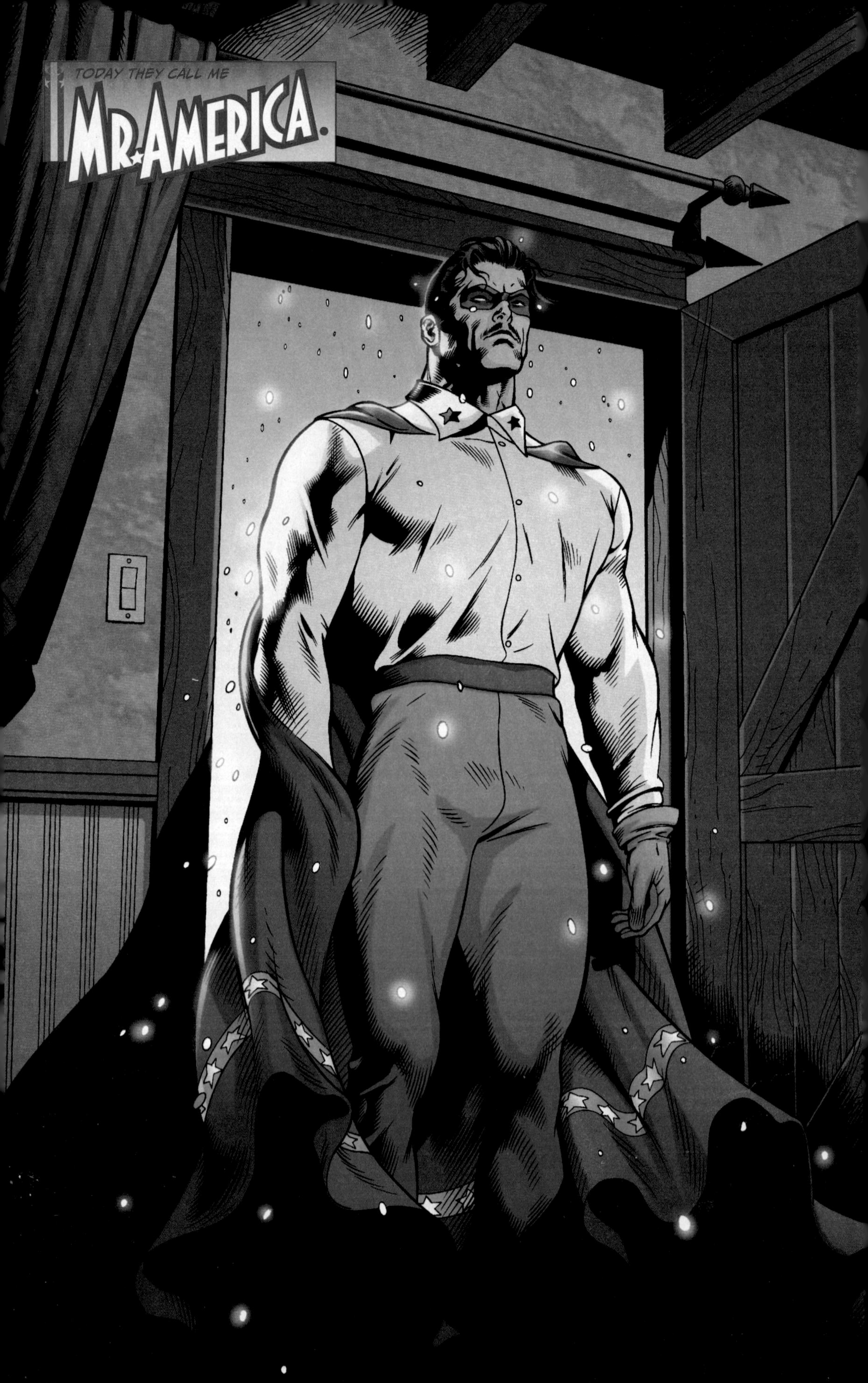
TODAY THEY CALL ME
MR. AMERICA.

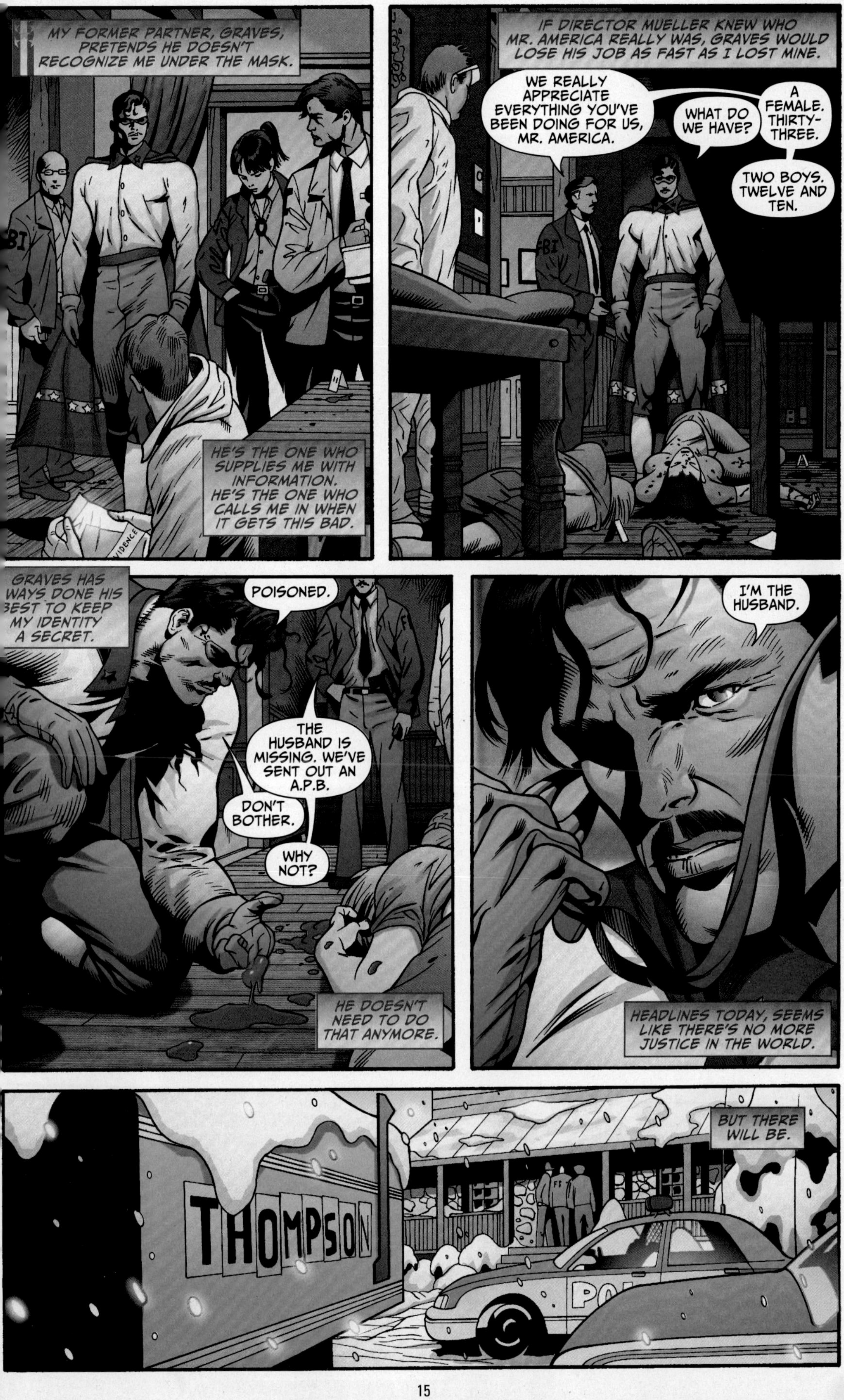

MY FORMER PARTNER, GRAVES, PRETENDS HE DOESN'T RECOGNIZE ME UNDER THE MASK.
HE'S THE ONE WHO SUPPLIES ME WITH INFORMATION. HE'S THE ONE WHO CALLS ME IN WHEN IT GETS THIS BAD.
IF DIRECTOR MUELLER KNEW WHO MR. AMERICA REALLY WAS, GRAVES WOULD LOSE HIS JOB AS FAST AS I LOST MINE.
WE REALLY APPRECIATE EVERYTHING YOU'VE BEEN DOING FOR US, MR. AMERICA.
WHAT DO WE HAVE?
A FEMALE. THIRTY-THREE.
TWO BOYS. TWELVE AND TEN.
GRAVES HAS WAYS DONE HIS BEST TO KEEP MY IDENTITY A SECRET.
POISONED.
THE HUSBAND IS MISSING. WE'VE SENT OUT AN A.P.B.
DON'T BOTHER.
WHY NOT?
HE DOESN'T NEED TO DO THAT ANYMORE.
I'M THE HUSBAND.
HEADLINES TODAY, SEEMS LIKE THERE'S NO MORE JUSTICE IN THE WORLD.
THOMPSON
BUT THERE WILL BE.

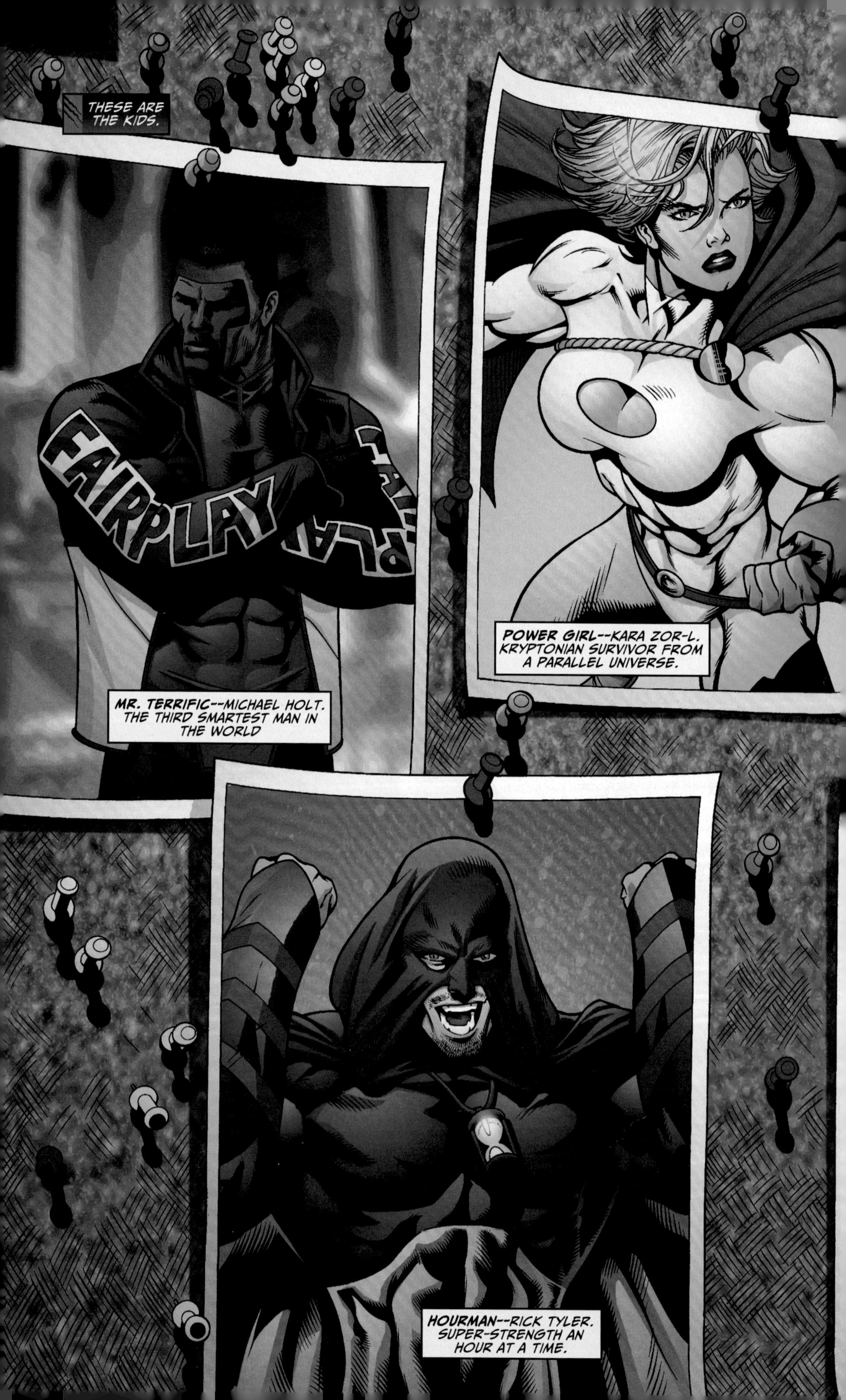
THESE ARE THE KIDS.
FAIRPLAY
MR. TERRIFIC--MICHAEL HOLT. THE THIRD SMARTEST MAN IN THE WORLD
POWER GIRL--KARA ZOR-L. KRYPTONIAN SURVIVOR FROM A PARALLEL UNIVERSE.
HOURMAN--RICK TYLER. SUPER-STRENGTH AN HOUR AT A TIME.

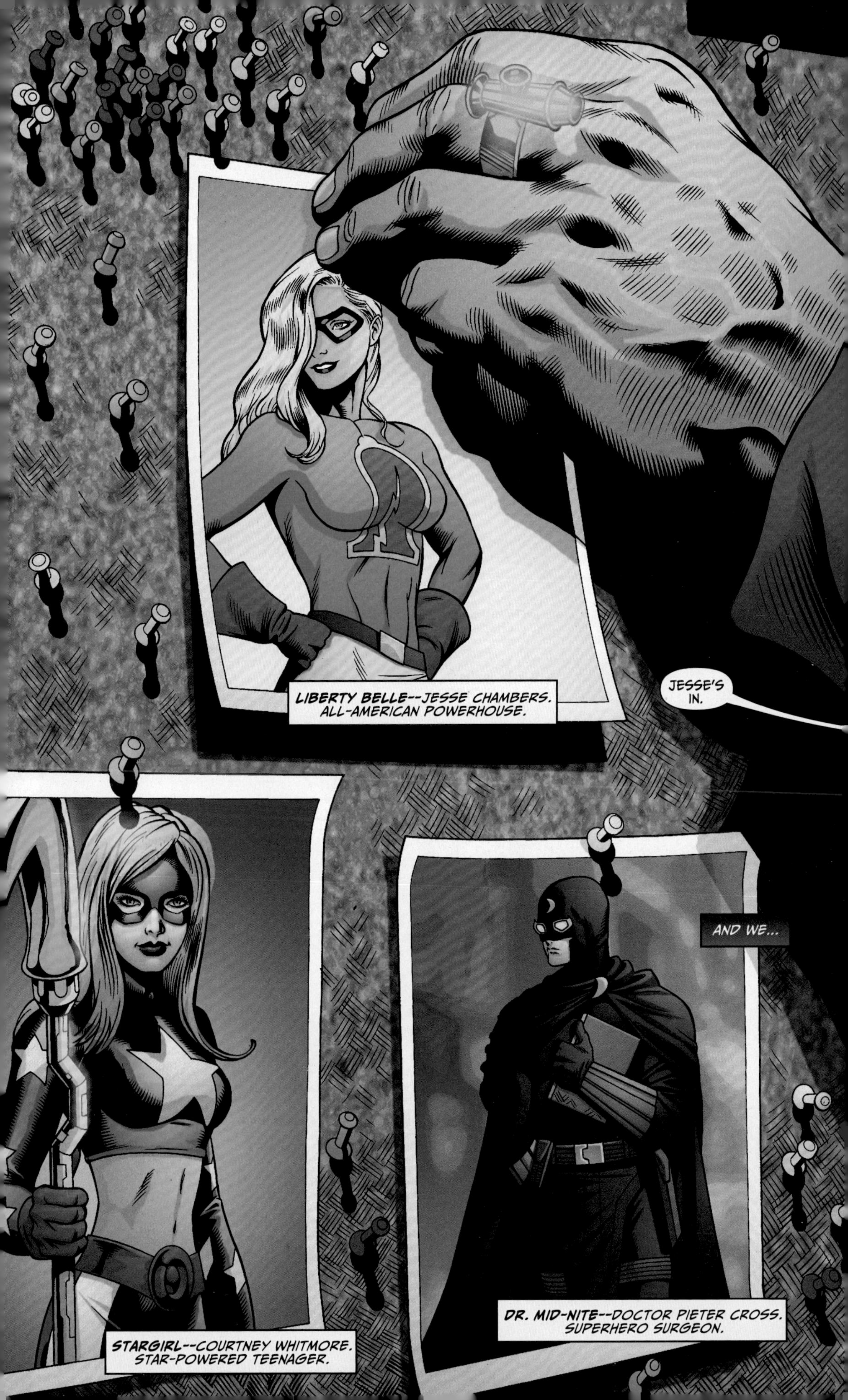
LIBERTY BELLE--JESSE CHAMBERS. ALL-AMERICAN POWERHOUSE.
JESSE'S IN.
AND WE...
STARGIRL--COURTNEY WHITMORE. STAR-POWERED TEENAGER.
DR. MID-NITE--DOCTOR PIETER CROSS. SUPERHERO SURGEON.

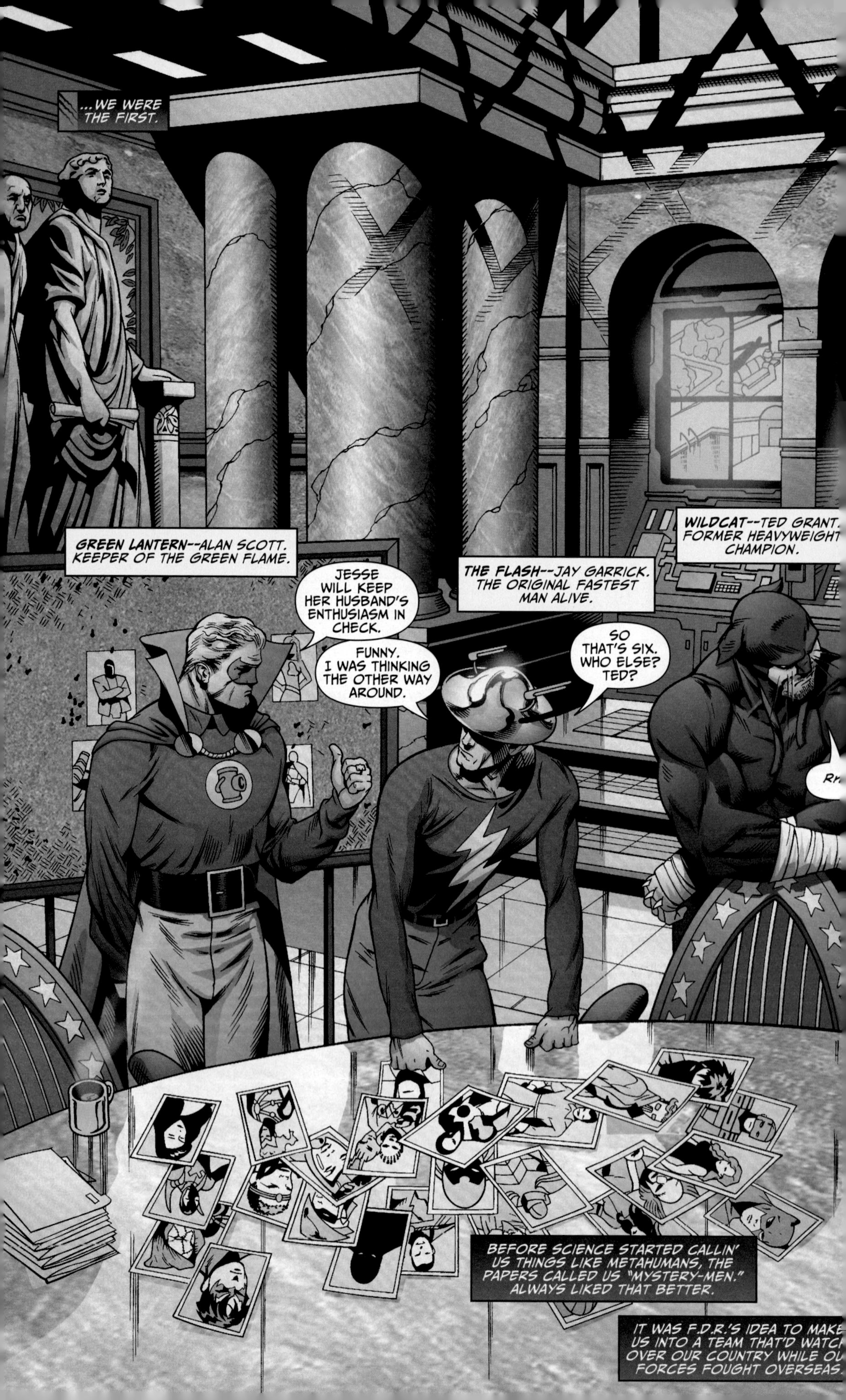
...WE WERE THE FIRST.
GREEN LANTERN--ALAN SCOTT. KEEPER OF THE GREEN FLAME.
JESSE WILL KEEP HER HUSBAND'S ENTHUSIASM IN CHECK.
FUNNY. I WAS THINKING THE OTHER WAY AROUND.
THE FLASH--JAY GARRICK. THE ORIGINAL FASTEST MAN ALIVE.
SO THAT'S SIX. WHO ELSE? TED?
WILDCAT--TED GRANT. FORMER HEAVYWEIGHT CHAMPION.
BEFORE SCIENCE STARTED CALLIN' US THINGS LIKE METAHUMANS, THE PAPERS CALLED US "MYSTERY-MEN." ALWAYS LIKED THAT BETTER.
IT WAS F.D.R.'S IDEA TO MAKE US INTO A TEAM THAT'D WATCH OVER OUR COUNTRY WHILE OUR FORCES FOUGHT OVERSEAS.

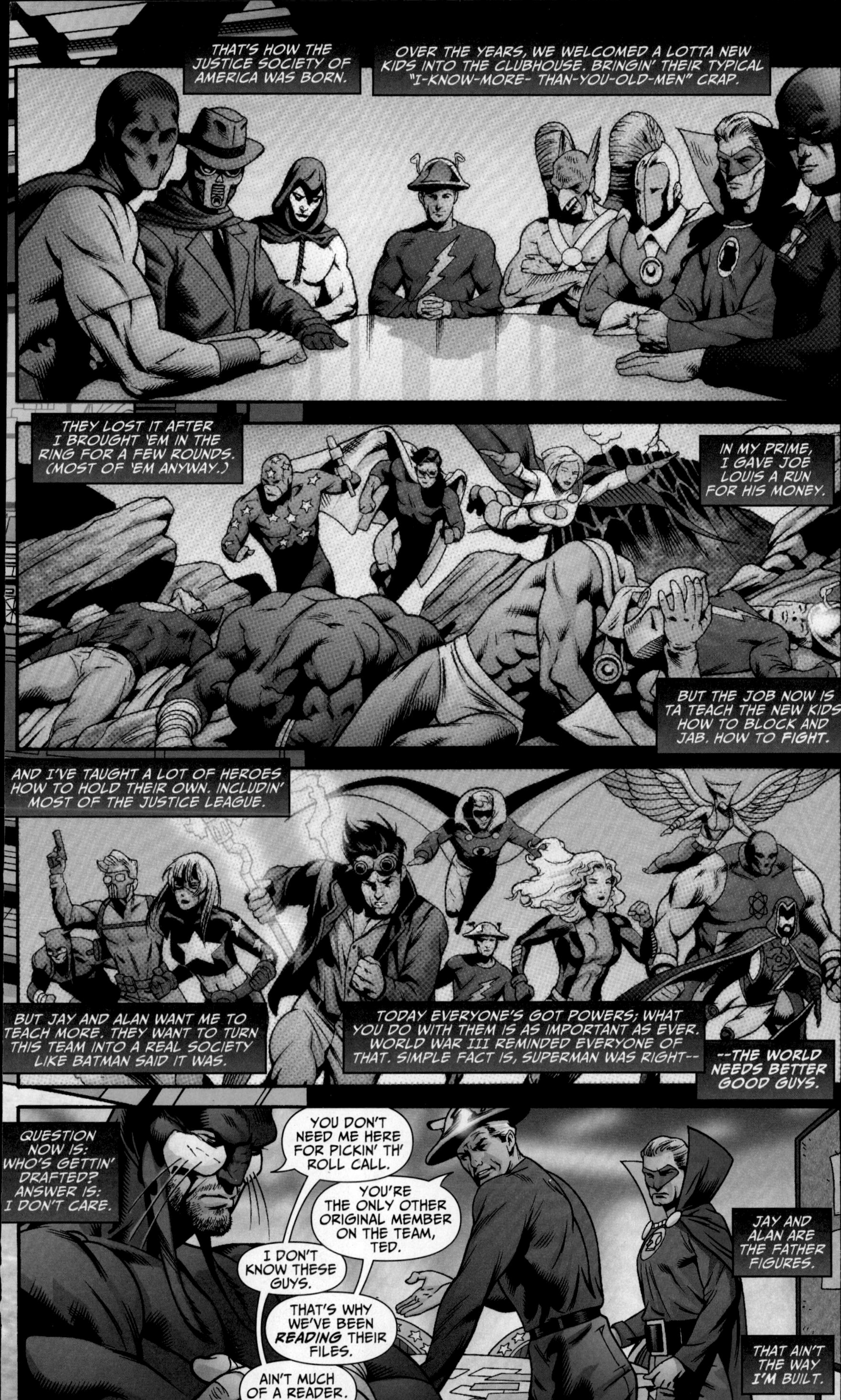
THAT'S HOW THE JUSTICE SOCIETY OF AMERICA WAS BORN.
OVER THE YEARS, WE WELCOMED A LOTTA NEW KIDS INTO THE CLUBHOUSE. BRINGIN' THEIR TYPICAL "I-KNOW-MORE- THAN-YOU-OLD-MEN" CRAP.
THEY LOST IT AFTER I BROUGHT 'EM IN THE RING FOR A FEW ROUNDS. (MOST OF 'EM ANYWAY.)
IN MY PRIME, I GAVE JOE LOUIS A RUN FOR HIS MONEY.
BUT THE JOB NOW IS TA TEACH THE NEW KIDS HOW TO BLOCK AND JAB. HOW TO FIGHT.
AND I'VE TAUGHT A LOT OF HEROES HOW TO HOLD THEIR OWN. INCLUDIN' MOST OF THE JUSTICE LEAGUE.
BUT JAY AND ALAN WANT ME TO TEACH MORE. THEY WANT TO TURN THIS TEAM INTO A REAL SOCIETY LIKE BATMAN SAID IT WAS.
TODAY EVERYONE'S GOT POWERS; WHAT YOU DO WITH THEM IS AS IMPORTANT AS EVER. WORLD WAR III REMINDED EVERYONE OF THAT. SIMPLE FACT IS, SUPERMAN WAS RIGHT--
--THE WORLD NEEDS BETTER GOOD GUYS.
QUESTION NOW IS: WHO'S GETTIN' DRAFTED? ANSWER IS: I DON'T CARE.
YOU DON'T NEED ME HERE FOR PICKIN' TH' ROLL CALL.
YOU'RE THE ONLY OTHER ORIGINAL MEMBER ON THE TEAM, TED.
I DON'T KNOW THESE GUYS.
THAT'S WHY WE'VE BEEN READING THEIR FILES.
AIN'T MUCH OF A READER.
JAY AND ALAN ARE THE FATHER FIGURES.
THAT AIN'T THE WAY I'M BUILT.

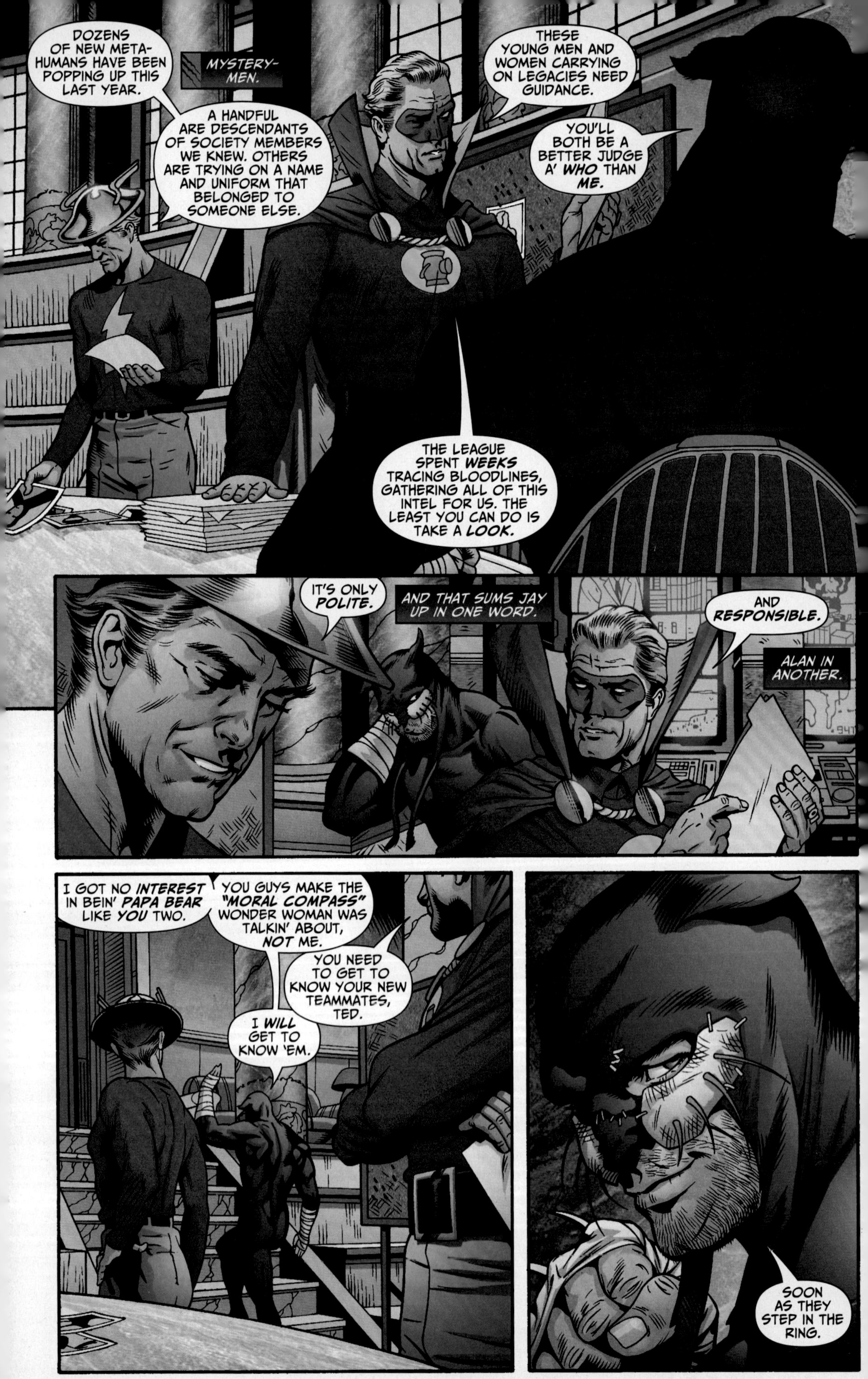
DOZENS OF NEW META-HUMANS HAVE BEEN POPPING UP THIS LAST YEAR.
MYSTERY-MEN.
A HANDFUL ARE DESCENDANTS OF SOCIETY MEMBERS WE KNEW. OTHERS ARE TRYING ON A NAME AND UNIFORM THAT BELONGED TO SOMEONE ELSE.
THESE YOUNG MEN AND WOMEN CARRYING ON LEGACIES NEED GUIDANCE.
YOU'LL BOTH BE A BETTER JUDGE A' WHO THAN ME.
THE LEAGUE SPENT WEEKS TRACING BLOODLINES, GATHERING ALL OF THIS INTEL FOR US. THE LEAST YOU CAN DO IS TAKE A LOOK.
IT'S ONLY POLITE.
AND THAT SUMS JAY UP IN ONE WORD.
AND RESPONSIBLE.
ALAN IN ANOTHER.
I GOT NO INTEREST IN BEIN' PAPA BEAR LIKE YOU TWO.
YOU GUYS MAKE THE "MORAL COMPASS" WONDER WOMAN WAS TALKIN' ABOUT, NOT ME.
YOU NEED TO GET TO KNOW YOUR NEW TEAMMATES, TED.
I WILL GET TO KNOW 'EM.
SOON AS THEY STEP IN THE RING.

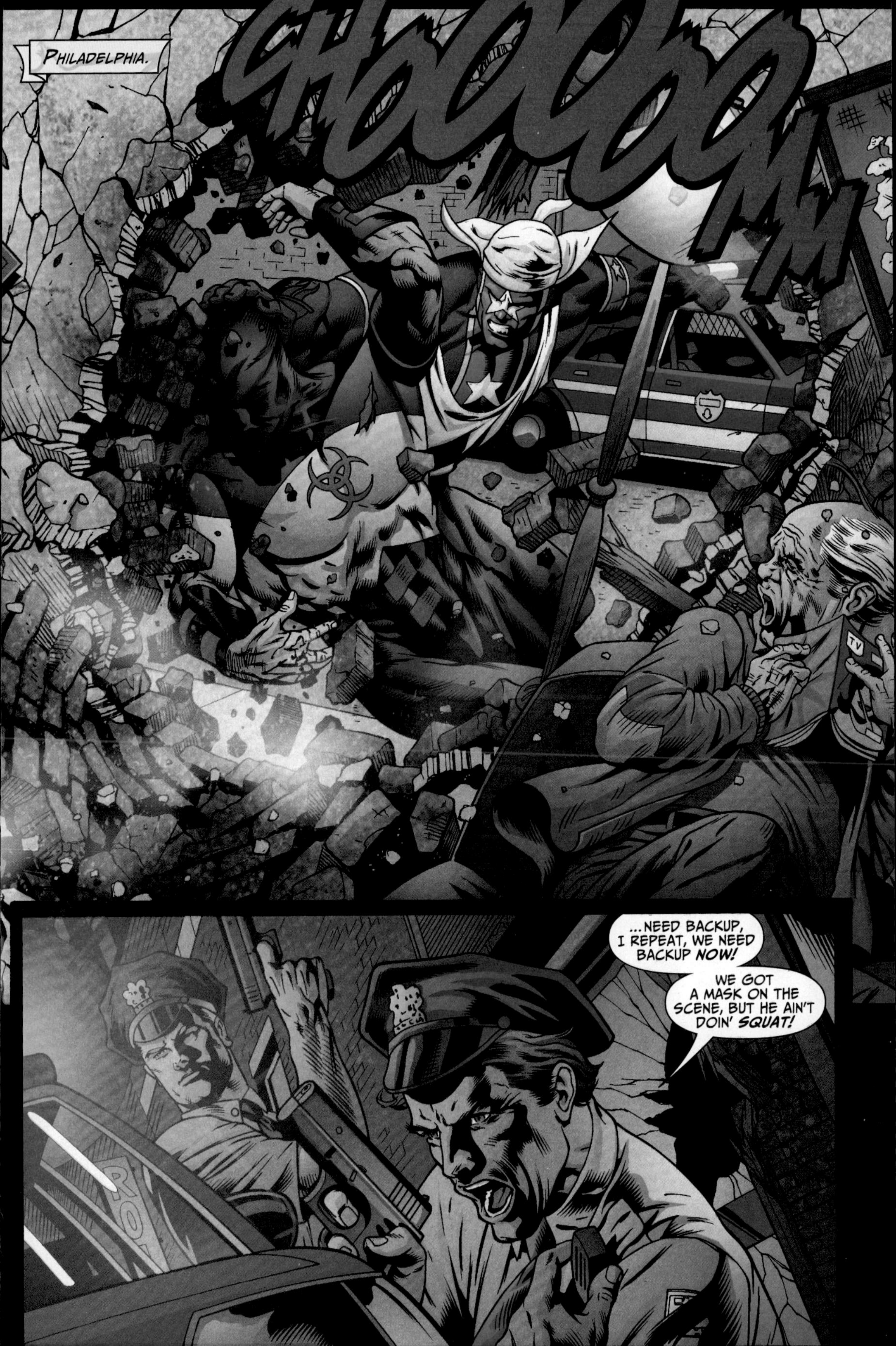
PHILADELPHIA.
...NEED BACKUP, I REPEAT, WE NEED BACKUP NOW!
WE GOT A MASK ON THE SCENE, BUT HE AIN'T DOIN' SQUAT!

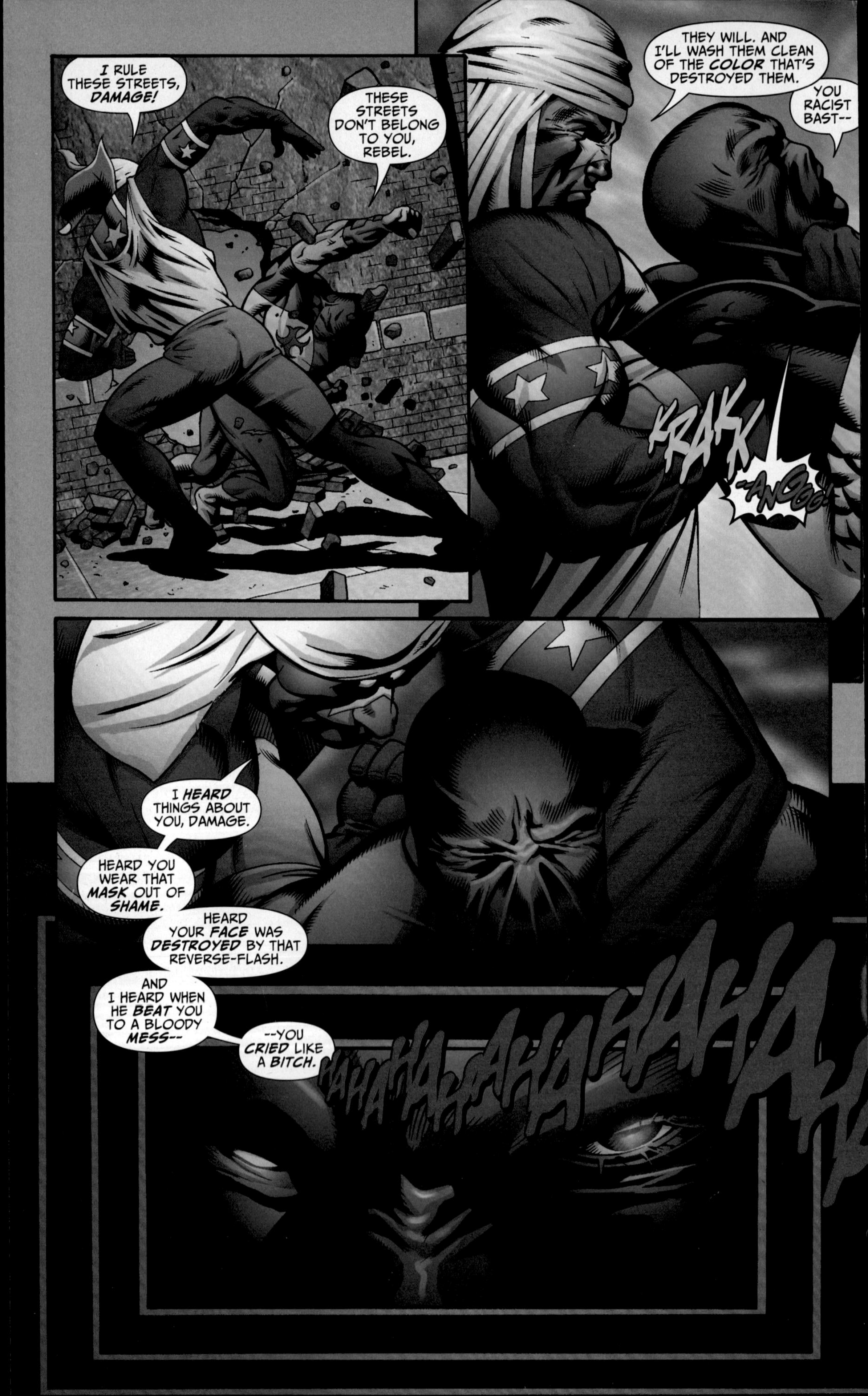
I RULE THESE STREETS, DAMAGE!
THESE STREETS DON'T BELONG TO YOU, REBEL.
THEY WILL. AND I'LL WASH THEM CLEAN OF THE COLOR THAT'S DESTROYED THEM.
YOU RACIST BAST--
KRAKK
--ANGGG!
I HEARD THINGS ABOUT YOU, DAMAGE.
HEARD YOU WEAR THAT MASK OUT OF SHAME.
HEARD YOUR FACE WAS DESTROYED BY THAT REVERSE-FLASH.
AND I HEARD WHEN HE BEAT YOU TO A BLOODY MESS--
--YOU CRIED LIKE A BITCH.
HAHAHAHAHAHAHA

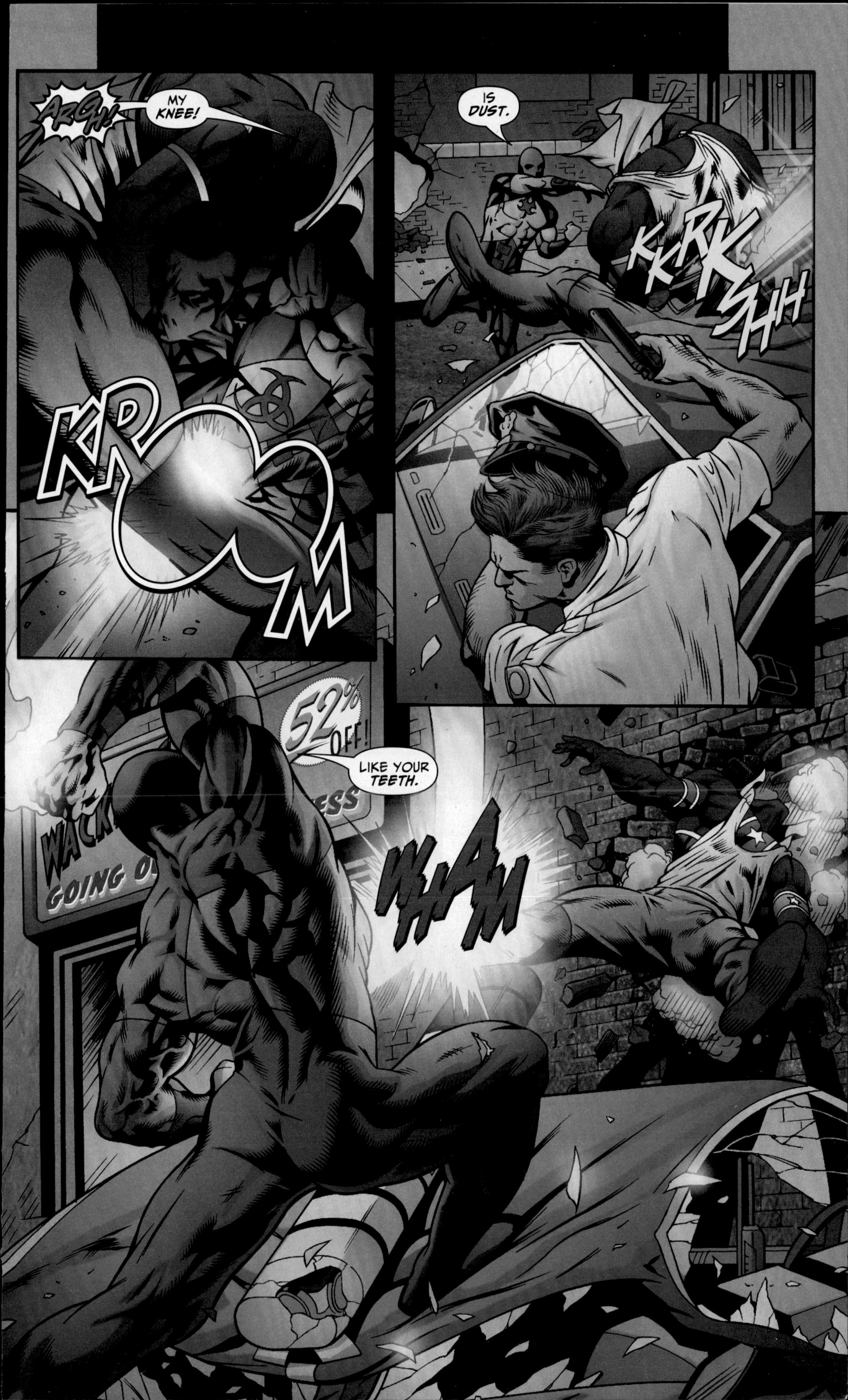

ARGH!
MY KNEE!
KROOM
IS DUST.
KKRKSHH
52% OFF!
LIKE YOUR TEETH.
WHAM
GOING O

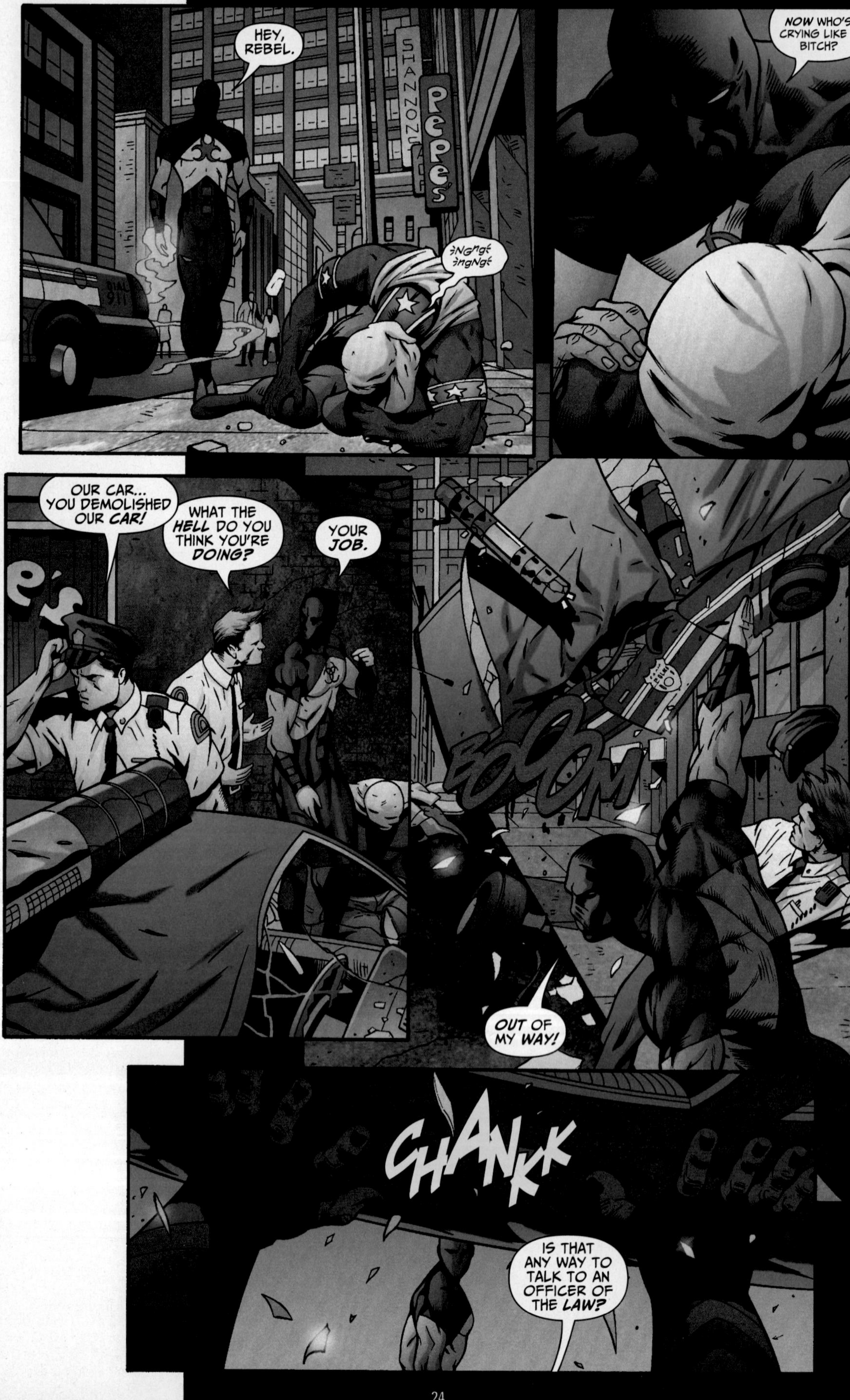
HEY, REBEL.
SHANNON'S
PEPE'S
NGNG NGNG
NOW WHO'S CRYING LIKE A BITCH?
OUR CAR... YOU DEMOLISHED OUR CAR!
WHAT THE HELL DO YOU THINK YOU'RE DOING?
YOUR JOB.
BOOOM
OUT OF MY WAY!
CHANKK
IS THAT ANY WAY TO TALK TO AN OFFICER OF THE LAW?

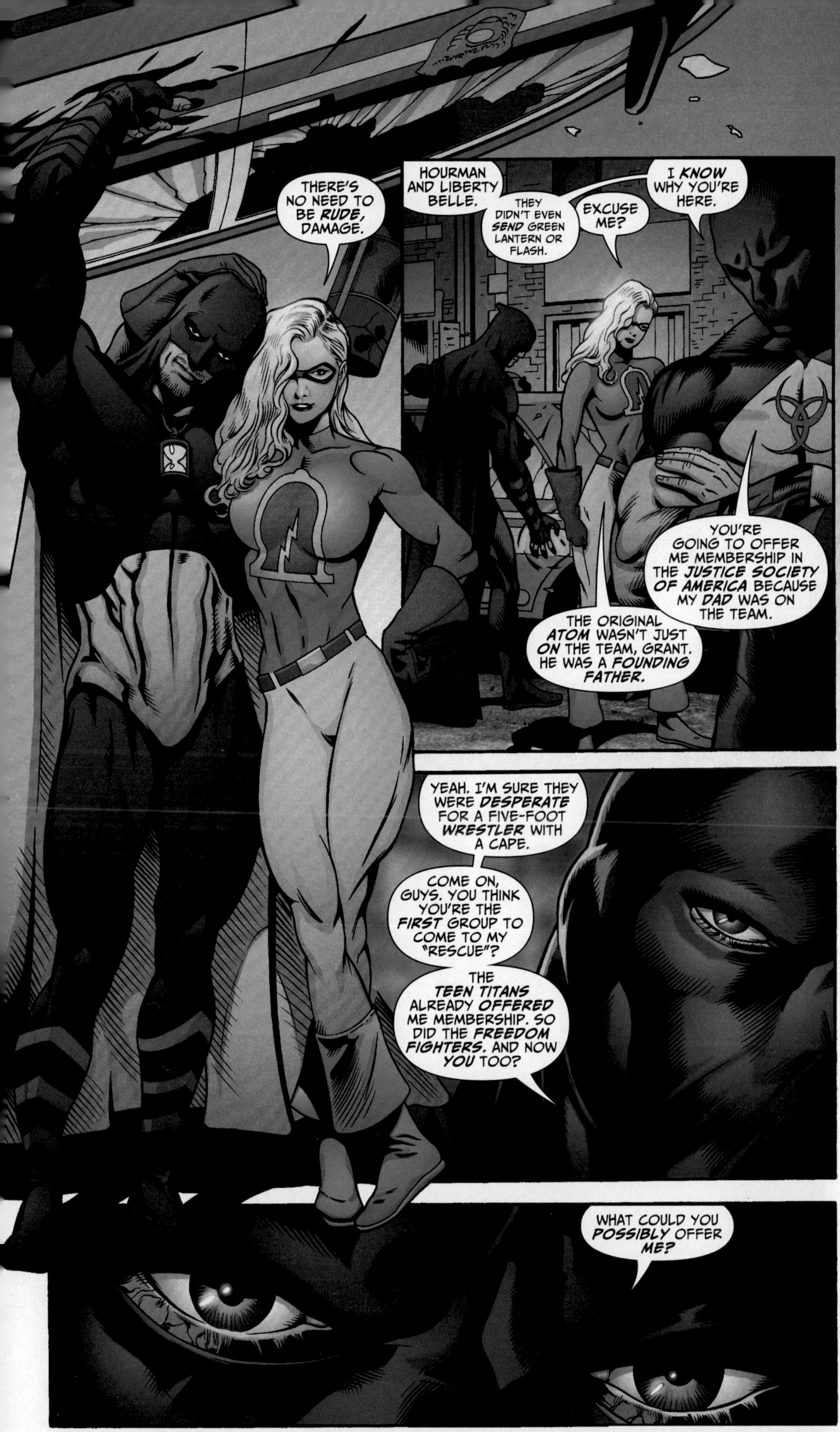
THERE'S NO NEED TO BE RUDE, DAMAGE.
HOURMAN AND LIBERTY BELLE.
THEY DIDN'T EVEN SEND GREEN LANTERN OR FLASH.
EXCUSE ME?
I KNOW WHY YOU'RE HERE.
YOU'RE GOING TO OFFER ME MEMBERSHIP IN THE JUSTICE SOCIETY OF AMERICA BECAUSE MY DAD WAS ON THE TEAM.
THE ORIGINAL ATOM WASN'T JUST ON THE TEAM, GRANT. HE WAS A FOUNDING FATHER.
YEAH. I'M SURE THEY WERE DESPERATE FOR A FIVE-FOOT WRESTLER WITH A CAPE.
COME ON, GUYS. YOU THINK YOU'RE THE FIRST GROUP TO COME TO MY "RESCUE"?
THE TEEN TITANS ALREADY OFFERED ME MEMBERSHIP. SO DID THE FREEDOM FIGHTERS. AND NOW YOU TOO?
WHAT COULD YOU POSSIBLY OFFER ME?

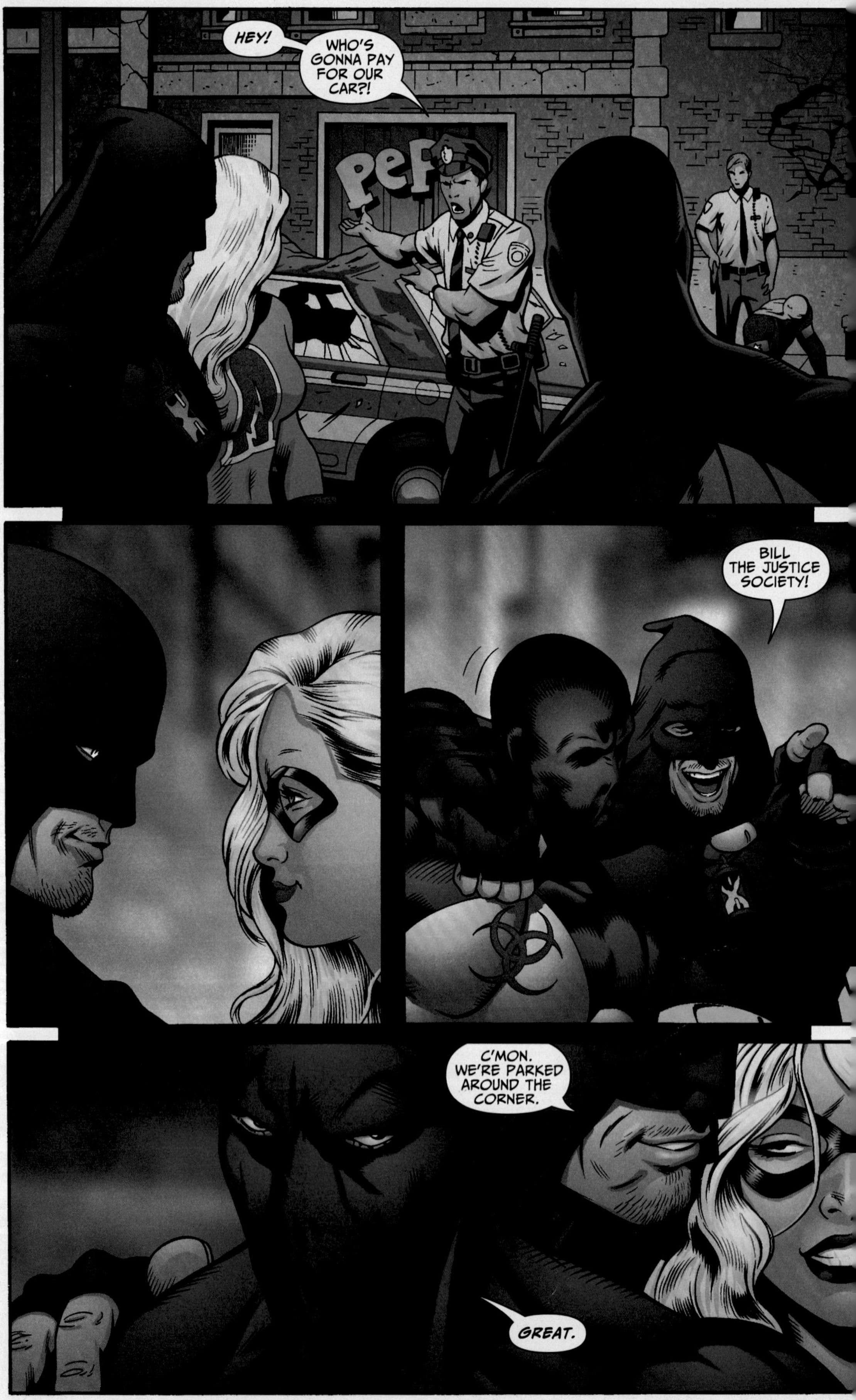
HEY!
WHO'S GONNA PAY FOR OUR CAR?!
BILL THE JUSTICE SOCIETY!
C'MON. WE'RE PARKED AROUND THE CORNER.
GREAT.

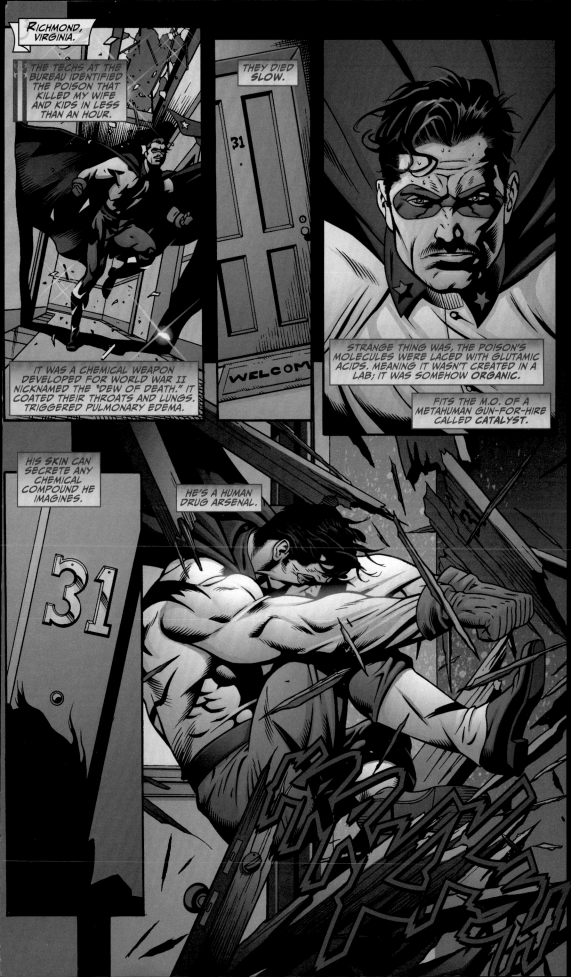

RICHMOND, VIRGINIA.

THE TECHS AT THE BUREAU IDENTIFIED THE POISON THAT KILLED MY WIFE AND KIDS IN LESS THAN AN HOUR.

THEY DIED SLOW.

IT WAS A CHEMICAL WEAPON DEVELOPED FOR WORLD WAR II NICKNAMED THE "DEW OF DEATH." IT COATED THEIR THROATS AND LUNGS. TRIGGERED PULMONARY EDEMA.

WELCOM

STRANGE THING WAS, THE POISON'S MOLECULES WERE LACED WITH GLUTAMIC ACIDS. MEANING IT WASN'T CREATED IN A LAB; IT WAS SOMEHOW ORGANIC.

FITS THE M.O. OF A METAHUMAN GUN-FOR-HIRE CALLED CATALYST.

HIS SKIN CAN SECRETE ANY CHEMICAL COMPOUND HE IMAGINES.

HE'S A HUMAN DRUG ARSENAL.

31

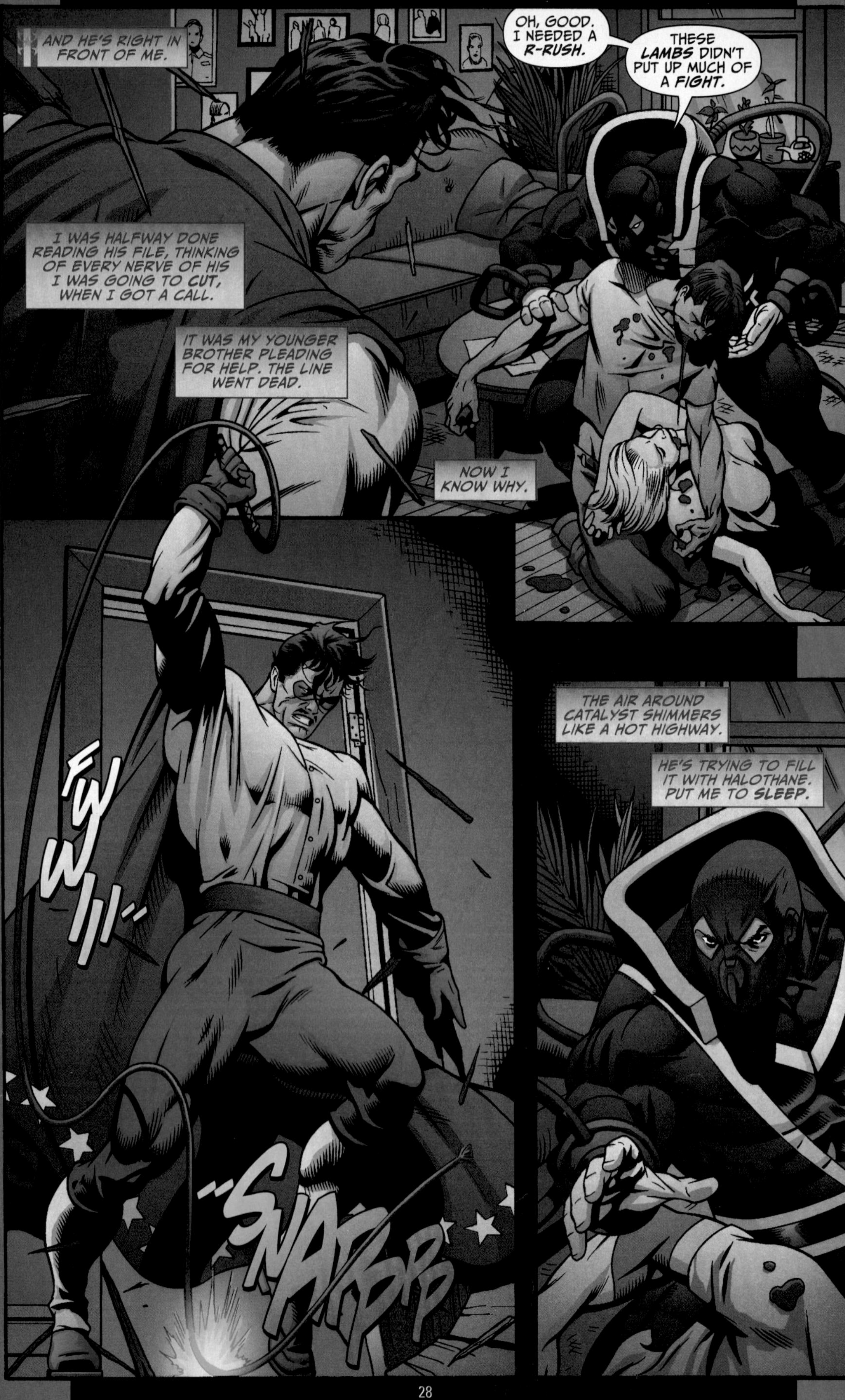
AND HE'S RIGHT IN FRONT OF ME.
OH, GOOD. I NEEDED A R-RUSH.
THESE LAMBS DIDN'T PUT UP MUCH OF A FIGHT.
I WAS HALFWAY DONE READING HIS FILE, THINKING OF EVERY NERVE OF HIS I WAS GOING TO CUT, WHEN I GOT A CALL.
IT WAS MY YOUNGER BROTHER PLEADING FOR HELP. THE LINE WENT DEAD.
NOW I KNOW WHY.
FWWIII--
--SNAPPP
THE AIR AROUND CATALYST SHIMMERS LIKE A HOT HIGHWAY.
HE'S TRYING TO FILL IT WITH HALOTHANE. PUT ME TO SLEEP.

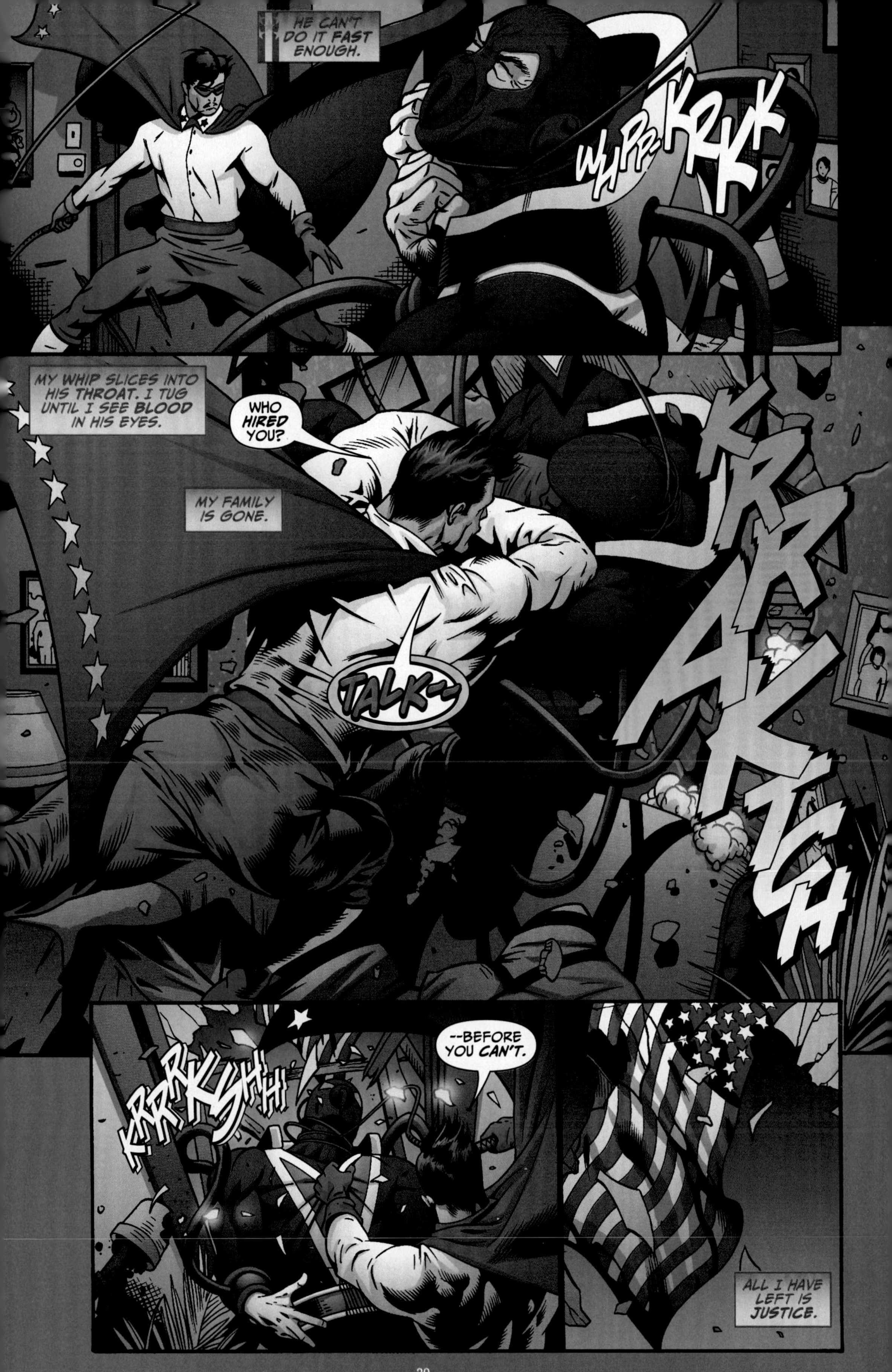

HE CAN'T DO IT FAST ENOUGH.
WHPP-KRKK
MY WHIP SLICES INTO HIS THROAT. I TUG UNTIL I SEE BLOOD IN HIS EYES.
WHO HIRED YOU?
MY FAMILY IS GONE.
TALK--
KRRAKKCH
KRRRKSHHH
--BEFORE YOU CAN'T.
ALL I HAVE LEFT IS JUSTICE.

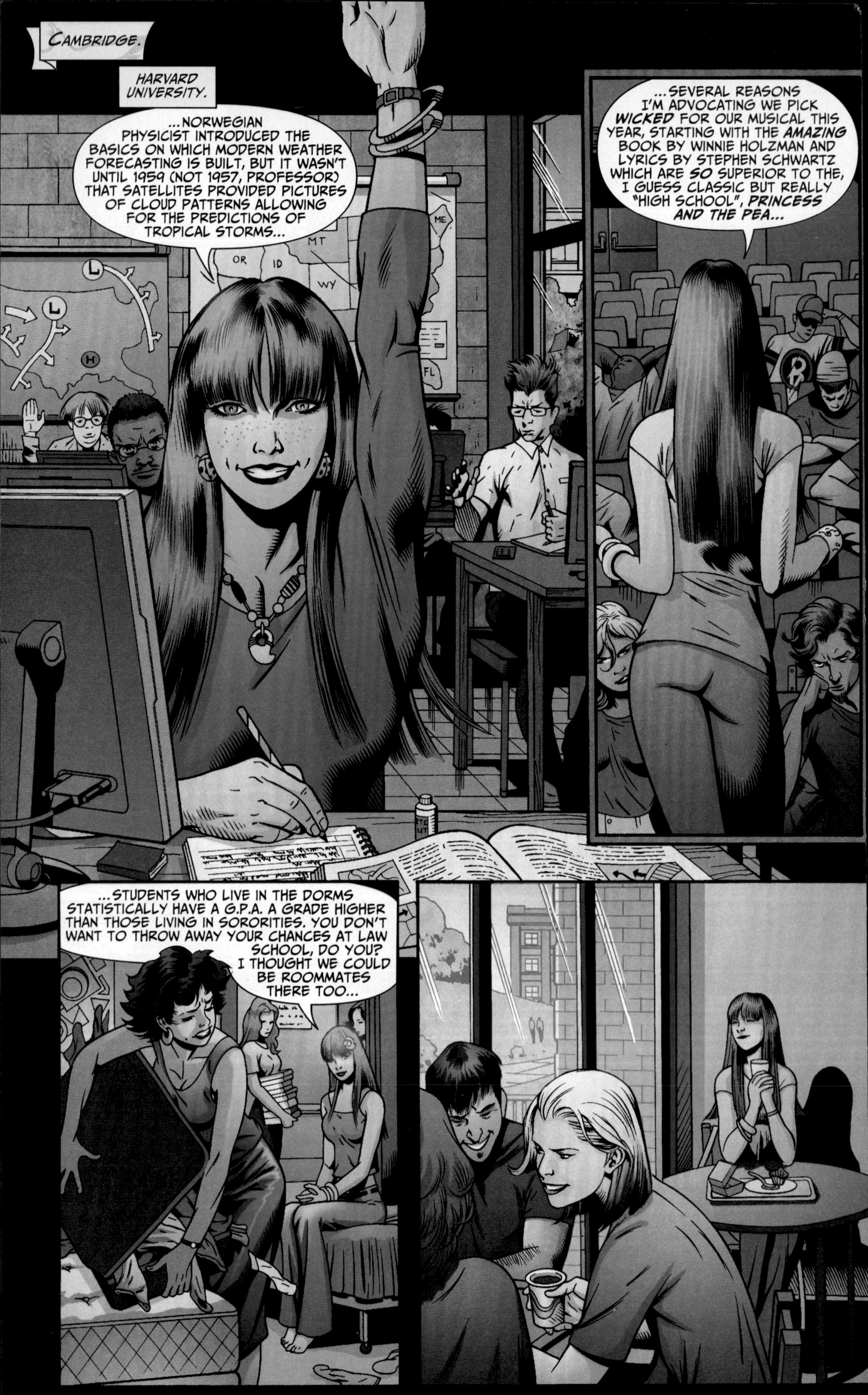
CAMBRIDGE.
HARVARD UNIVERSITY.
...NORWEGIAN PHYSICIST INTRODUCED THE BASICS ON WHICH MODERN WEATHER FORECASTING IS BUILT, BUT IT WASN'T UNTIL 1959 (NOT 1957, PROFESSOR) THAT SATELLITES PROVIDED PICTURES OF CLOUD PATTERNS ALLOWING FOR THE PREDICTIONS OF TROPICAL STORMS...
...SEVERAL REASONS I'M ADVOCATING WE PICK WICKED FOR OUR MUSICAL THIS YEAR, STARTING WITH THE AMAZING BOOK BY WINNIE HOLZMAN AND LYRICS BY STEPHEN SCHWARTZ WHICH ARE SO SUPERIOR TO THE, I GUESS CLASSIC BUT REALLY "HIGH SCHOOL", PRINCESS AND THE PEA...
...STUDENTS WHO LIVE IN THE DORMS STATISTICALLY HAVE A G.P.A. A GRADE HIGHER THAN THOSE LIVING IN SORORITIES. YOU DON'T WANT TO THROW AWAY YOUR CHANCES AT LAW SCHOOL, DO YOU? I THOUGHT WE COULD BE ROOMMATES THERE TOO...

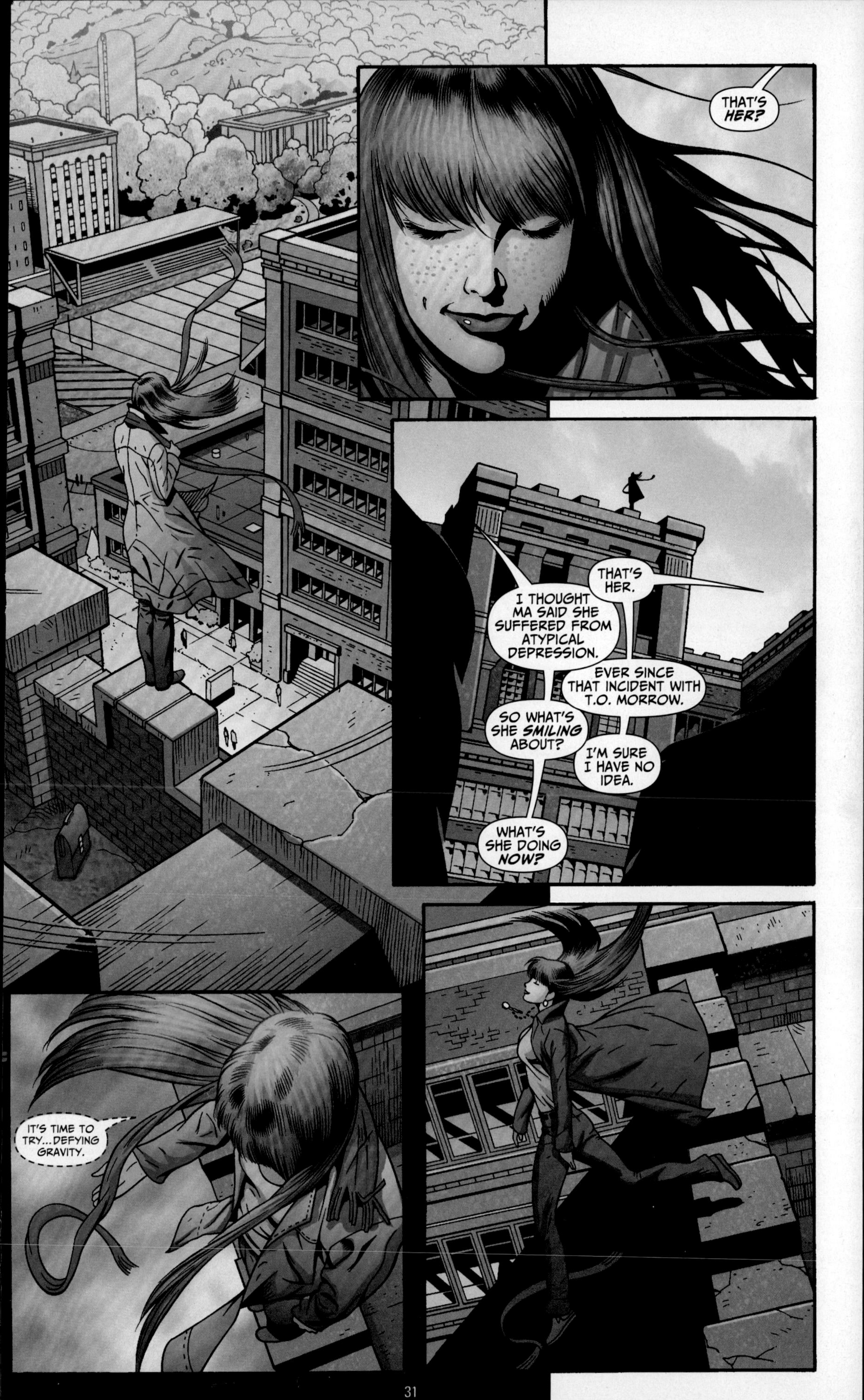
THAT'S HER?
I THOUGHT MA SAID SHE SUFFERED FROM ATYPICAL DEPRESSION.
THAT'S HER.
EVER SINCE THAT INCIDENT WITH T.O. MORROW.
SO WHAT'S SHE SMILING ABOUT?
I'M SURE I HAVE NO IDEA.
WHAT'S SHE DOING NOW?
IT'S TIME TO TRY...DEFYING GRAVITY.

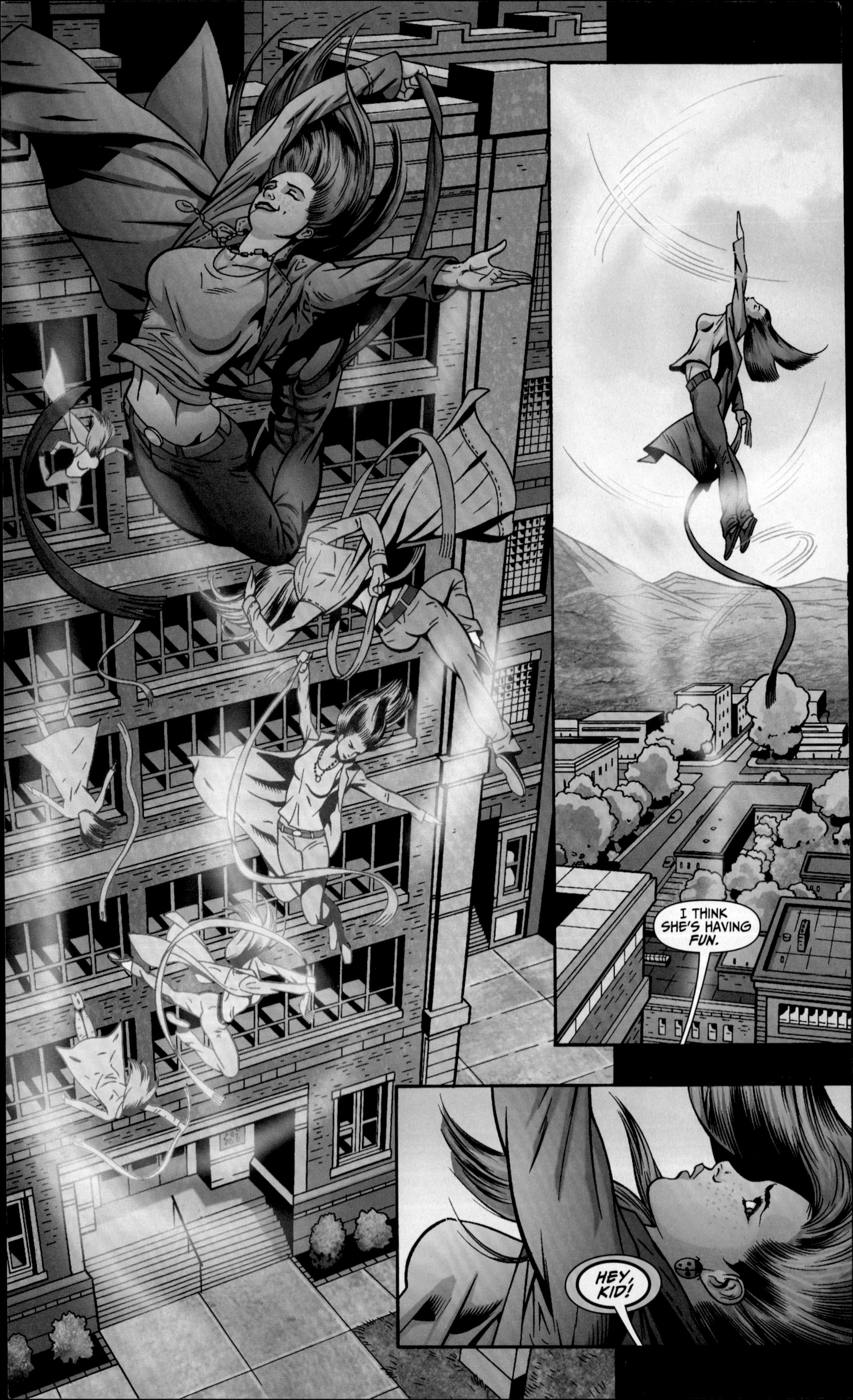
I THINK SHE'S HAVING FUN.
HEY, KID!

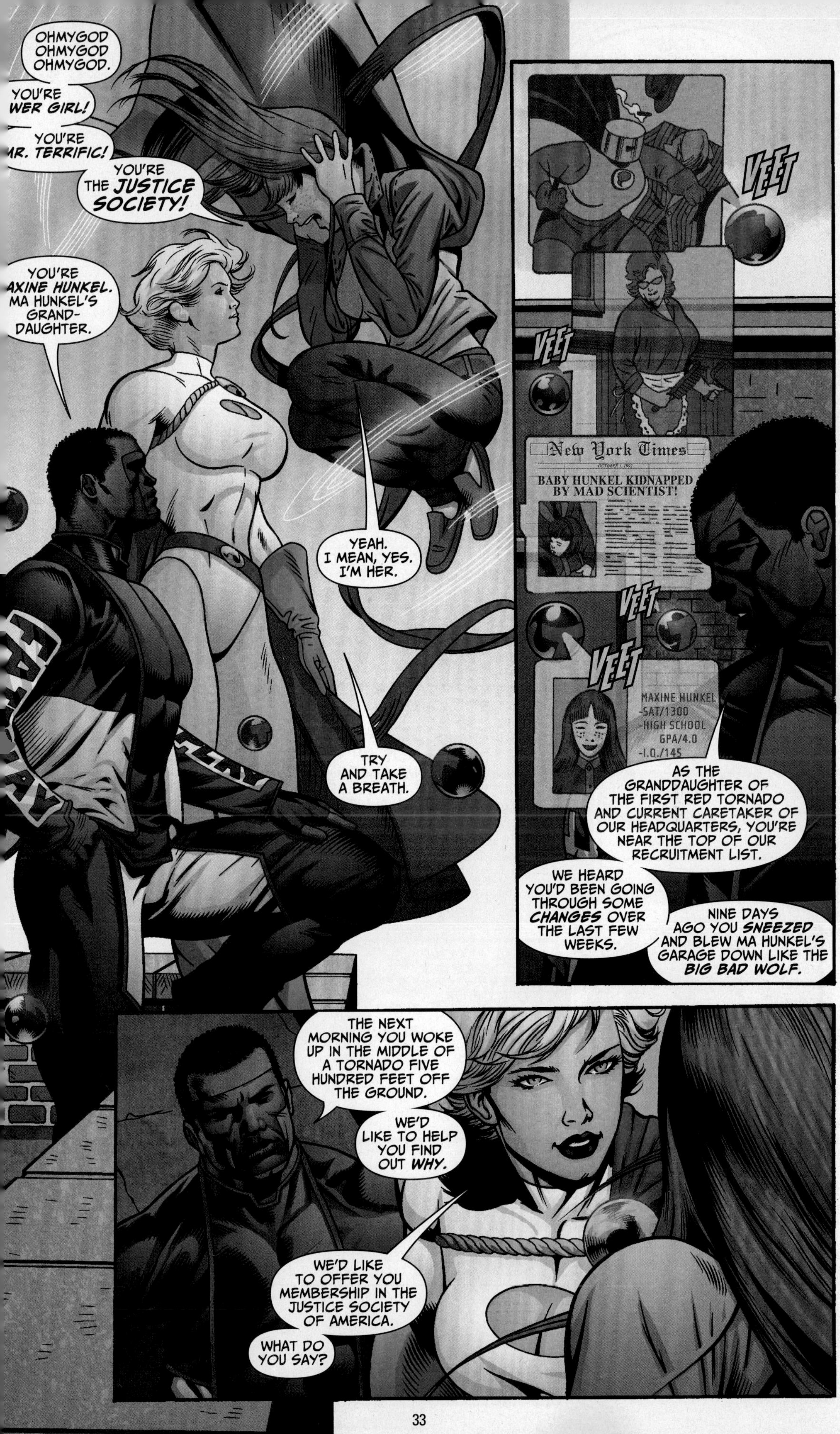
OHMYGOD OHMYGOD OHMYGOD.
YOU'RE WER GIRL!
YOU'RE R. TERRIFIC!
YOU'RE THE JUSTICE SOCIETY!
YOU'RE AXINE HUNKEL. MA HUNKEL'S GRAND-DAUGHTER.
YEAH. I MEAN, YES. I'M HER.
TRY AND TAKE A BREATH.
VEET
VEET
New York Times
BABY HUNKEL KIDNAPPED BY MAD SCIENTIST!
VEET
VEET
MAXINE HUNKEL
-SAT/1300
-HIGH SCHOOL
GPA/4.0
-I.Q./145
AS THE GRANDDAUGHTER OF THE FIRST RED TORNADO AND CURRENT CARETAKER OF OUR HEADQUARTERS, YOU'RE NEAR THE TOP OF OUR RECRUITMENT LIST.
WE HEARD YOU'D BEEN GOING THROUGH SOME CHANGES OVER THE LAST FEW WEEKS.
NINE DAYS AGO YOU SNEEZED AND BLEW MA HUNKEL'S GARAGE DOWN LIKE THE BIG BAD WOLF.
THE NEXT MORNING YOU WOKE UP IN THE MIDDLE OF A TORNADO FIVE HUNDRED FEET OFF THE GROUND.
WE'D LIKE TO HELP YOU FIND OUT WHY.
WE'D LIKE TO OFFER YOU MEMBERSHIP IN THE JUSTICE SOCIETY OF AMERICA.
WHAT DO YOU SAY?

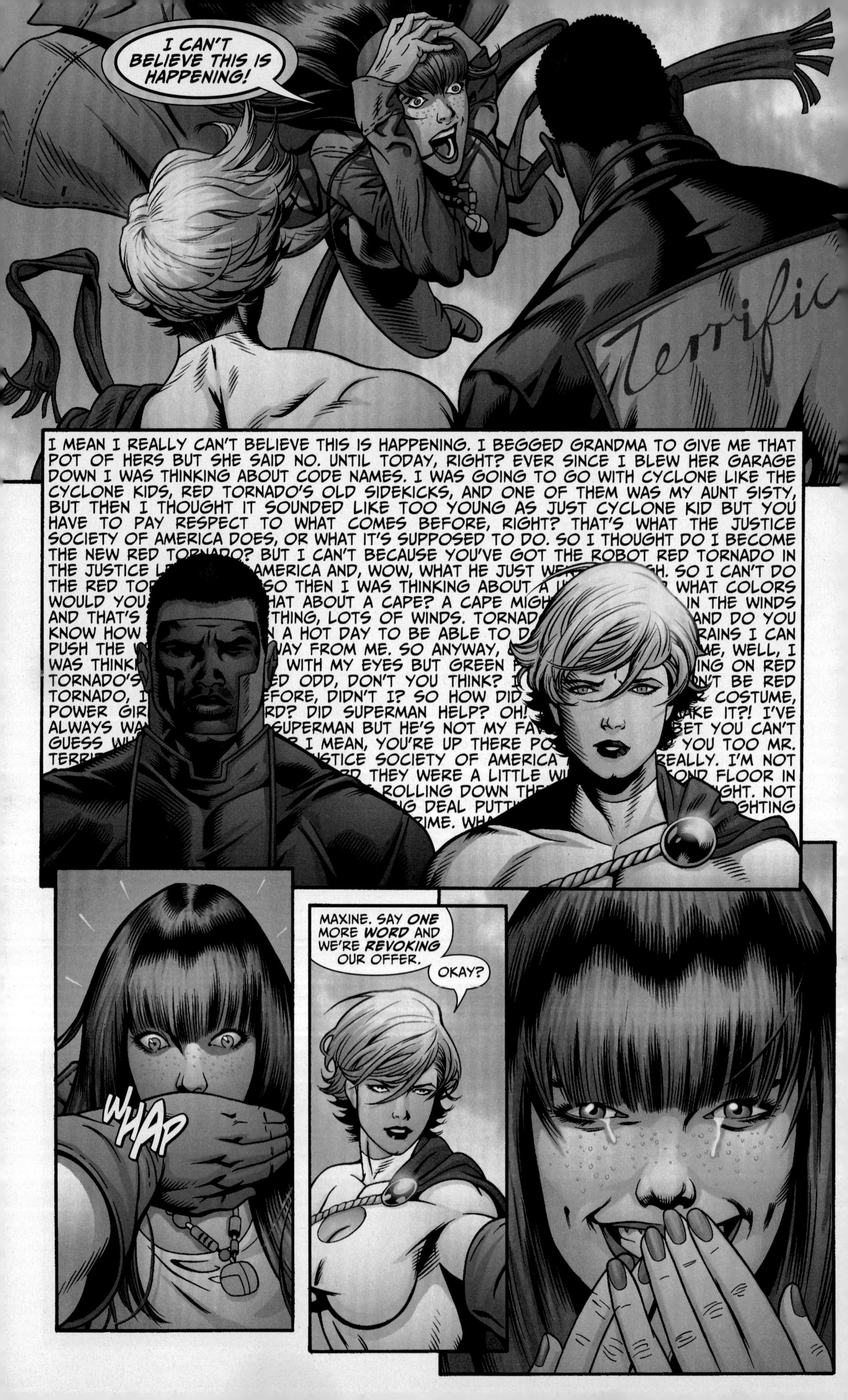
I CAN'T BELIEVE THIS IS HAPPENING!
Terrific
I MEAN I REALLY CAN'T BELIEVE THIS IS HAPPENING. I BEGGED GRANDMA TO GIVE ME THAT
POT OF HERS BUT SHE SAID NO. UNTIL TODAY, RIGHT? EVER SINCE I BLEW HER GARAGE
DOWN I WAS THINKING ABOUT CODE NAMES. I WAS GOING TO GO WITH CYCLONE LIKE THE
CYCLONE KIDS, RED TORNADO'S OLD SIDEKICKS, AND ONE OF THEM WAS MY AUNT SISTY,
BUT THEN I THOUGHT IT SOUNDED LIKE TOO YOUNG AS JUST CYCLONE KID BUT YOU
HAVE TO PAY RESPECT TO WHAT COMES BEFORE, RIGHT? THAT'S WHAT THE JUSTICE
SOCIETY OF AMERICA DOES, OR WHAT IT'S SUPPOSED TO DO. SO I THOUGHT DO I BECOME
THE NEW RED TORNADO? BUT I CAN'T BECAUSE YOU'VE GOT THE ROBOT RED TORNADO IN
THE JUSTICE AMERICA AND, WOW, WHAT HE JUST SO I CAN'T DO
THE RED SO THEN I WAS THINKING ABOUT A WHAT COLORS
WOULD A CAPE? A CAPE IN THE WINDS
AND THAT'S THING, LOTS OF WINDS. AND DO YOU
KNOW HOW A HOT DAY TO BE ABLE TO RAINS I CAN
PUSH THE WAY FROM ME. SO ANYWAY, WELL, I
WAS WITH MY EYES BUT GREEN ON RED
TORNADO'S ODD, DON'T YOU THINK? BE RED
TORNADO, DIDN'T I? SO HOW DID COSTUME,
POWER DID SUPERMAN HELP? OH! I'VE
ALWAYS SUPERMAN BUT HE'S NOT MY BET YOU CAN'T
GUESS I MEAN, YOU'RE UP THERE YOU TOO MR.
SOCIETY OF AMERICA REALLY. I'M NOT
THEY WERE A LITTLE FLOOR IN
ROLLING DOWN NOT
DEAL
MAXINE. SAY ONE MORE WORD AND WE'RE REVOKING OUR OFFER.
OKAY?
WHAP

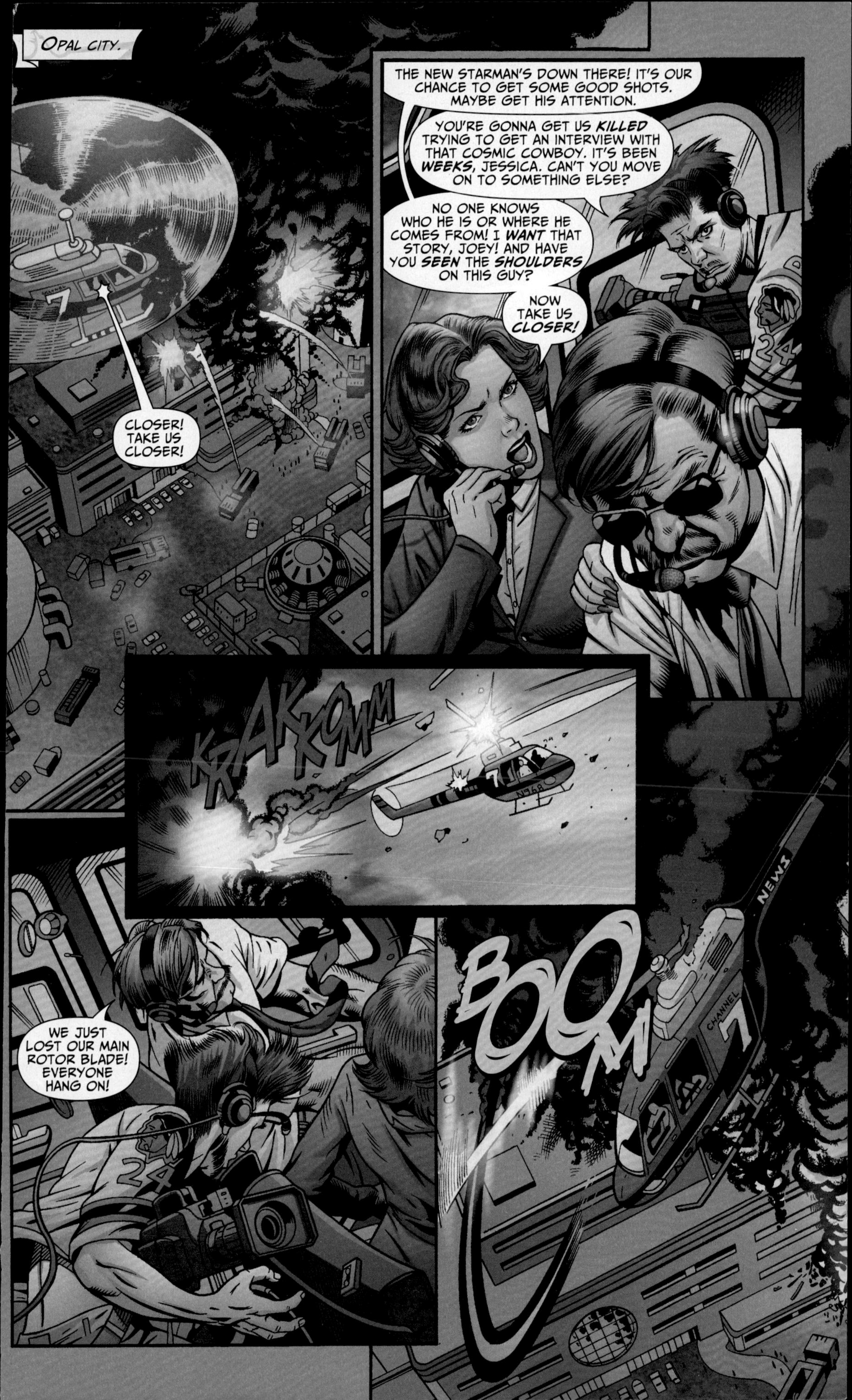
OPAL CITY.
CLOSER! TAKE US CLOSER!
THE NEW STARMAN'S DOWN THERE! IT'S OUR CHANCE TO GET SOME GOOD SHOTS. MAYBE GET HIS ATTENTION.
YOU'RE GONNA GET US KILLED TRYING TO GET AN INTERVIEW WITH THAT COSMIC COWBOY. IT'S BEEN WEEKS, JESSICA. CAN'T YOU MOVE ON TO SOMETHING ELSE?
NO ONE KNOWS WHO HE IS OR WHERE HE COMES FROM! I WANT THAT STORY, JOEY! AND HAVE YOU SEEN THE SHOULDERS ON THIS GUY?
NOW TAKE US CLOSER!
KRAKKOMM
WE JUST LOST OUR MAIN ROTOR BLADE! EVERYONE HANG ON!
BOOM
NEWS
CHANNEL 7

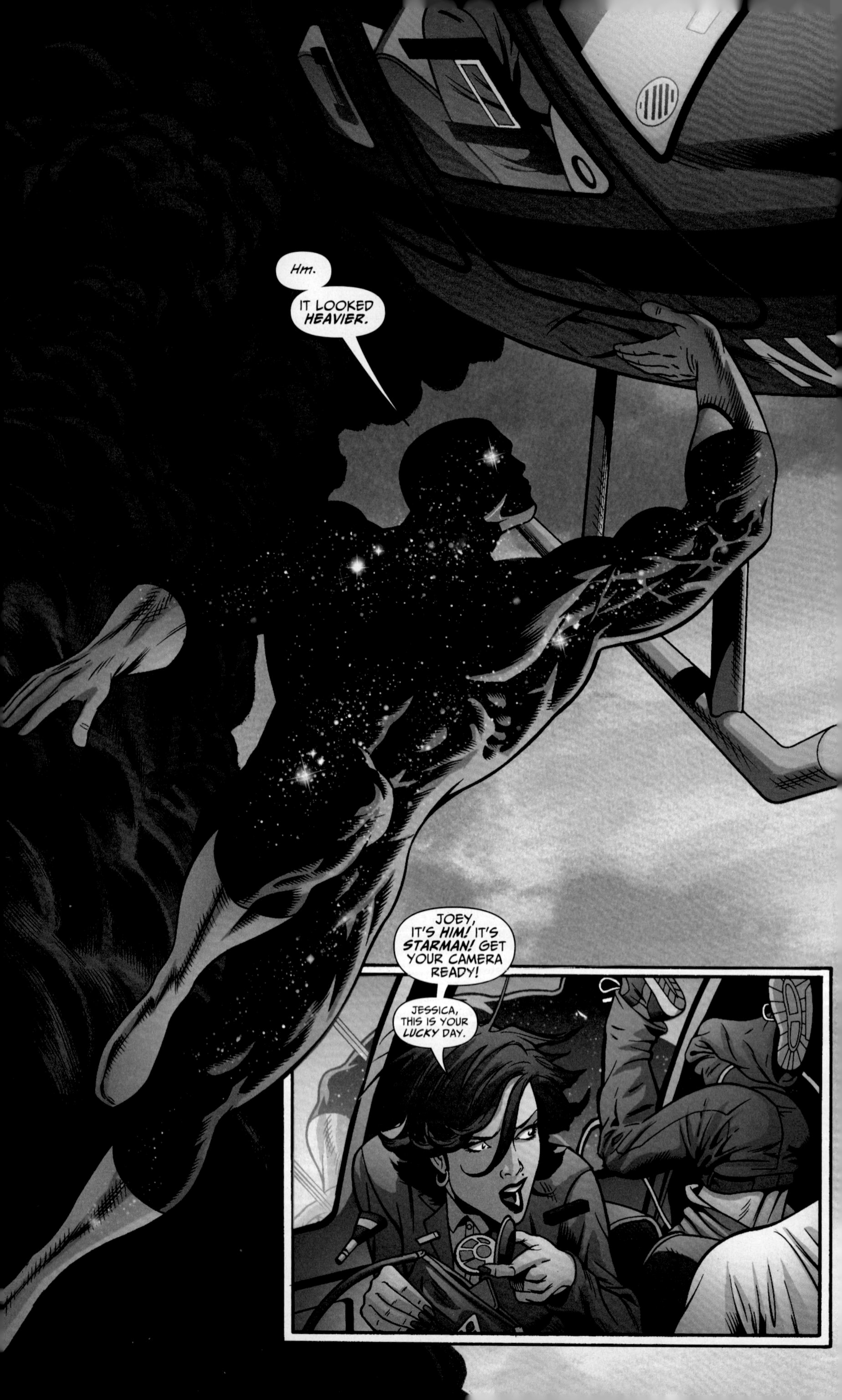
Hm.
IT LOOKED HEAVIER.
JOEY, IT'S HIM! IT'S STARMAN! GET YOUR CAMERA READY!
JESSICA, THIS IS YOUR LUCKY DAY.

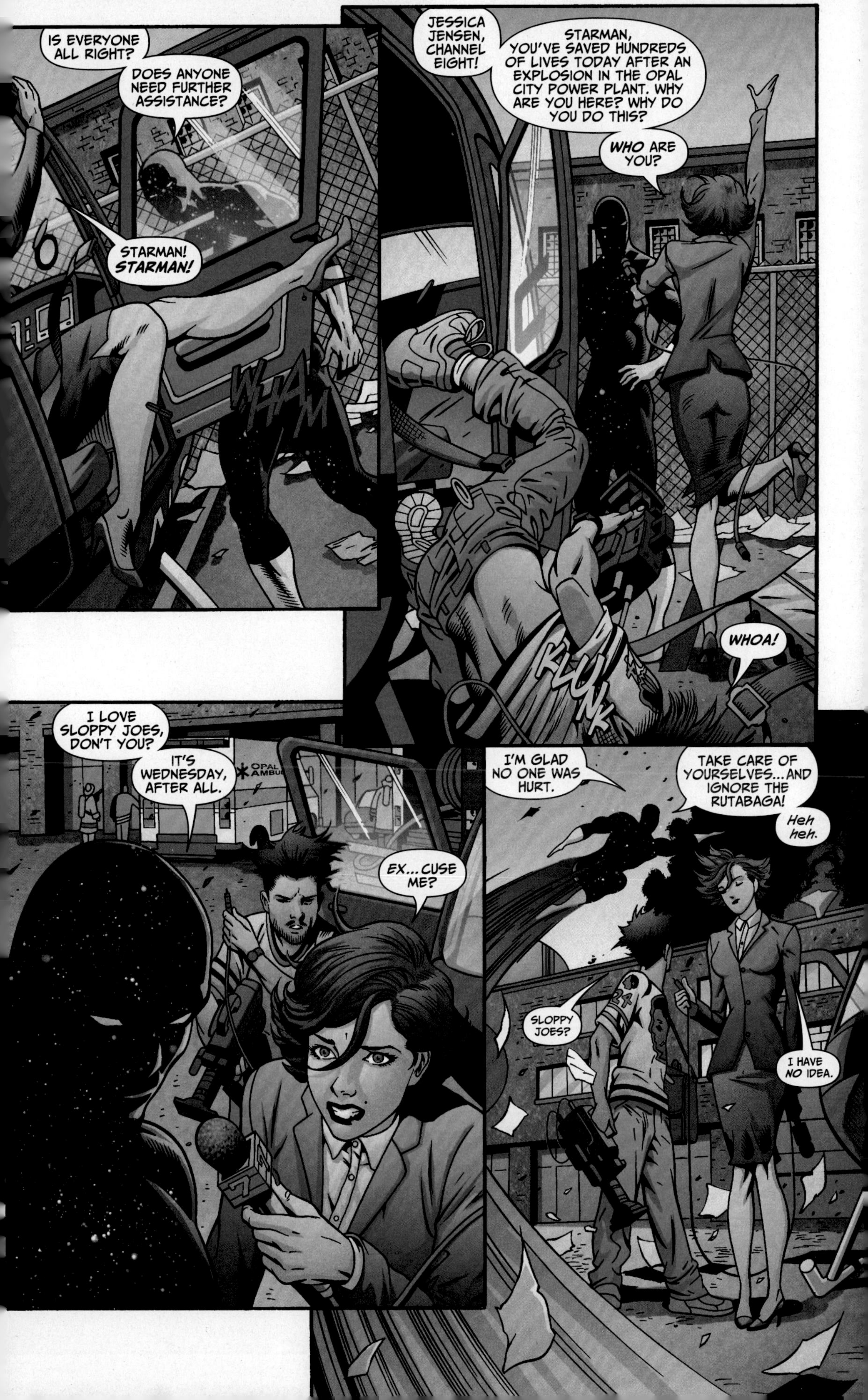
IS EVERYONE ALL RIGHT?
DOES ANYONE NEED FURTHER ASSISTANCE?
STARMAN! STARMAN!
WHAM
JESSICA JENSEN, CHANNEL EIGHT!
STARMAN, YOU'VE SAVED HUNDREDS OF LIVES TODAY AFTER AN EXPLOSION IN THE OPAL CITY POWER PLANT. WHY ARE YOU HERE? WHY DO YOU DO THIS?
WHO ARE YOU?
WHOA!
KLUNK
I LOVE SLOPPY JOES, DON'T YOU?
IT'S WEDNESDAY, AFTER ALL.
EX...CUSE ME?
I'M GLAD NO ONE WAS HURT.
TAKE CARE OF YOURSELVES...AND IGNORE THE RUTABAGA!
Heh heh.
SLOPPY JOES?
I HAVE NO IDEA.

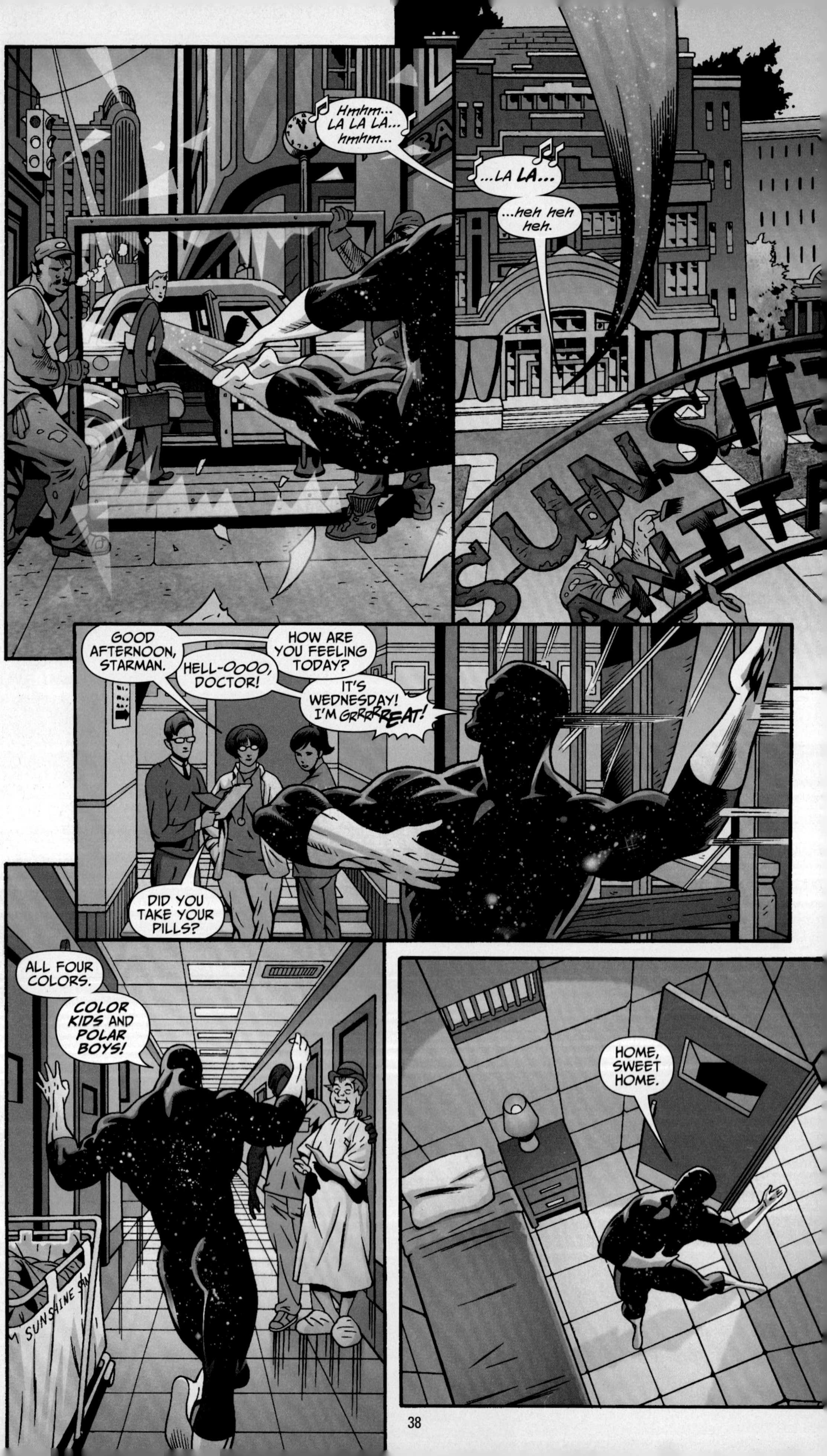
Hmhm... LA LA LA... hmhm...
...LA LA...
...heh heh heh.
SUNSHINE
GOOD AFTERNOON, STARMAN.
HELL-OOOO, DOCTOR!
HOW ARE YOU FEELING TODAY?
IT'S WEDNESDAY! I'M GRRRREAT!
DID YOU TAKE YOUR PILLS?
ALL FOUR COLORS.
COLOR KIDS AND POLAR BOYS!
SUNSHINE
HOME, SWEET HOME.

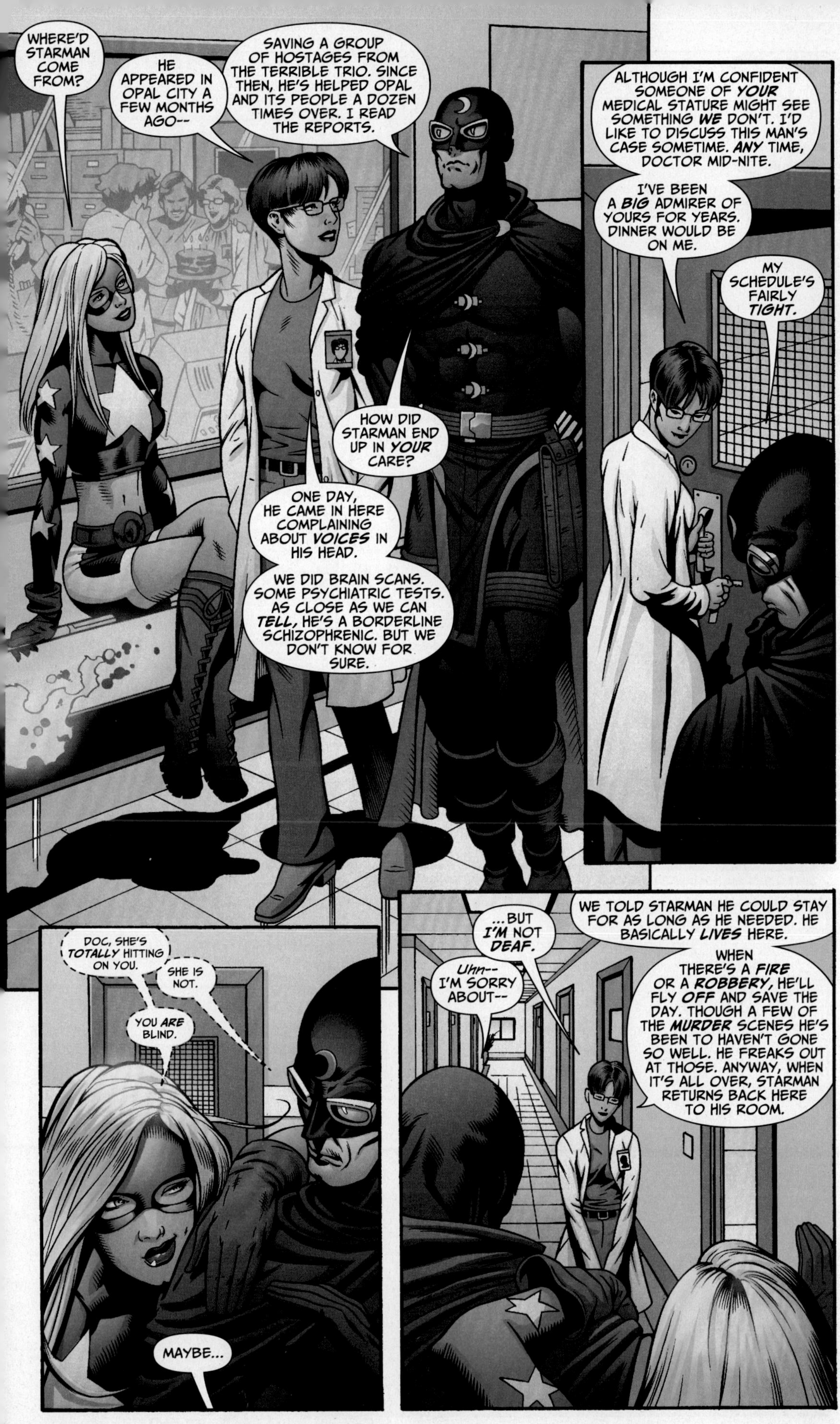
WHERE'D STARMAN COME FROM?
HE APPEARED IN OPAL CITY A FEW MONTHS AGO--
SAVING A GROUP OF HOSTAGES FROM THE TERRIBLE TRIO. SINCE THEN, HE'S HELPED OPAL AND ITS PEOPLE A DOZEN TIMES OVER. I READ THE REPORTS.
HOW DID STARMAN END UP IN YOUR CARE?
ONE DAY, HE CAME IN HERE COMPLAINING ABOUT VOICES IN HIS HEAD.
WE DID BRAIN SCANS. SOME PSYCHIATRIC TESTS. AS CLOSE AS WE CAN TELL, HE'S A BORDERLINE SCHIZOPHRENIC. BUT WE DON'T KNOW FOR SURE.
ALTHOUGH I'M CONFIDENT SOMEONE OF YOUR MEDICAL STATURE MIGHT SEE SOMETHING WE DON'T. I'D LIKE TO DISCUSS THIS MAN'S CASE SOMETIME. ANY TIME, DOCTOR MID-NITE.
I'VE BEEN A BIG ADMIRER OF YOURS FOR YEARS. DINNER WOULD BE ON ME.
MY SCHEDULE'S FAIRLY TIGHT.
DOC, SHE'S TOTALLY HITTING ON YOU.
SHE IS NOT.
YOU ARE BLIND.
MAYBE...
WE TOLD STARMAN HE COULD STAY FOR AS LONG AS HE NEEDED. HE BASICALLY LIVES HERE.
WHEN THERE'S A FIRE OR A ROBBERY, HE'LL FLY OFF AND SAVE THE DAY. THOUGH A FEW OF THE MURDER SCENES HE'S BEEN TO HAVEN'T GONE SO WELL. HE FREAKS OUT AT THOSE. ANYWAY, WHEN IT'S ALL OVER, STARMAN RETURNS BACK HERE TO HIS ROOM.
...BUT I'M NOT DEAF.
Uhn-- I'M SORRY ABOUT--

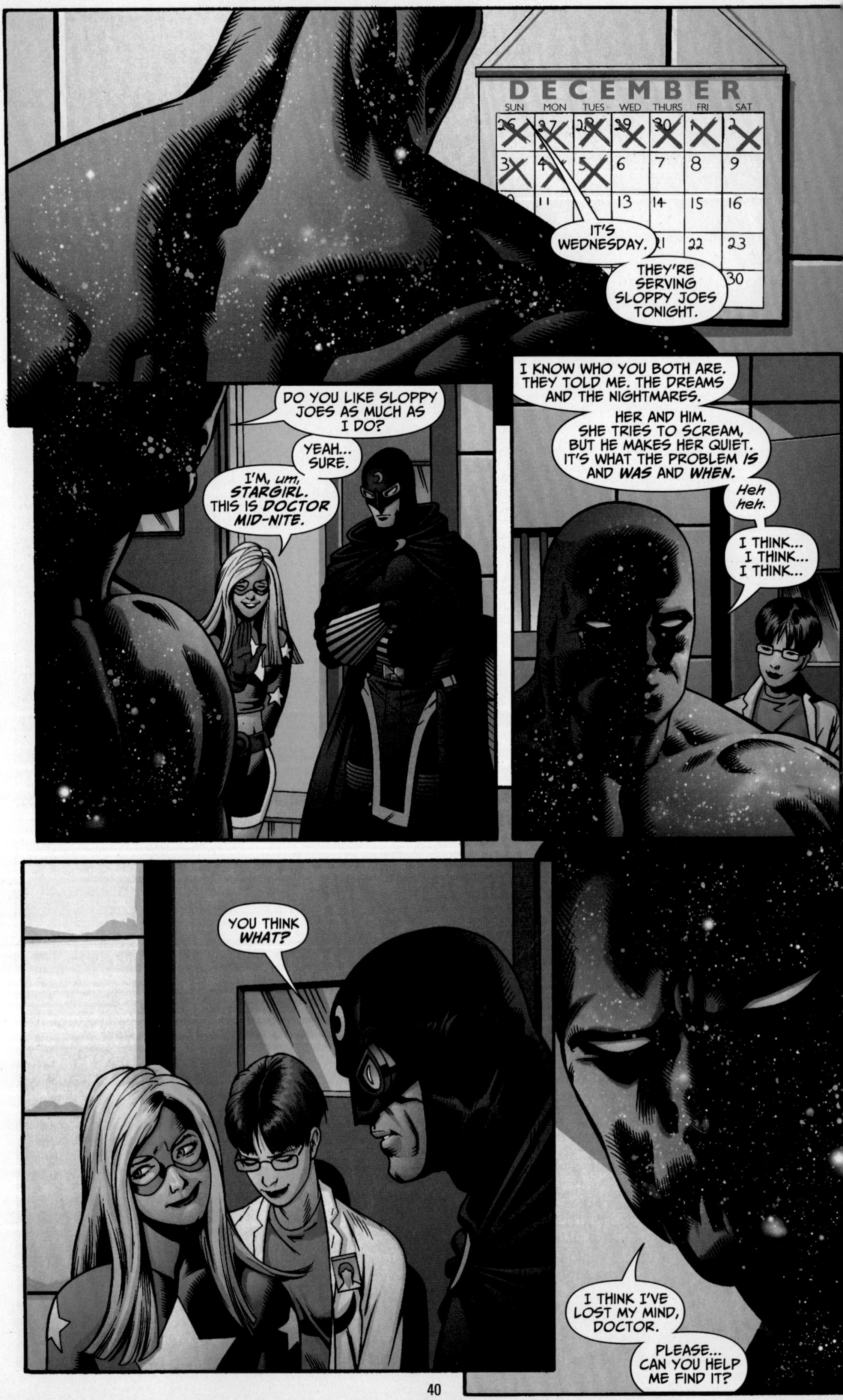
DECEMBER
SUN MON TUES WED THURS FRI SAT
IT'S WEDNESDAY.
THEY'RE SERVING SLOPPY JOES TONIGHT.
DO YOU LIKE SLOPPY JOES AS MUCH AS I DO?
YEAH... SURE.
I'M, *um*, **STARGIRL.** THIS IS **DOCTOR MID-NITE.**
I KNOW WHO YOU BOTH ARE. THEY TOLD ME. THE DREAMS AND THE NIGHTMARES.
HER AND HIM. SHE TRIES TO SCREAM, BUT HE MAKES HER QUIET. IT'S WHAT THE PROBLEM ***IS*** AND ***WAS*** AND ***WHEN.***
Heh heh.
I THINK... I THINK... I THINK...
YOU THINK ***WHAT?***
I THINK I'VE LOST MY MIND, DOCTOR.
PLEASE... CAN YOU HELP ME FIND IT?

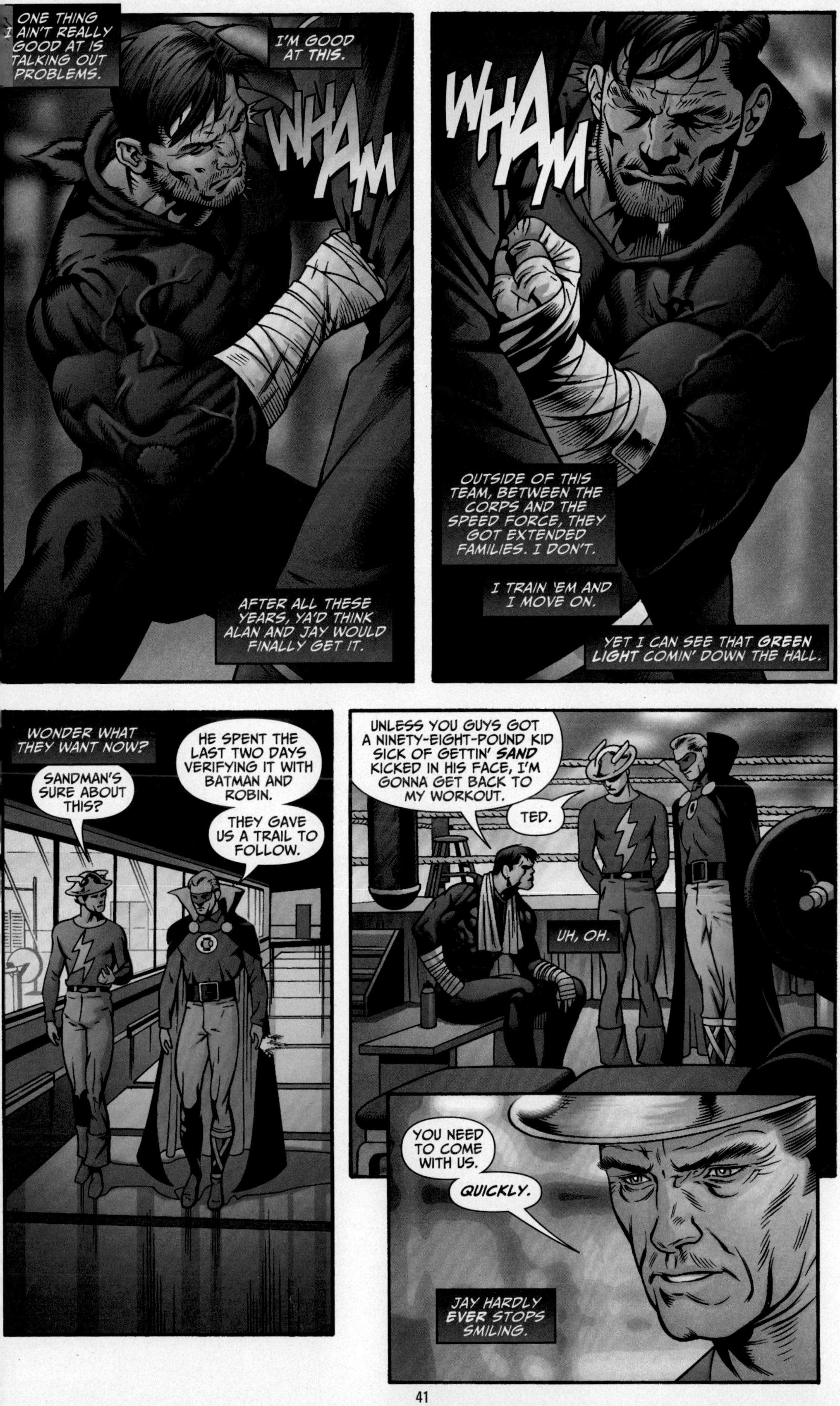
ONE THING I AIN'T REALLY GOOD AT IS TALKING OUT PROBLEMS.
I'M GOOD AT THIS.
WHAM
AFTER ALL THESE YEARS, YA'D THINK ALAN AND JAY WOULD FINALLY GET IT.
WHAM
OUTSIDE OF THIS TEAM, BETWEEN THE CORPS AND THE SPEED FORCE, THEY GOT EXTENDED FAMILIES. I DON'T.
I TRAIN 'EM AND I MOVE ON.
YET I CAN SEE THAT GREEN LIGHT COMIN' DOWN THE HALL.
WONDER WHAT THEY WANT NOW?
SANDMAN'S SURE ABOUT THIS?
HE SPENT THE LAST TWO DAYS VERIFYING IT WITH BATMAN AND ROBIN.
THEY GAVE US A TRAIL TO FOLLOW.
UNLESS YOU GUYS GOT A NINETY-EIGHT-POUND KID SICK OF GETTIN' SAND KICKED IN HIS FACE, I'M GONNA GET BACK TO MY WORKOUT.
TED.
UH, OH.
YOU NEED TO COME WITH US.
QUICKLY.
JAY HARDLY EVER STOPS SMILING.

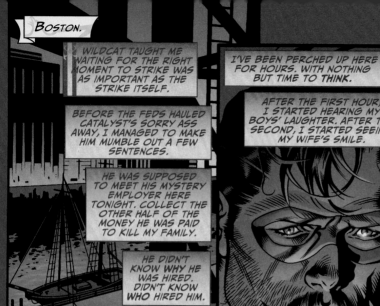

BOSTON.

WILDCAT TAUGHT ME WAITING FOR THE RIGHT MOMENT TO STRIKE WAS AS IMPORTANT AS THE STRIKE ITSELF.

BEFORE THE FEDS HAULED CATALYST'S SORRY ASS AWAY, I MANAGED TO MAKE HIM MUMBLE OUT A FEW SENTENCES.

HE WAS SUPPOSED TO MEET HIS MYSTERY EMPLOYER HERE TONIGHT. COLLECT THE OTHER HALF OF THE MONEY HE WAS PAID TO KILL MY FAMILY.

HE DIDN'T KNOW WHY HE WAS HIRED. DIDN'T KNOW WHO HIRED HIM.

I'VE BEEN PERCHED UP HERE FOR HOURS. WITH NOTHING BUT TIME TO THINK.

AFTER THE FIRST HOUR, I STARTED HEARING MY BOYS' LAUGHTER. AFTER THE SECOND, I STARTED SEEING MY WIFE'S SMILE.

MY EYES AND EARS ARE PLAYING TRICKS ON ME.

MY GOD...

...THEY'RE REALLY GONE.

GOOD EVENING, THOMPSON.

I'M ALONE.

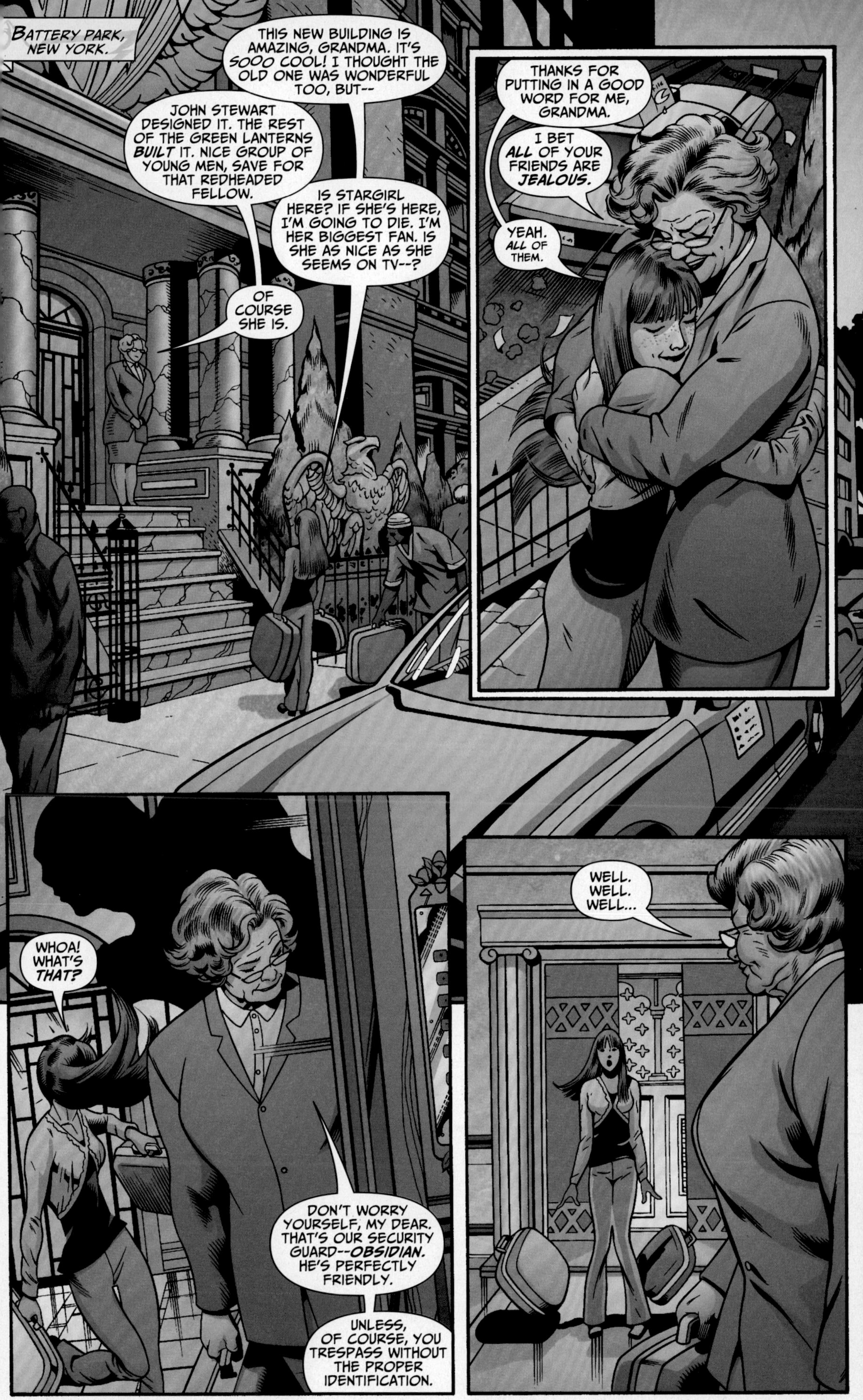
BATTERY PARK, NEW YORK.
THIS NEW BUILDING IS AMAZING, GRANDMA. IT'S SOOO COOL! I THOUGHT THE OLD ONE WAS WONDERFUL TOO, BUT--
JOHN STEWART DESIGNED IT. THE REST OF THE GREEN LANTERNS BUILT IT. NICE GROUP OF YOUNG MEN, SAVE FOR THAT REDHEADED FELLOW.
IS STARGIRL HERE? IF SHE'S HERE, I'M GOING TO DIE. I'M HER BIGGEST FAN. IS SHE AS NICE AS SHE SEEMS ON TV--?
OF COURSE SHE IS.
THANKS FOR PUTTING IN A GOOD WORD FOR ME, GRANDMA.
I BET ALL OF YOUR FRIENDS ARE JEALOUS.
YEAH. ALL OF THEM.
WHOA! WHAT'S THAT?
DON'T WORRY YOURSELF, MY DEAR. THAT'S OUR SECURITY GUARD--OBSIDIAN. HE'S PERFECTLY FRIENDLY.
UNLESS, OF COURSE, YOU TRESPASS WITHOUT THE PROPER IDENTIFICATION.
WELL. WELL. WELL...

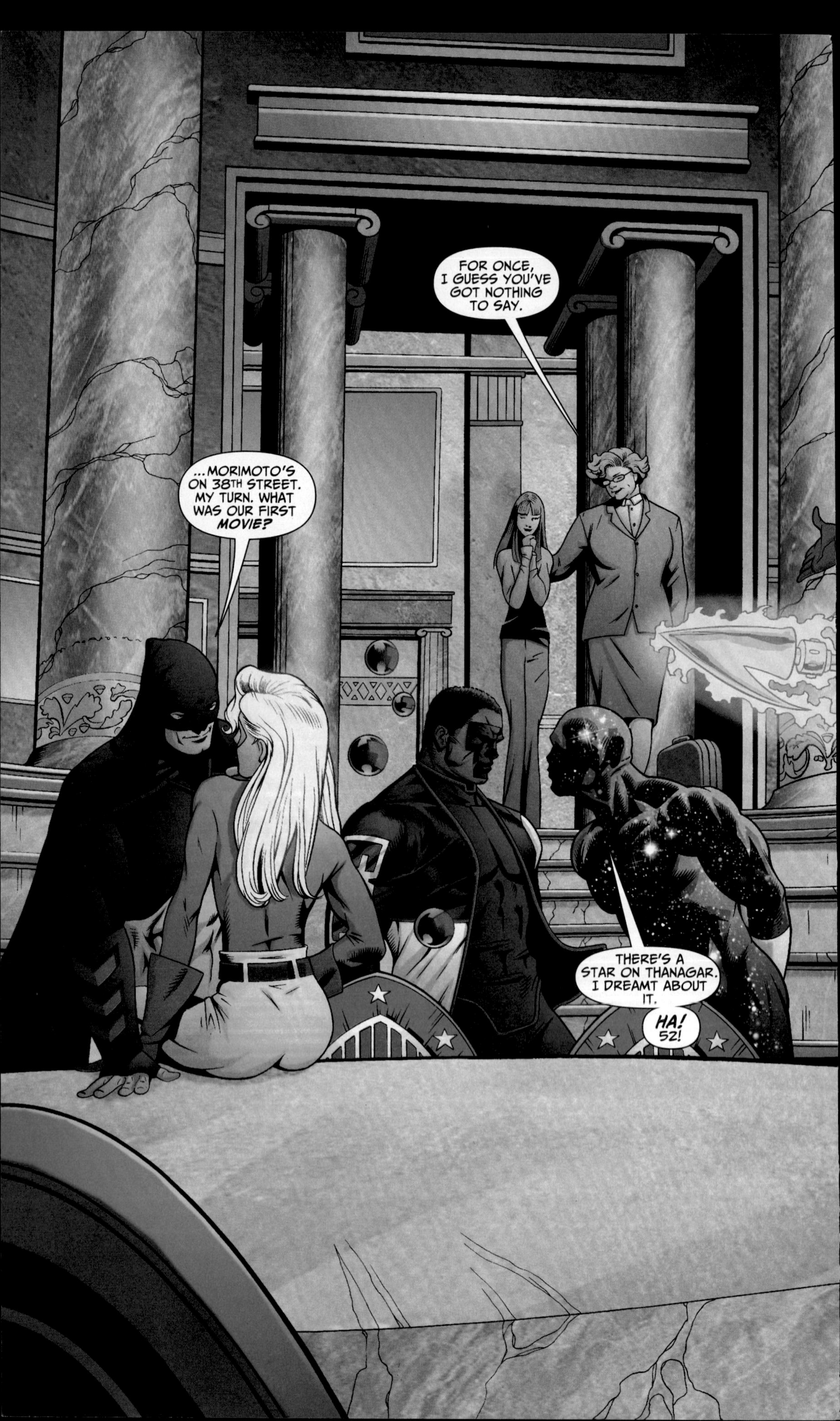
FOR ONCE, I GUESS YOU'VE GOT NOTHING TO SAY.
...MORIMOTO'S ON 38TH STREET. MY TURN. WHAT WAS OUR FIRST *MOVIE?*
THERE'S A STAR ON THANAGAR. I DREAMT ABOUT IT.
HA! 52!

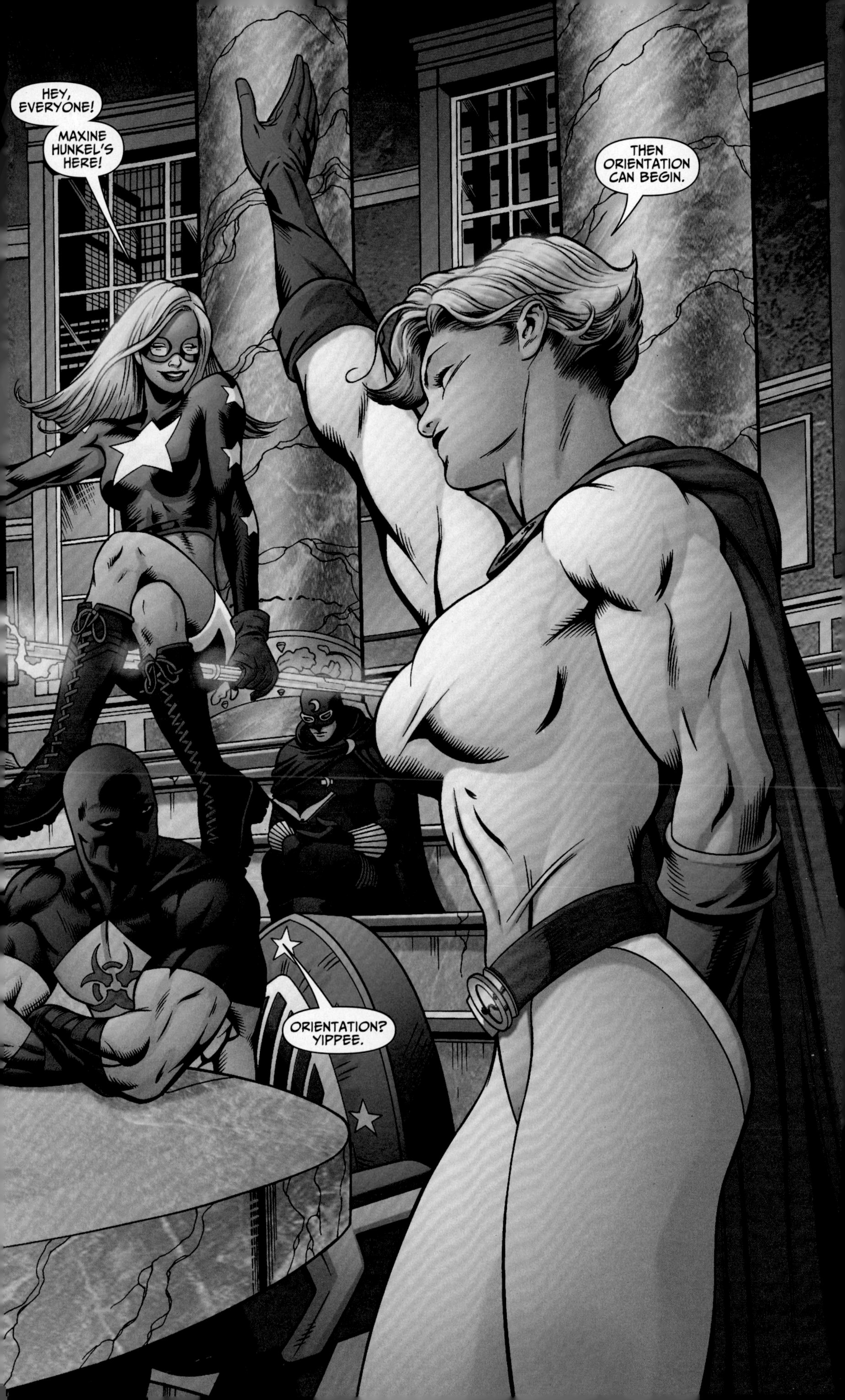
HEY, EVERYONE!
MAXINE HUNKEL'S HERE!
THEN ORIENTATION CAN BEGIN.
ORIENTATION? YIPPEE.

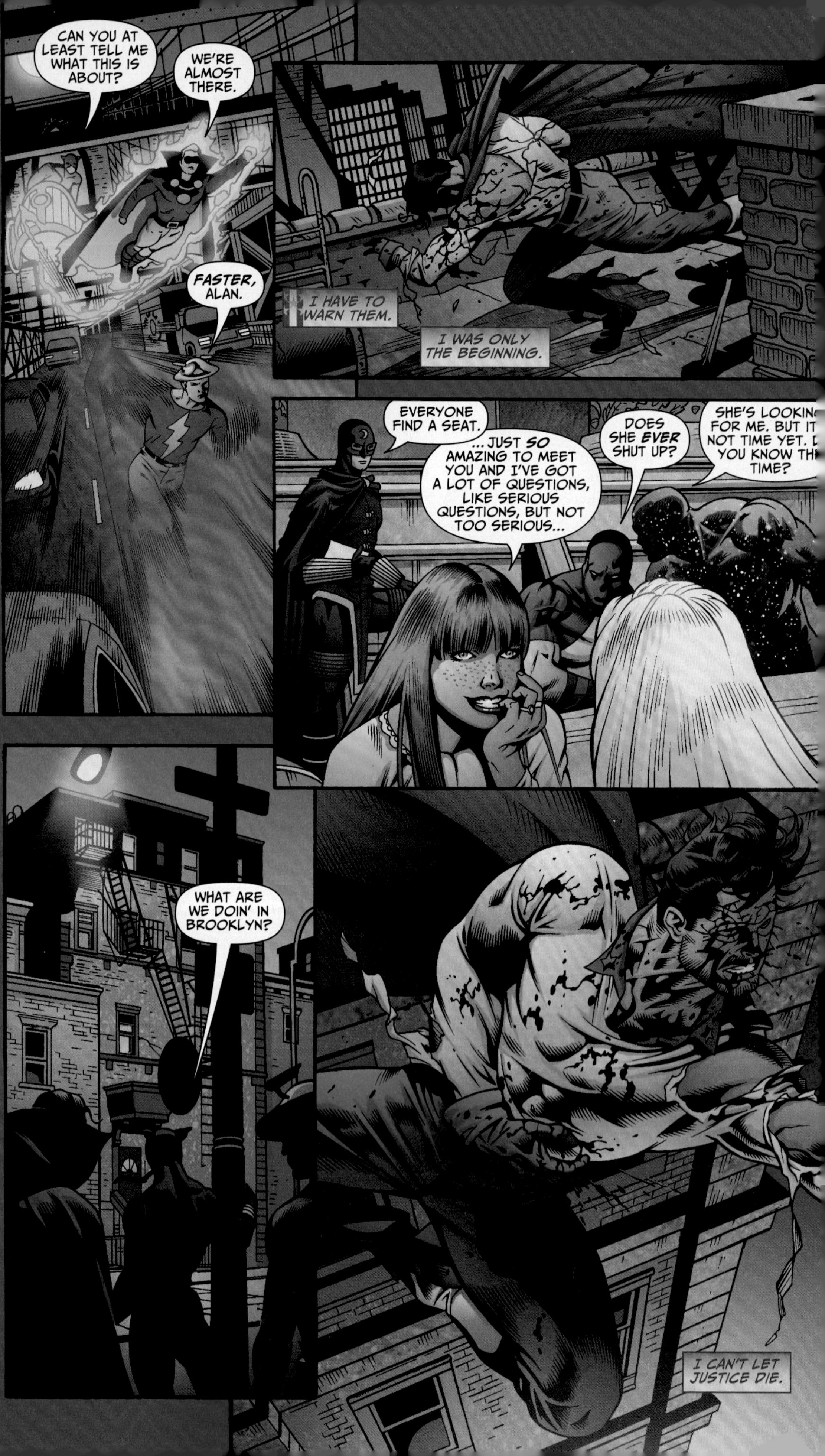
CAN YOU AT LEAST TELL ME WHAT THIS IS ABOUT?
WE'RE ALMOST THERE.
FASTER, ALAN.
I HAVE TO WARN THEM.
I WAS ONLY THE BEGINNING.
EVERYONE FIND A SEAT.
...JUST SO AMAZING TO MEET YOU AND I'VE GOT A LOT OF QUESTIONS, LIKE SERIOUS QUESTIONS, BUT NOT TOO SERIOUS...
DOES SHE EVER SHUT UP?
SHE'S LOOKIN FOR ME. BUT IT NOT TIME YET. YOU KNOW TH TIME?
WHAT ARE WE DOIN' IN BROOKLYN?
I CAN'T LET JUSTICE DIE.

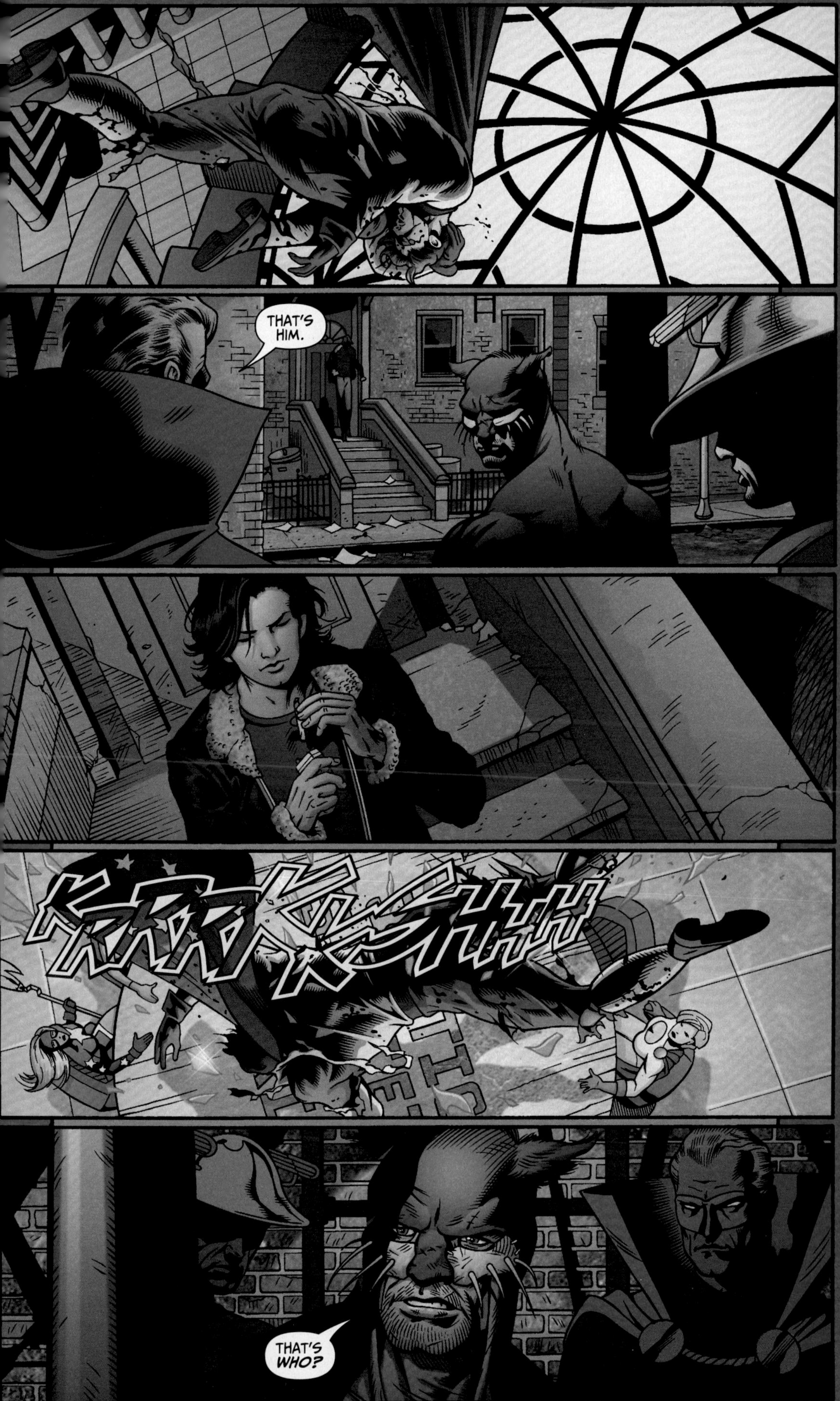
THAT'S HIM.
KRRRKKSHHH
THAT'S WHO?

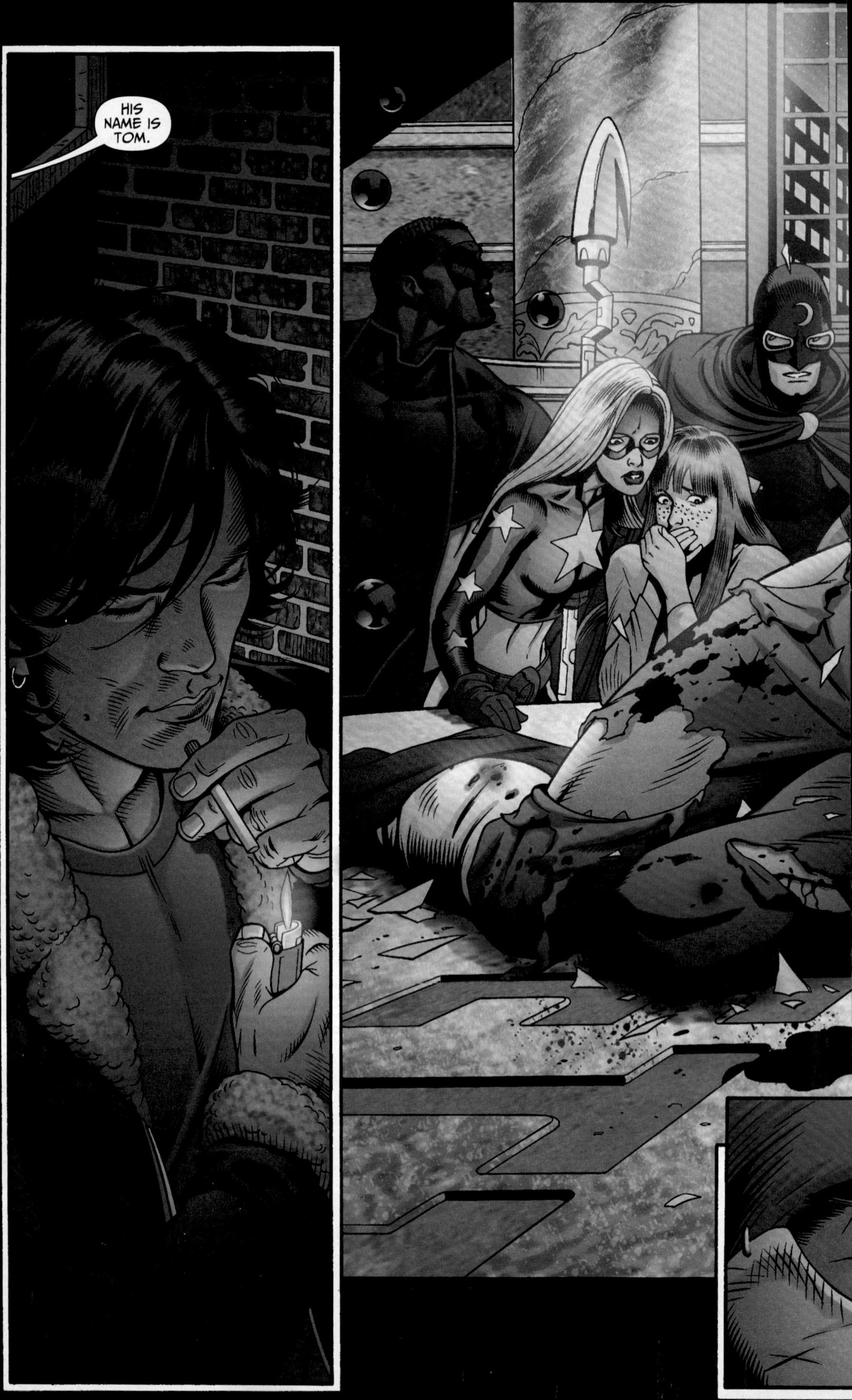
HIS NAME IS TOM.

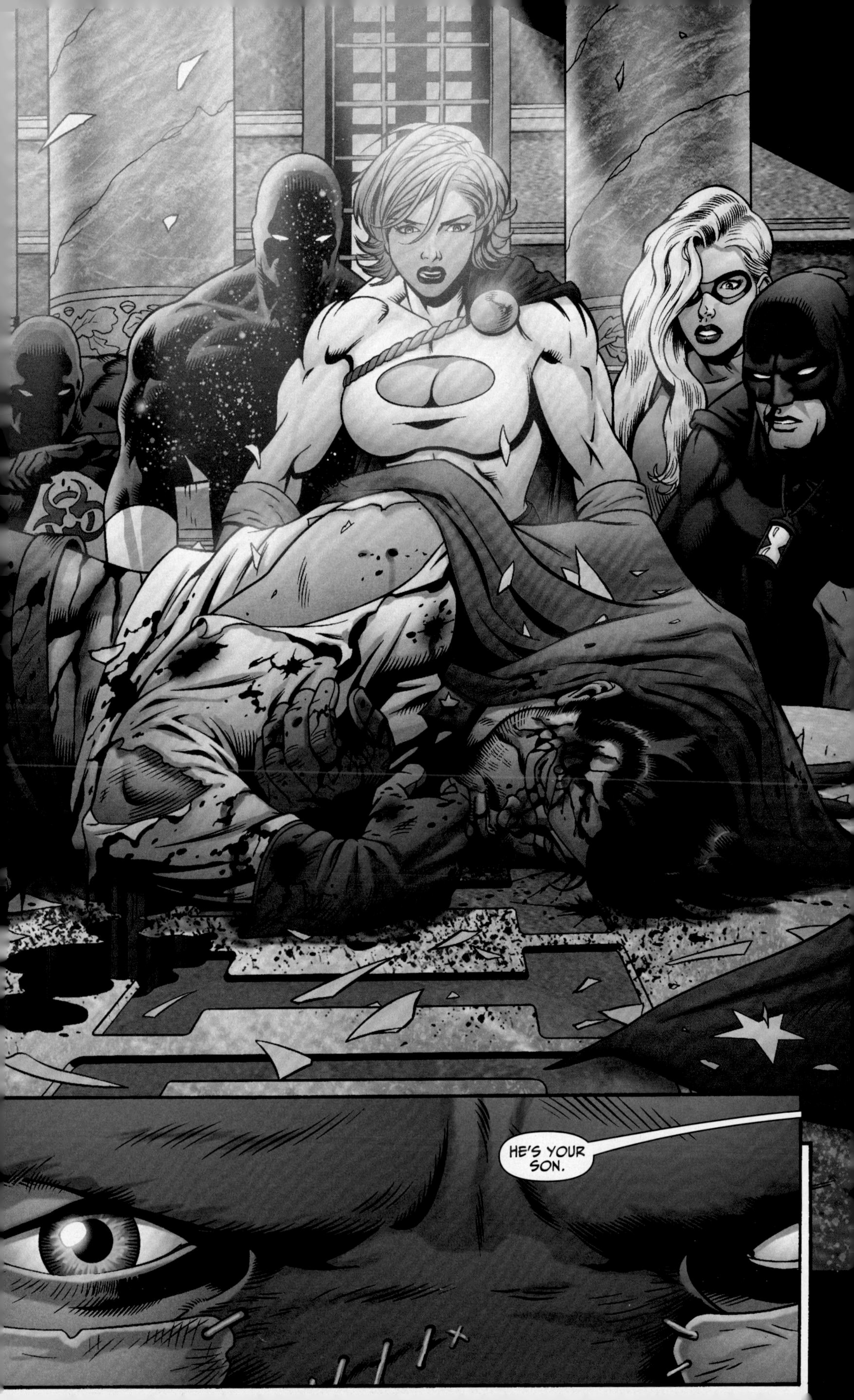
HE'S YOUR SON.

JUSTICE SOCIETY OF AMERICA
of AMERICA

THE NEXT AGE

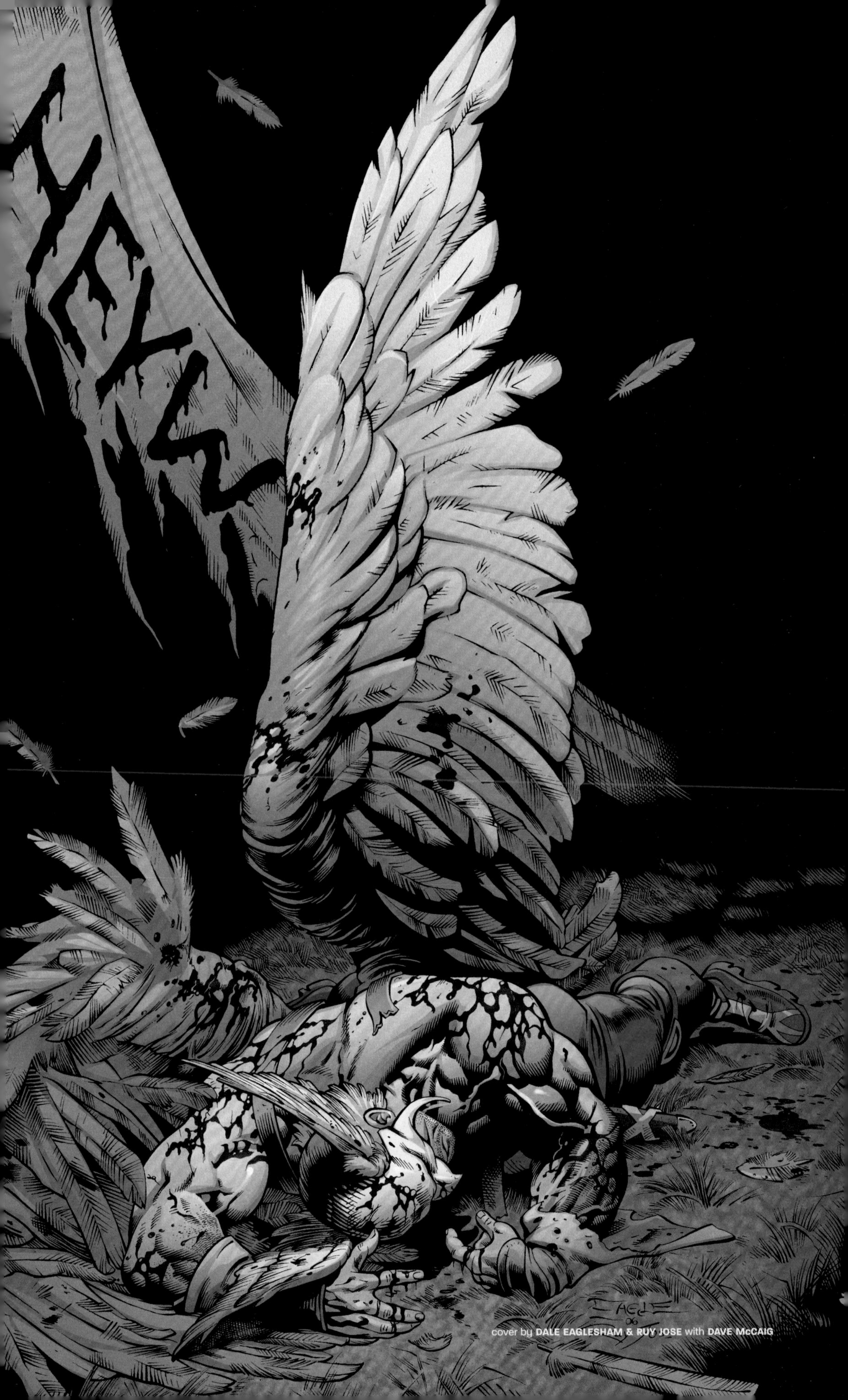

cover by **DALE EAGLESHAM & RUY JOSE** with **DAVE McCAIG**

THE NEXT AGE

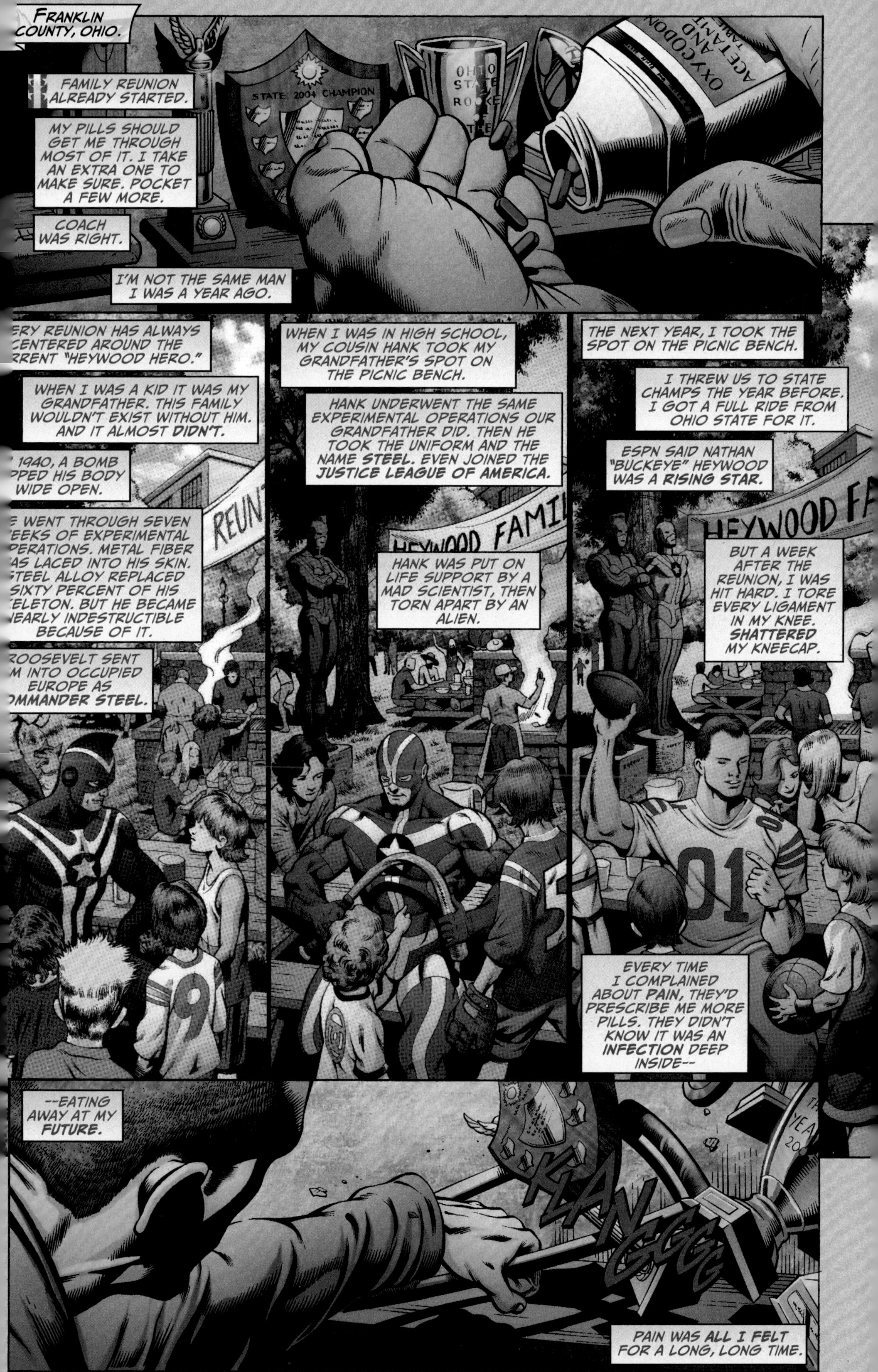

FRANKLIN COUNTY, OHIO.
FAMILY REUNION ALREADY STARTED.
MY PILLS SHOULD GET ME THROUGH MOST OF IT. I TAKE AN EXTRA ONE TO MAKE SURE. POCKET A FEW MORE.
COACH WAS RIGHT.
I'M NOT THE SAME MAN I WAS A YEAR AGO.
STATE 2004 CHAMPION
OHIO STATE
OXYCODON
ERY REUNION HAS ALWAYS CENTERED AROUND THE RRENT "HEYWOOD HERO."
WHEN I WAS A KID IT WAS MY GRANDFATHER. THIS FAMILY WOULDN'T EXIST WITHOUT HIM. AND IT ALMOST DIDN'T.
1940, A BOMB PPED HIS BODY WIDE OPEN.
E WENT THROUGH SEVEN EEKS OF EXPERIMENTAL PERATIONS. METAL FIBER AS LACED INTO HIS SKIN. STEEL ALLOY REPLACED SIXTY PERCENT OF HIS KELETON. BUT HE BECAME NEARLY INDESTRUCTIBLE BECAUSE OF IT.
ROOSEVELT SENT M INTO OCCUPIED EUROPE AS OMMANDER STEEL.
REUN
WHEN I WAS IN HIGH SCHOOL, MY COUSIN HANK TOOK MY GRANDFATHER'S SPOT ON THE PICNIC BENCH.
HANK UNDERWENT THE SAME EXPERIMENTAL OPERATIONS OUR GRANDFATHER DID. THEN HE TOOK THE UNIFORM AND THE NAME STEEL. EVEN JOINED THE JUSTICE LEAGUE OF AMERICA.
HEYWOOD FAMI
HANK WAS PUT ON LIFE SUPPORT BY A MAD SCIENTIST, THEN TORN APART BY AN ALIEN.
THE NEXT YEAR, I TOOK THE SPOT ON THE PICNIC BENCH.
I THREW US TO STATE CHAMPS THE YEAR BEFORE. I GOT A FULL RIDE FROM OHIO STATE FOR IT.
ESPN SAID NATHAN "BUCKEYE" HEYWOOD WAS A RISING STAR.
HEYWOOD FA
BUT A WEEK AFTER THE REUNION, I WAS HIT HARD. I TORE EVERY LIGAMENT IN MY KNEE. SHATTERED MY KNEECAP.
01
EVERY TIME I COMPLAINED ABOUT PAIN, THEY'D PRESCRIBE ME MORE PILLS. THEY DIDN'T KNOW IT WAS AN INFECTION DEEP INSIDE--
--EATING AWAY AT MY FUTURE.
KLANGGG
PAIN WAS ALL I FELT FOR A LONG, LONG TIME.

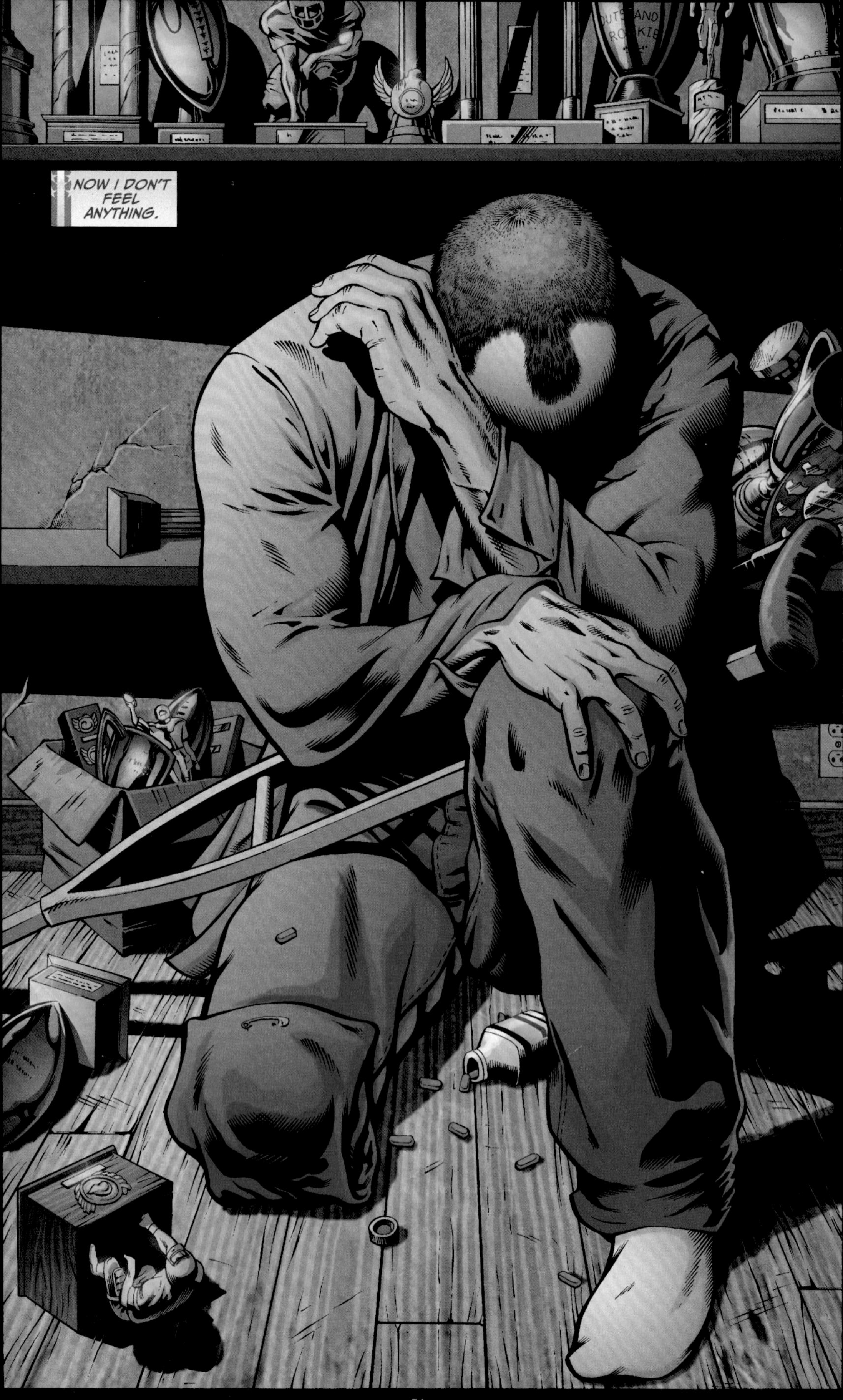
NOW I DON'T FEEL ANYTHING.

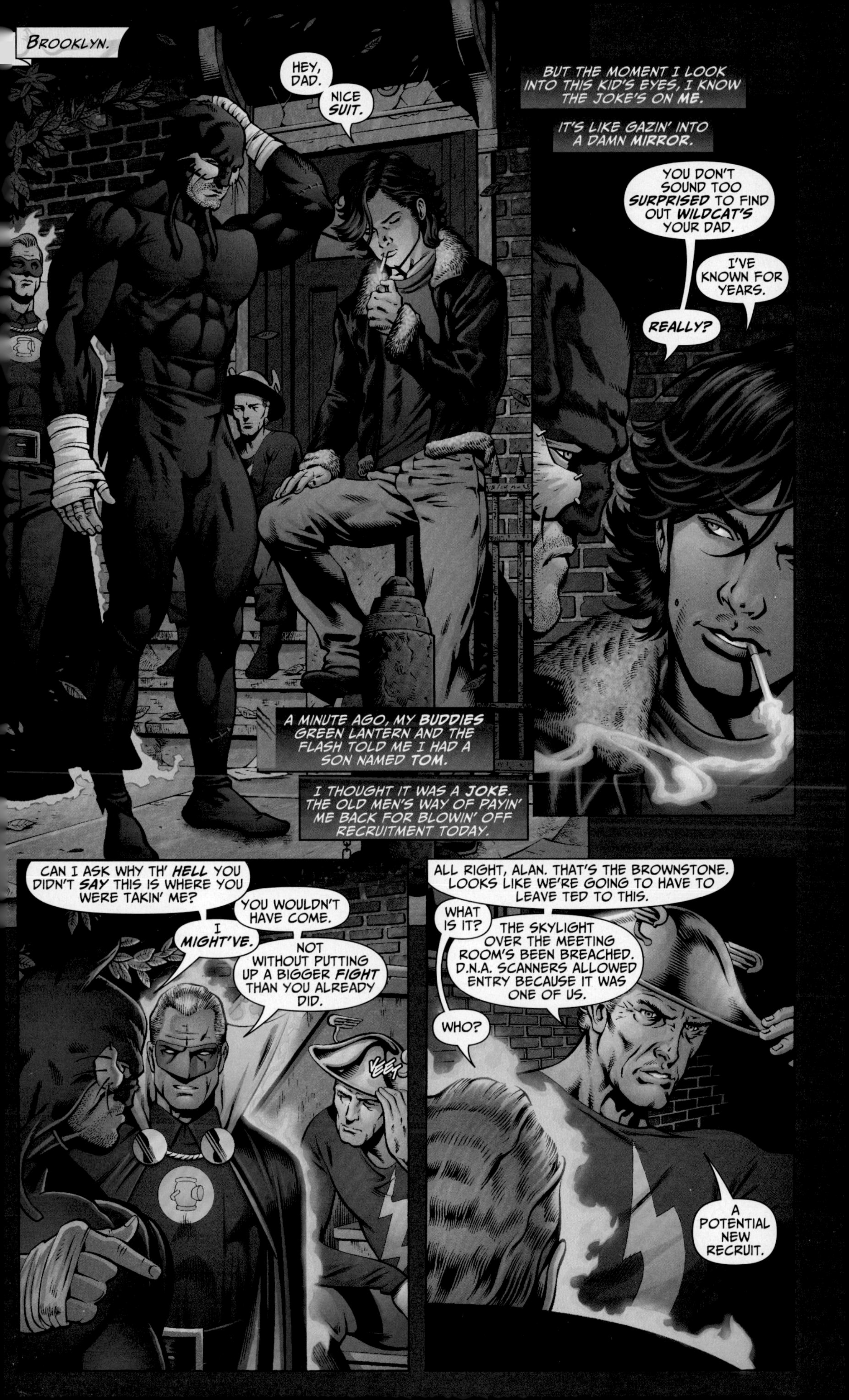
BROOKLYN.
HEY, DAD.
NICE SUIT.
A MINUTE AGO, MY BUDDIES GREEN LANTERN AND THE FLASH TOLD ME I HAD A SON NAMED TOM.
I THOUGHT IT WAS A JOKE. THE OLD MEN'S WAY OF PAYIN' ME BACK FOR BLOWIN' OFF RECRUITMENT TODAY.
BUT THE MOMENT I LOOK INTO THIS KID'S EYES, I KNOW THE JOKE'S ON ME.
IT'S LIKE GAZIN' INTO A DAMN MIRROR.
YOU DON'T SOUND TOO SURPRISED TO FIND OUT WILDCAT'S YOUR DAD.
I'VE KNOWN FOR YEARS.
REALLY?
CAN I ASK WHY TH' HELL YOU DIDN'T SAY THIS IS WHERE YOU WERE TAKIN' ME?
YOU WOULDN'T HAVE COME.
I MIGHT'VE.
NOT WITHOUT PUTTING UP A BIGGER FIGHT THAN YOU ALREADY DID.
VEEV
ALL RIGHT, ALAN. THAT'S THE BROWNSTONE. LOOKS LIKE WE'RE GOING TO HAVE TO LEAVE TED TO THIS.
WHAT IS IT?
THE SKYLIGHT OVER THE MEETING ROOM'S BEEN BREACHED. D.N.A. SCANNERS ALLOWED ENTRY BECAUSE IT WAS ONE OF US.
WHO?
A POTENTIAL NEW RECRUIT.

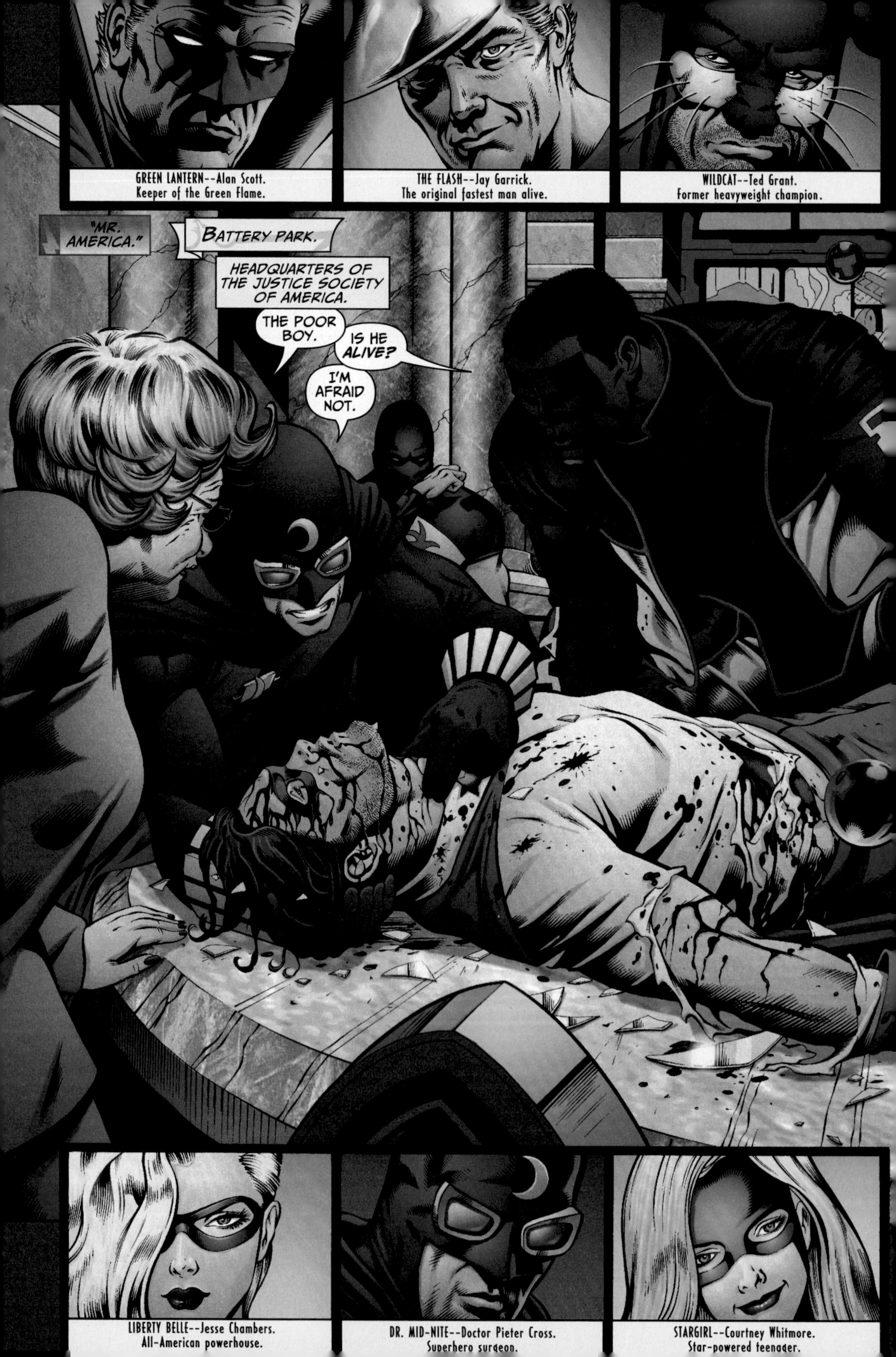
GREEN LANTERN--Alan Scott.
Keeper of the Green Flame.
THE FLASH--Jay Garrick.
The original fastest man alive.
WILDCAT--Ted Grant.
Former heavyweight champion.
"MR. AMERICA."
BATTERY PARK.
HEADQUARTERS OF THE JUSTICE SOCIETY OF AMERICA.
THE POOR BOY.
IS HE ALIVE?
I'M AFRAID NOT.
LIBERTY BELLE--Jesse Chambers.
All-American powerhouse.
DR. MID-NITE--Doctor Pieter Cross.
Superhero surgeon.
STARGIRL--Courtney Whitmore.
Star-powered teenager.

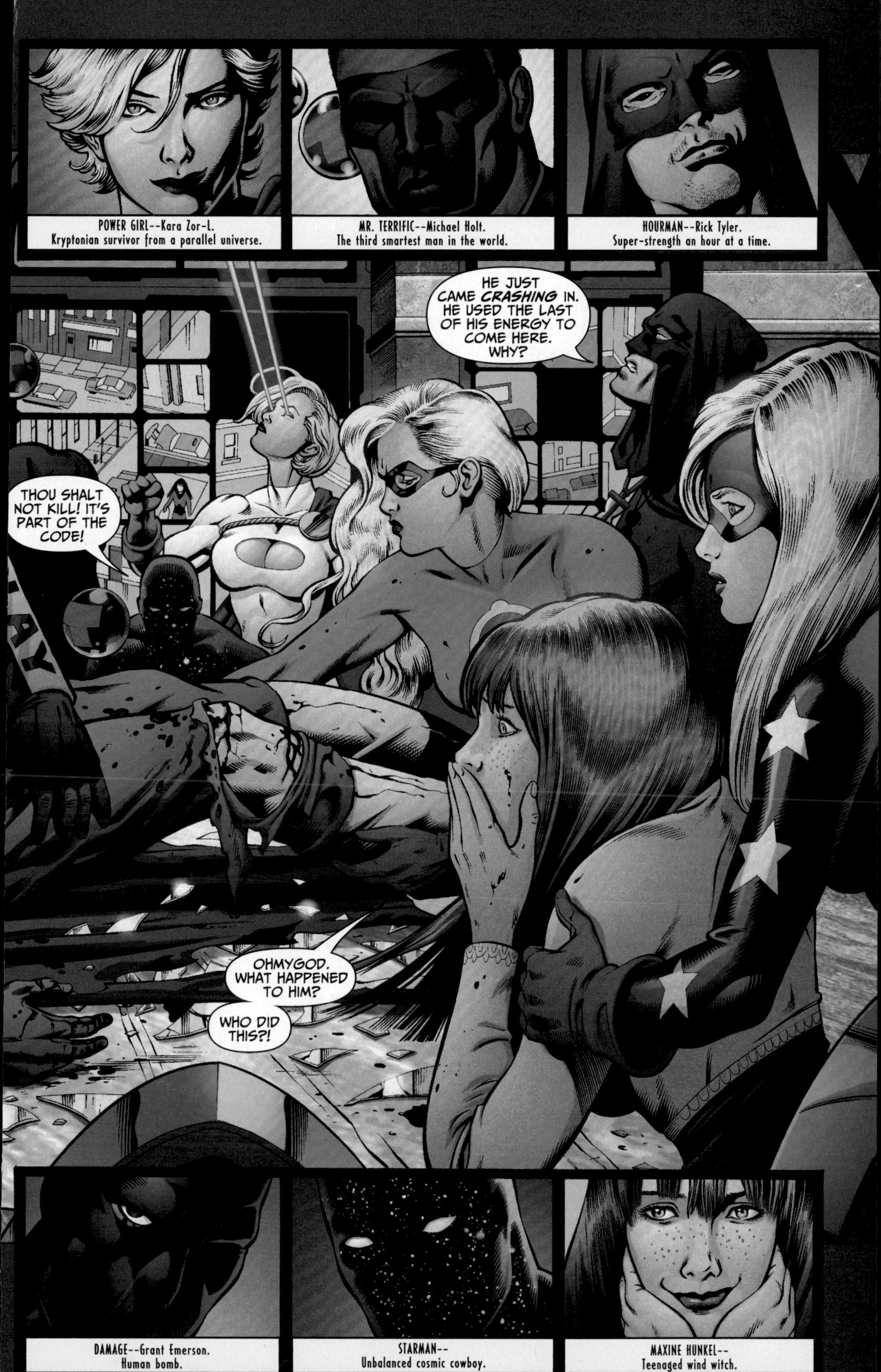
POWER GIRL--Kara Zor-L.
Kryptonian survivor from a parallel universe.
MR. TERRIFIC--Michael Holt.
The third smartest man in the world.
HOURMAN--Rick Tyler.
Super-strength an hour at a time.
HE JUST CAME CRASHING IN. HE USED THE LAST OF HIS ENERGY TO COME HERE. WHY?
THOU SHALT NOT KILL! IT'S PART OF THE CODE!
OHMYGOD. WHAT HAPPENED TO HIM?
WHO DID THIS?!
DAMAGE--Grant Emerson.
Human bomb.
STARMAN--
Unbalanced cosmic cowboy.
MAXINE HUNKEL--
Teenaged wind witch.

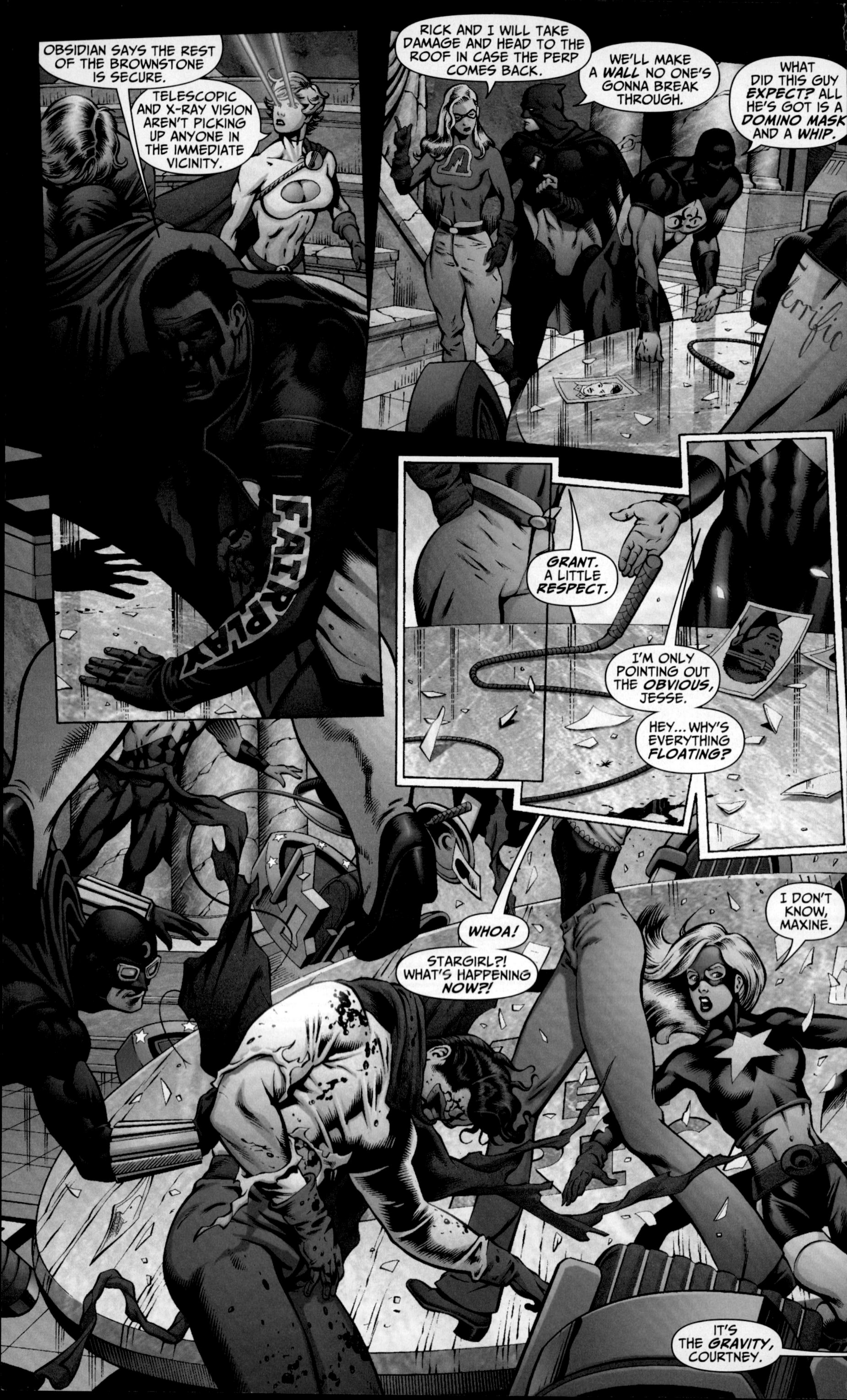

OBSIDIAN SAYS THE REST OF THE BROWNSTONE IS SECURE.
TELESCOPIC AND X-RAY VISION AREN'T PICKING UP ANYONE IN THE IMMEDIATE VICINITY.
RICK AND I WILL TAKE DAMAGE AND HEAD TO THE ROOF IN CASE THE PERP COMES BACK.
WE'LL MAKE A WALL NO ONE'S GONNA BREAK THROUGH.
WHAT DID THIS GUY EXPECT? ALL HE'S GOT IS A DOMINO MASK AND A WHIP.
FAIRPLAY
GRANT. A LITTLE RESPECT.
I'M ONLY POINTING OUT THE OBVIOUS, JESSE.
HEY... WHY'S EVERYTHING FLOATING?
WHOA!
STARGIRL?! WHAT'S HAPPENING NOW?!
I DON'T KNOW, MAXINE.
IT'S THE GRAVITY, COURTNEY.

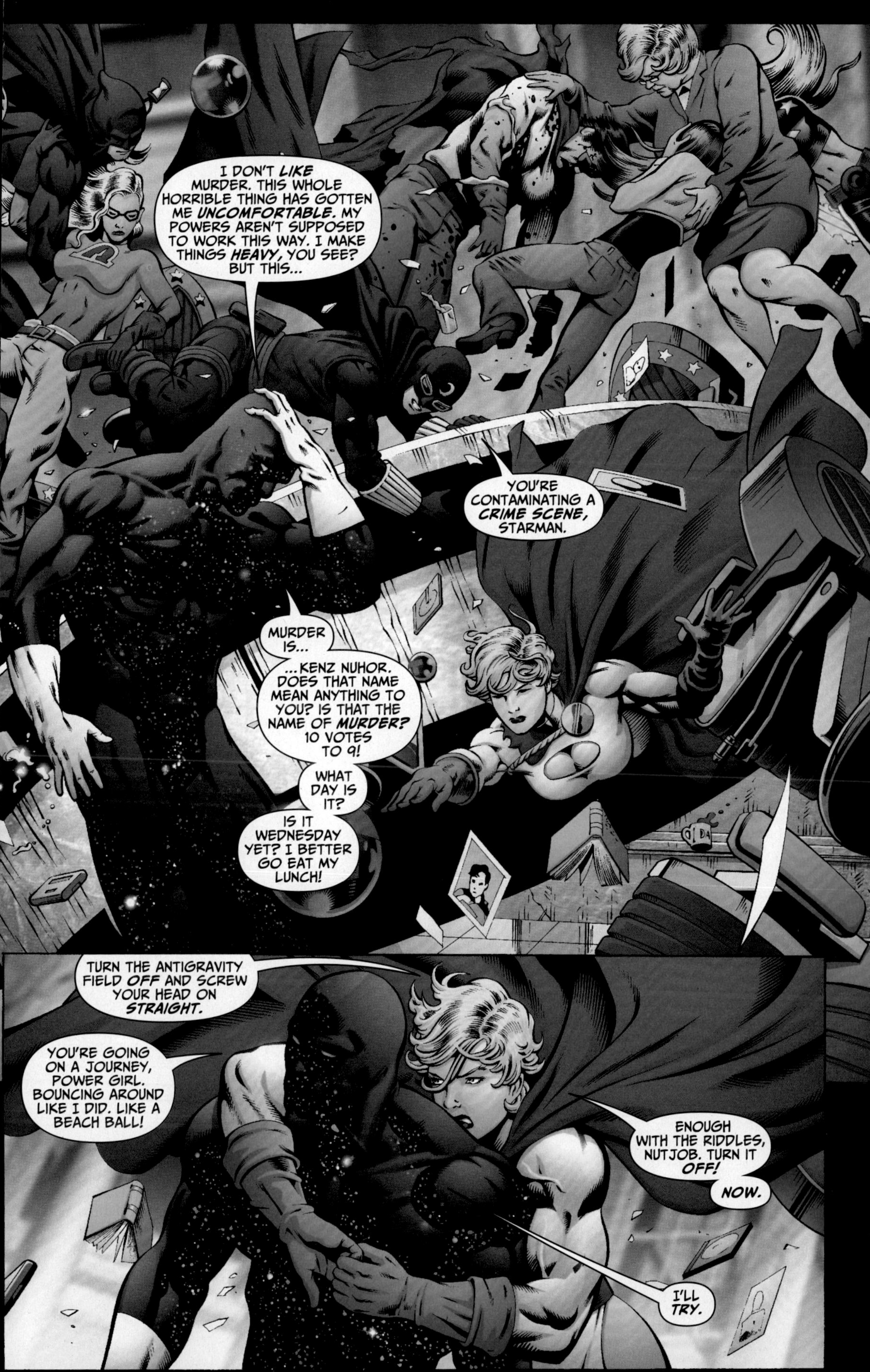

I DON'T *LIKE* MURDER. THIS WHOLE HORRIBLE THING HAS GOTTEN ME *UNCOMFORTABLE.* MY POWERS AREN'T SUPPOSED TO WORK THIS WAY. I MAKE THINGS *HEAVY,* YOU SEE? BUT THIS...
YOU'RE CONTAMINATING A *CRIME SCENE,* STARMAN.
MURDER IS...
...KENZ NUHOR. DOES THAT NAME MEAN ANYTHING TO YOU? IS THAT THE NAME OF *MURDER?* 10 VOTES TO 9!
WHAT DAY IS IT?
IS IT WEDNESDAY YET? I BETTER GO EAT MY LUNCH!
TURN THE ANTIGRAVITY FIELD *OFF* AND SCREW YOUR HEAD ON *STRAIGHT.*
YOU'RE GOING ON A JOURNEY, POWER GIRL. BOUNCING AROUND LIKE I DID. LIKE A BEACH BALL!
ENOUGH WITH THE RIDDLES, NUTJOB. TURN IT *OFF!*
NOW.
I'LL *TRY.*

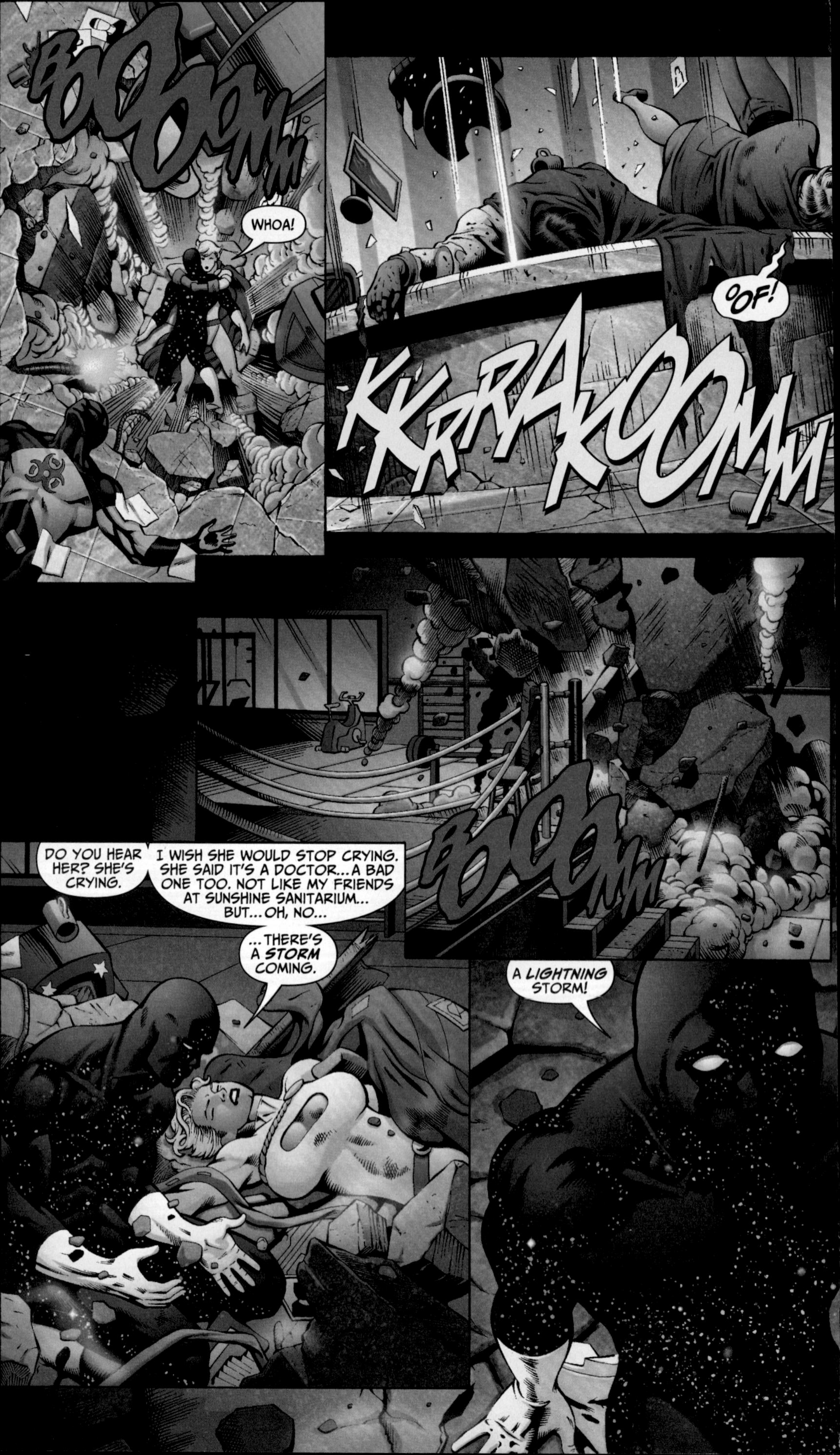
BOOOOMM
WHOA!
OOF!
KRRRAKOOMM
BOOOMM
DO YOU HEAR HER? SHE'S CRYING.
I WISH SHE WOULD STOP CRYING. SHE SAID IT'S A DOCTOR... A BAD ONE TOO. NOT LIKE MY FRIENDS AT SUNSHINE SANITARIUM... BUT... OH, NO...
...THERE'S A STORM COMING.
A LIGHTNING STORM!

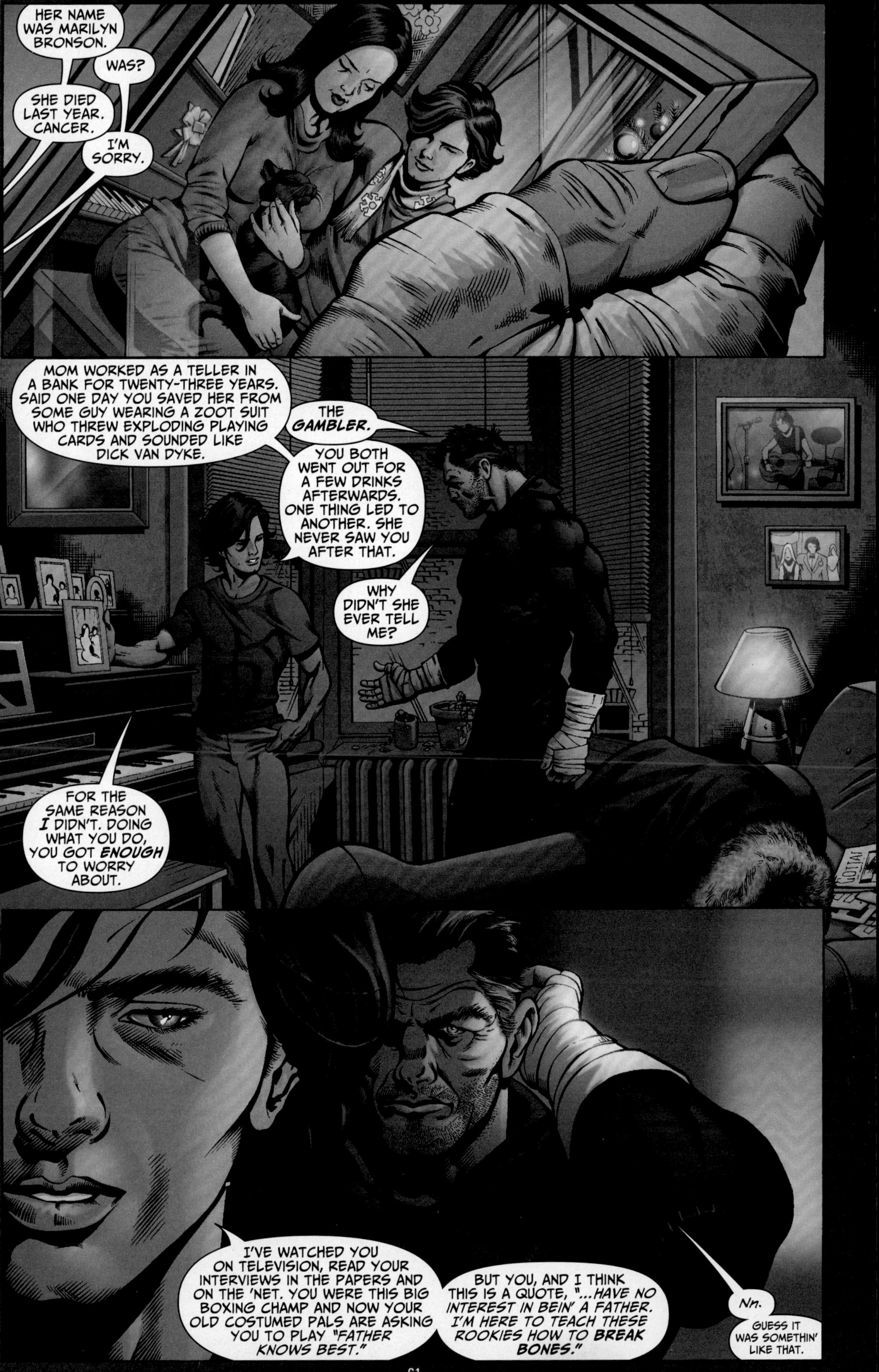
HER NAME WAS MARILYN BRONSON.
WAS?
SHE DIED LAST YEAR. CANCER.
I'M SORRY.
MOM WORKED AS A TELLER IN A BANK FOR TWENTY-THREE YEARS. SAID ONE DAY YOU SAVED HER FROM SOME GUY WEARING A ZOOT SUIT WHO THREW EXPLODING PLAYING CARDS AND SOUNDED LIKE DICK VAN DYKE.
THE *GAMBLER.*
YOU BOTH WENT OUT FOR A FEW DRINKS AFTERWARDS. ONE THING LED TO ANOTHER. SHE NEVER SAW YOU AFTER THAT.
WHY DIDN'T SHE EVER TELL ME?
FOR THE SAME REASON *I* DIDN'T. DOING WHAT YOU DO, YOU GOT ***ENOUGH*** TO WORRY ABOUT.
I'VE WATCHED YOU ON TELEVISION, READ YOUR INTERVIEWS IN THE PAPERS AND ON THE 'NET. YOU WERE THIS BIG BOXING CHAMP AND NOW YOUR OLD COSTUMED PALS ARE ASKING YOU TO PLAY *"FATHER KNOWS BEST."*
BUT YOU, AND I THINK THIS IS A QUOTE, *"...HAVE NO INTEREST IN BEIN' A FATHER. I'M HERE TO TEACH THESE ROOKIES HOW TO* ***BREAK BONES."***
Nn.
GUESS IT WAS SOMETHIN' LIKE THAT.

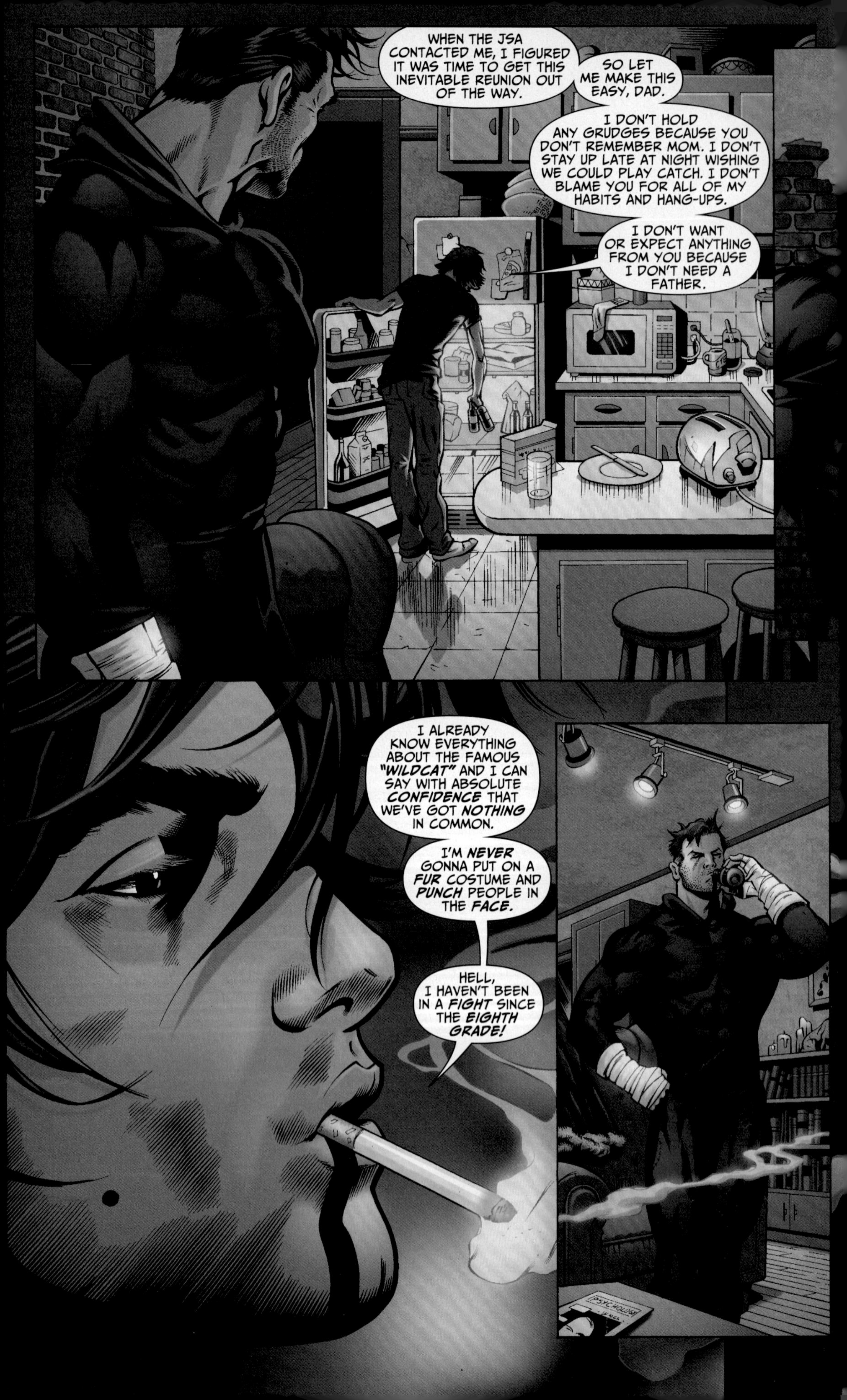
WHEN THE JSA CONTACTED ME, I FIGURED IT WAS TIME TO GET THIS INEVITABLE REUNION OUT OF THE WAY.
SO LET ME MAKE THIS EASY, DAD.
I DON'T HOLD ANY GRUDGES BECAUSE YOU DON'T REMEMBER MOM. I DON'T STAY UP LATE AT NIGHT WISHING WE COULD PLAY CATCH. I DON'T BLAME YOU FOR ALL OF MY HABITS AND HANG-UPS.
I DON'T WANT OR EXPECT ANYTHING FROM YOU BECAUSE I DON'T NEED A FATHER.
I ALREADY KNOW EVERYTHING ABOUT THE FAMOUS "WILDCAT" AND I CAN SAY WITH ABSOLUTE CONFIDENCE THAT WE'VE GOT NOTHING IN COMMON.
I'M NEVER GONNA PUT ON A FUR COSTUME AND PUNCH PEOPLE IN THE FACE.
HELL, I HAVEN'T BEEN IN A FIGHT SINCE THE EIGHTH GRADE!

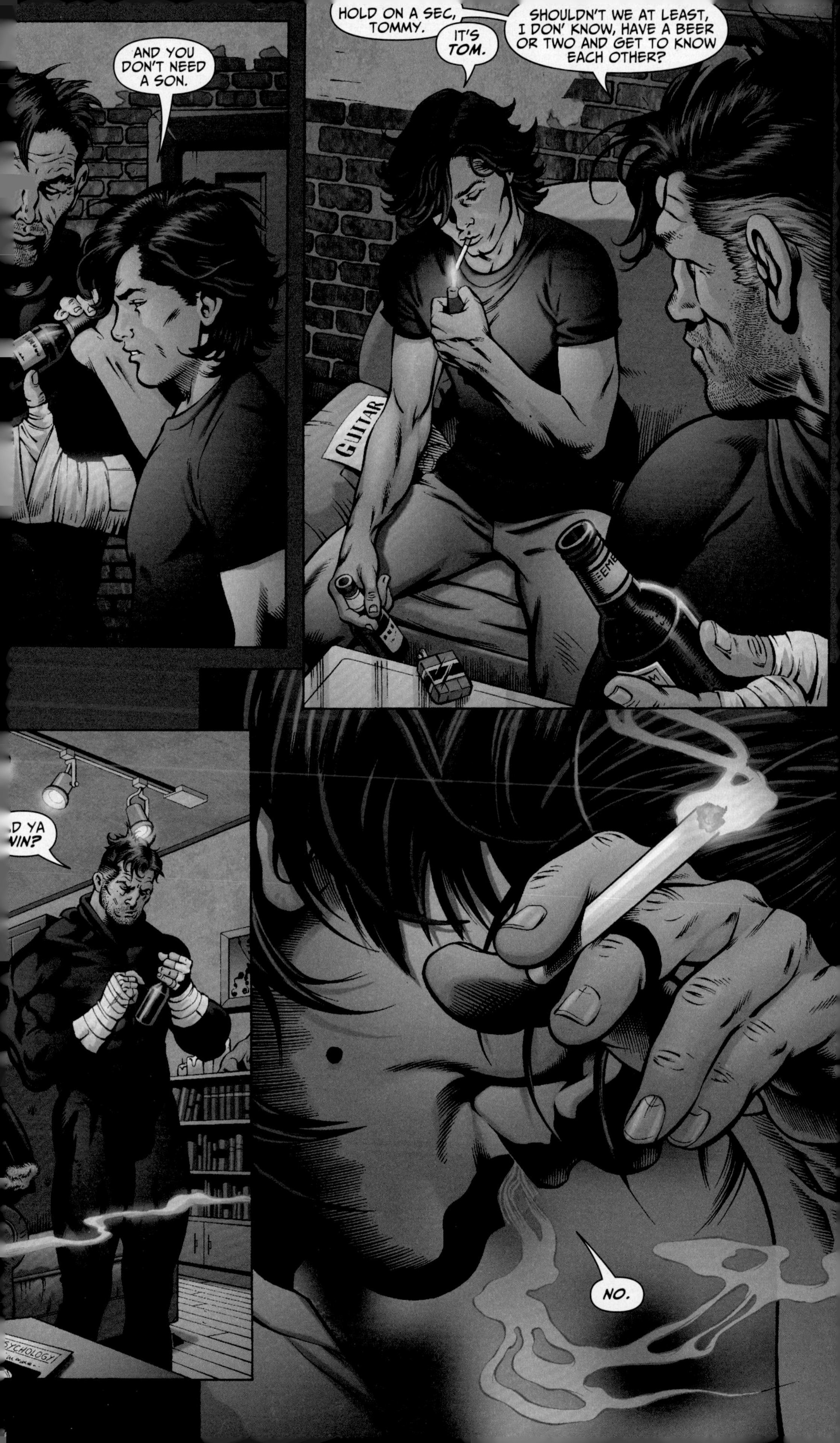
AND YOU DON'T NEED A SON.
HOLD ON A SEC, TOMMY.
IT'S TOM.
SHOULDN'T WE AT LEAST, I DON' KNOW, HAVE A BEER OR TWO AND GET TO KNOW EACH OTHER?
GUITAR
NO.

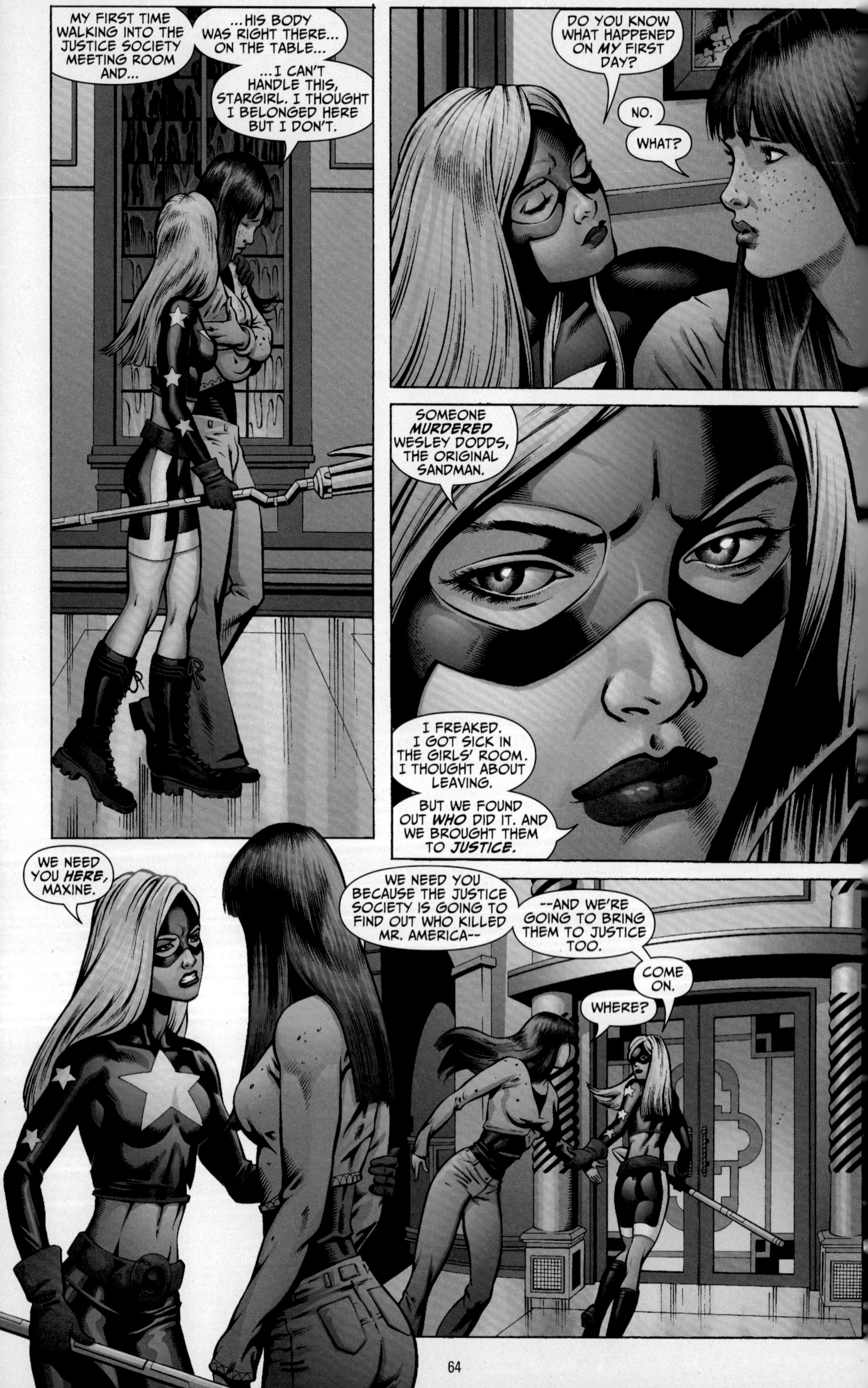
MY FIRST TIME WALKING INTO THE JUSTICE SOCIETY MEETING ROOM AND...
...HIS BODY WAS RIGHT THERE... ON THE TABLE...
...I CAN'T HANDLE THIS, STARGIRL. I THOUGHT I BELONGED HERE BUT I DON'T.
DO YOU KNOW WHAT HAPPENED ON MY FIRST DAY?
NO.
WHAT?
SOMEONE MURDERED WESLEY DODDS, THE ORIGINAL SANDMAN.
I FREAKED. I GOT SICK IN THE GIRLS' ROOM. I THOUGHT ABOUT LEAVING.
BUT WE FOUND OUT WHO DID IT. AND WE BROUGHT THEM TO JUSTICE.
WE NEED YOU HERE, MAXINE.
WE NEED YOU BECAUSE THE JUSTICE SOCIETY IS GOING TO FIND OUT WHO KILLED MR. AMERICA--
--AND WE'RE GOING TO BRING THEM TO JUSTICE TOO.
COME ON.
WHERE?

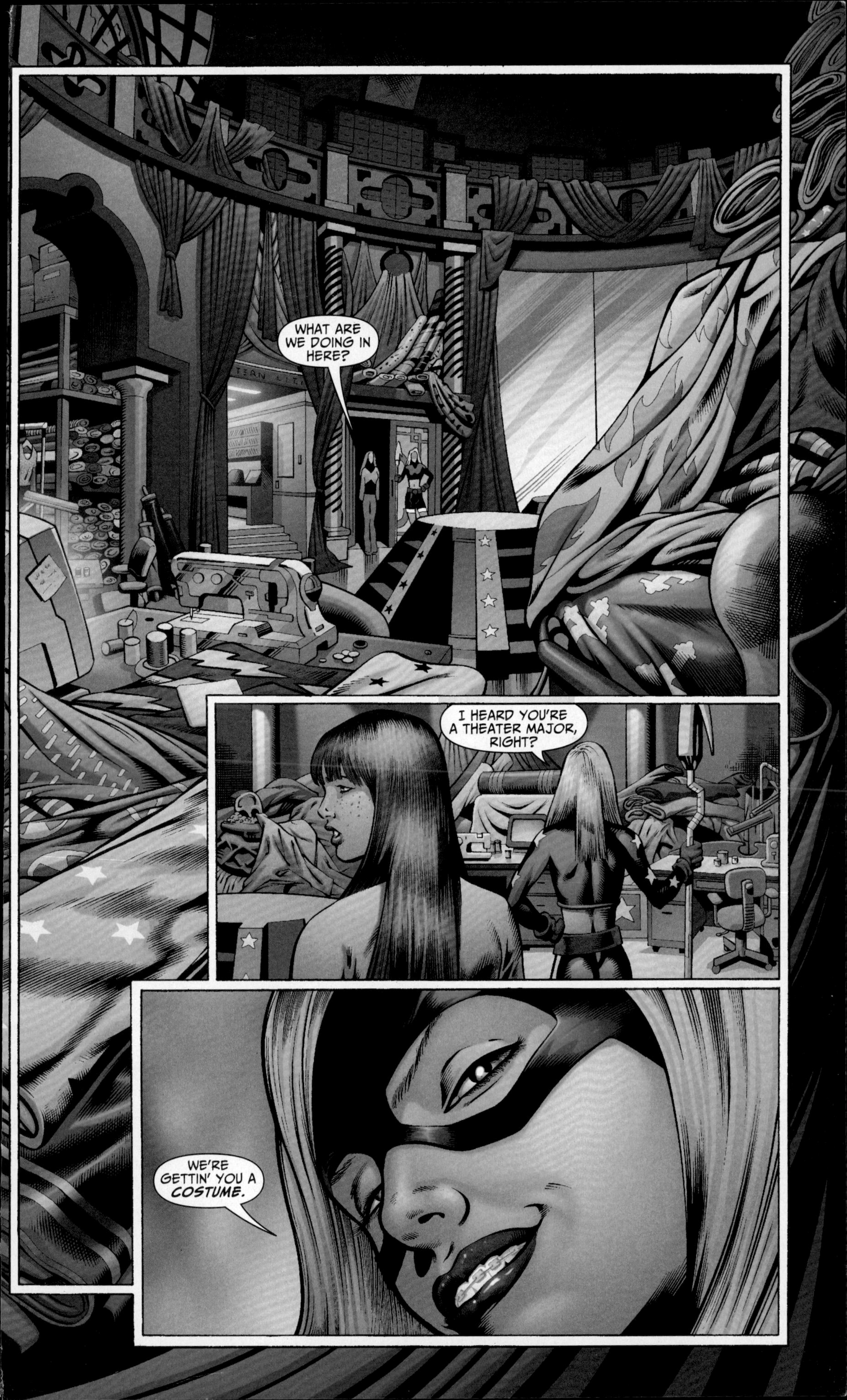
WHAT ARE WE DOING IN HERE?
I HEARD YOU'RE A THEATER MAJOR, RIGHT?
WE'RE GETTIN' YOU A *COSTUME.*

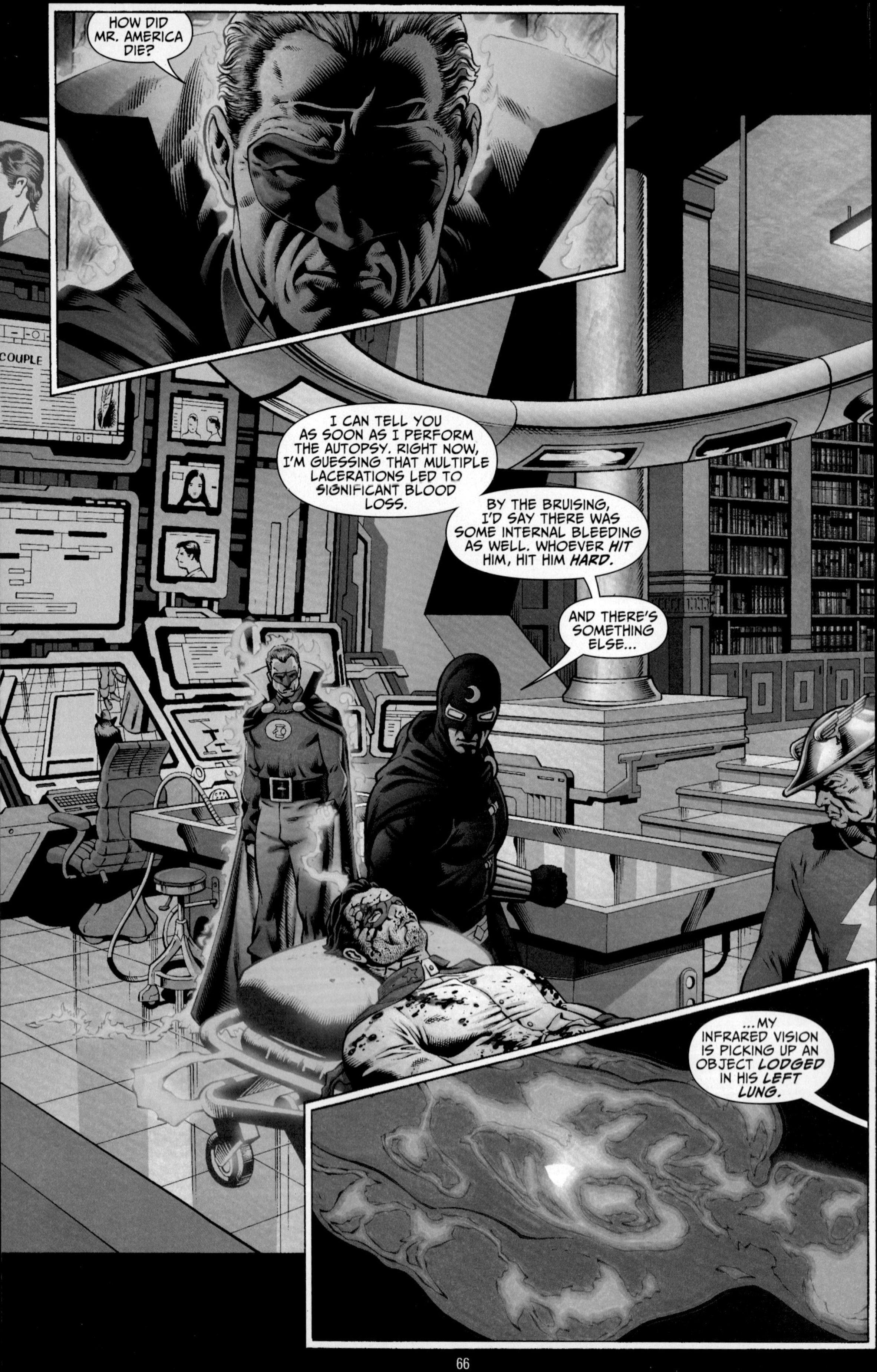
HOW DID MR. AMERICA DIE?
COUPLE
I CAN TELL YOU AS SOON AS I PERFORM THE AUTOPSY. RIGHT NOW, I'M GUESSING THAT MULTIPLE LACERATIONS LED TO SIGNIFICANT BLOOD LOSS.
BY THE BRUISING, I'D SAY THERE WAS SOME INTERNAL BLEEDING AS WELL. WHOEVER *HIT* HIM, HIT HIM *HARD.*
AND THERE'S SOMETHING ELSE...
...MY INFRARED VISION IS PICKING UP AN OBJECT *LODGED* IN HIS *LEFT LUNG.*

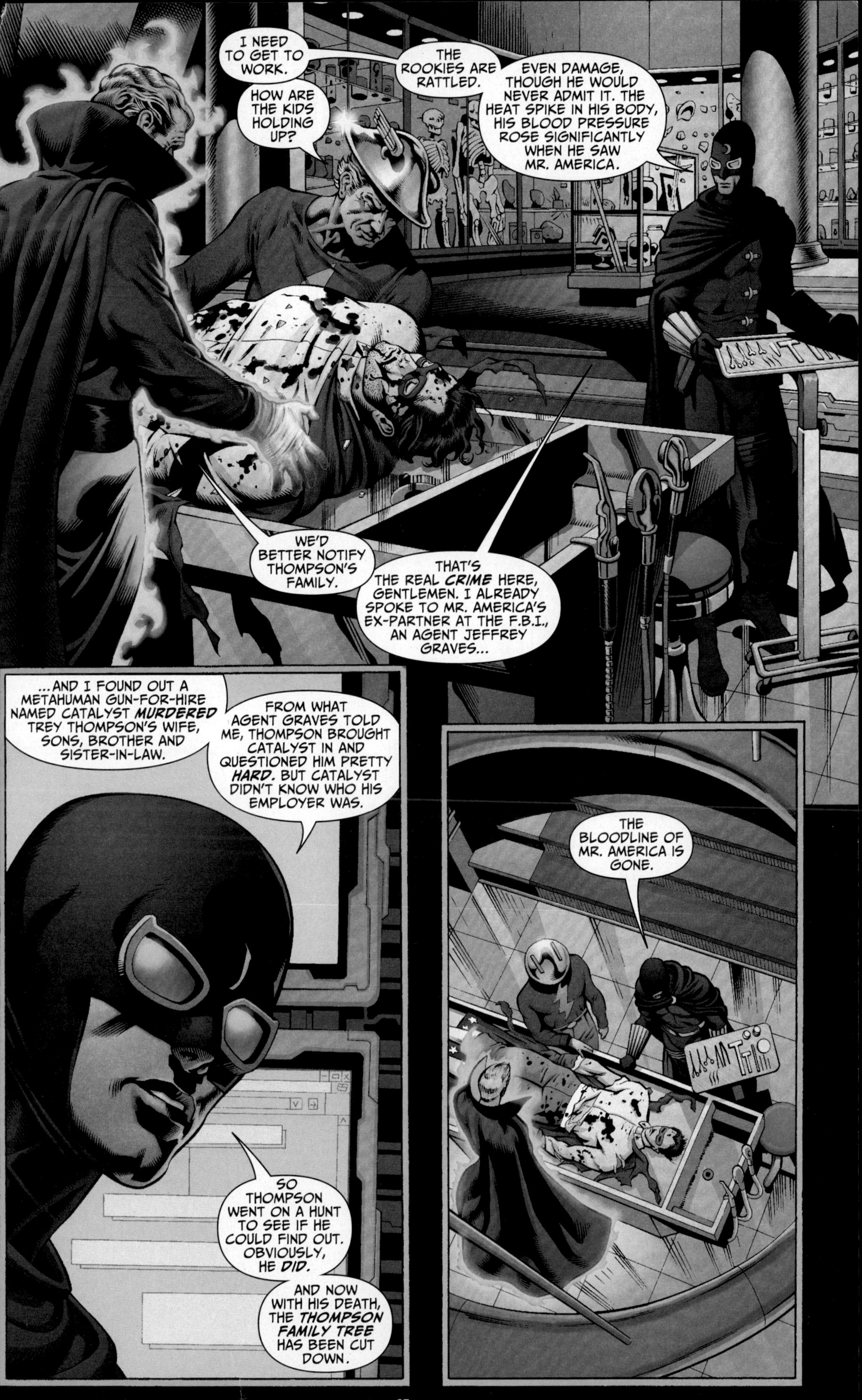
I NEED TO GET TO WORK.
HOW ARE THE KIDS HOLDING UP?
THE ROOKIES ARE RATTLED.
EVEN DAMAGE, THOUGH HE WOULD NEVER ADMIT IT. THE HEAT SPIKE IN HIS BODY, HIS BLOOD PRESSURE ROSE SIGNIFICANTLY WHEN HE SAW MR. AMERICA.
WE'D BETTER NOTIFY THOMPSON'S FAMILY.
THAT'S THE REAL CRIME HERE, GENTLEMEN. I ALREADY SPOKE TO MR. AMERICA'S EX-PARTNER AT THE F.B.I., AN AGENT JEFFREY GRAVES...
...AND I FOUND OUT A METAHUMAN GUN-FOR-HIRE NAMED CATALYST MURDERED TREY THOMPSON'S WIFE, SONS, BROTHER AND SISTER-IN-LAW.
FROM WHAT AGENT GRAVES TOLD ME, THOMPSON BROUGHT CATALYST IN AND QUESTIONED HIM PRETTY HARD. BUT CATALYST DIDN'T KNOW WHO HIS EMPLOYER WAS.
SO THOMPSON WENT ON A HUNT TO SEE IF HE COULD FIND OUT. OBVIOUSLY, HE DID.
AND NOW WITH HIS DEATH, THE THOMPSON FAMILY TREE HAS BEEN CUT DOWN.
THE BLOODLINE OF MR. AMERICA IS GONE.

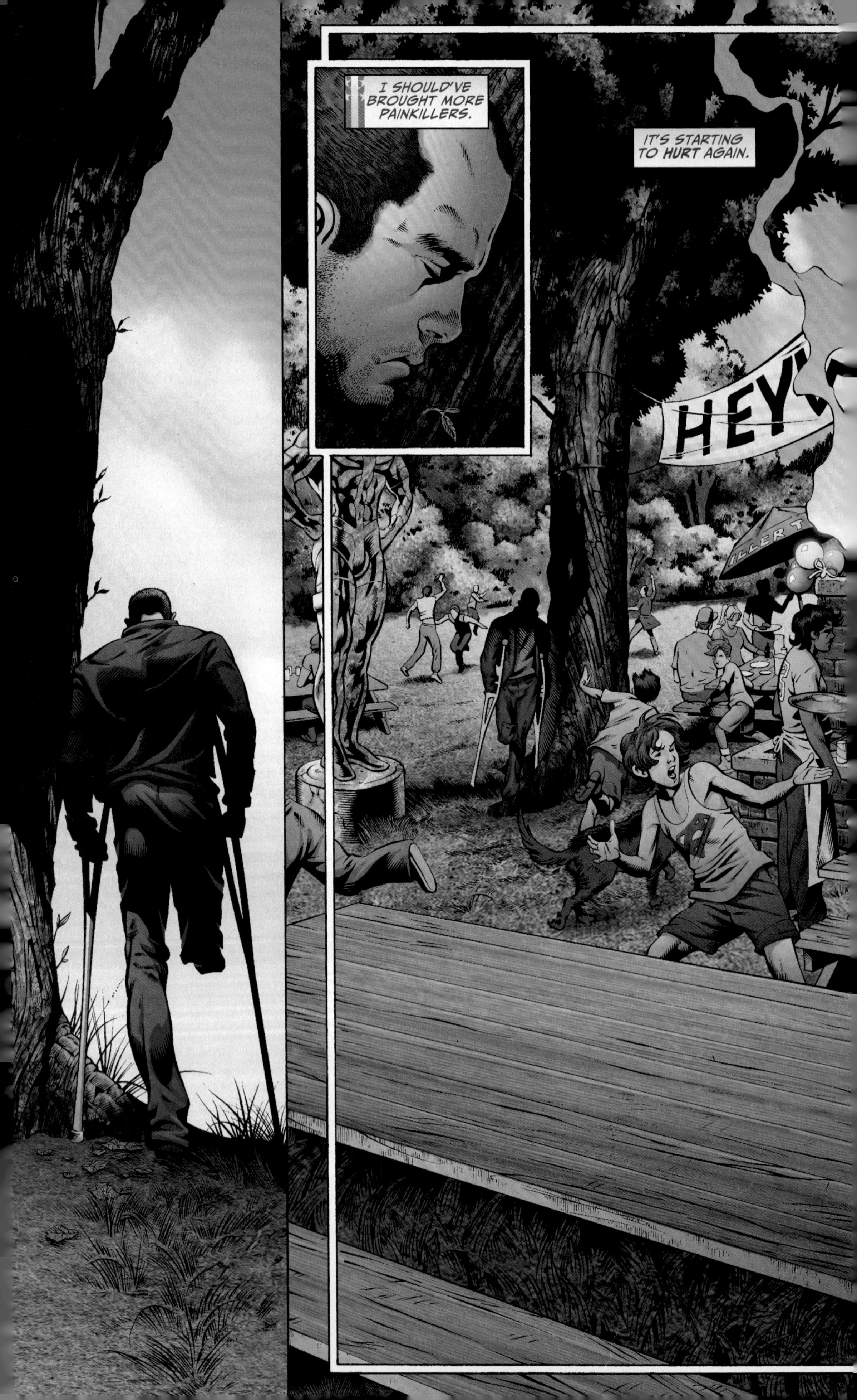
I SHOULD'VE BROUGHT MORE PAINKILLERS.
IT'S STARTING TO HURT AGAIN.
HEY

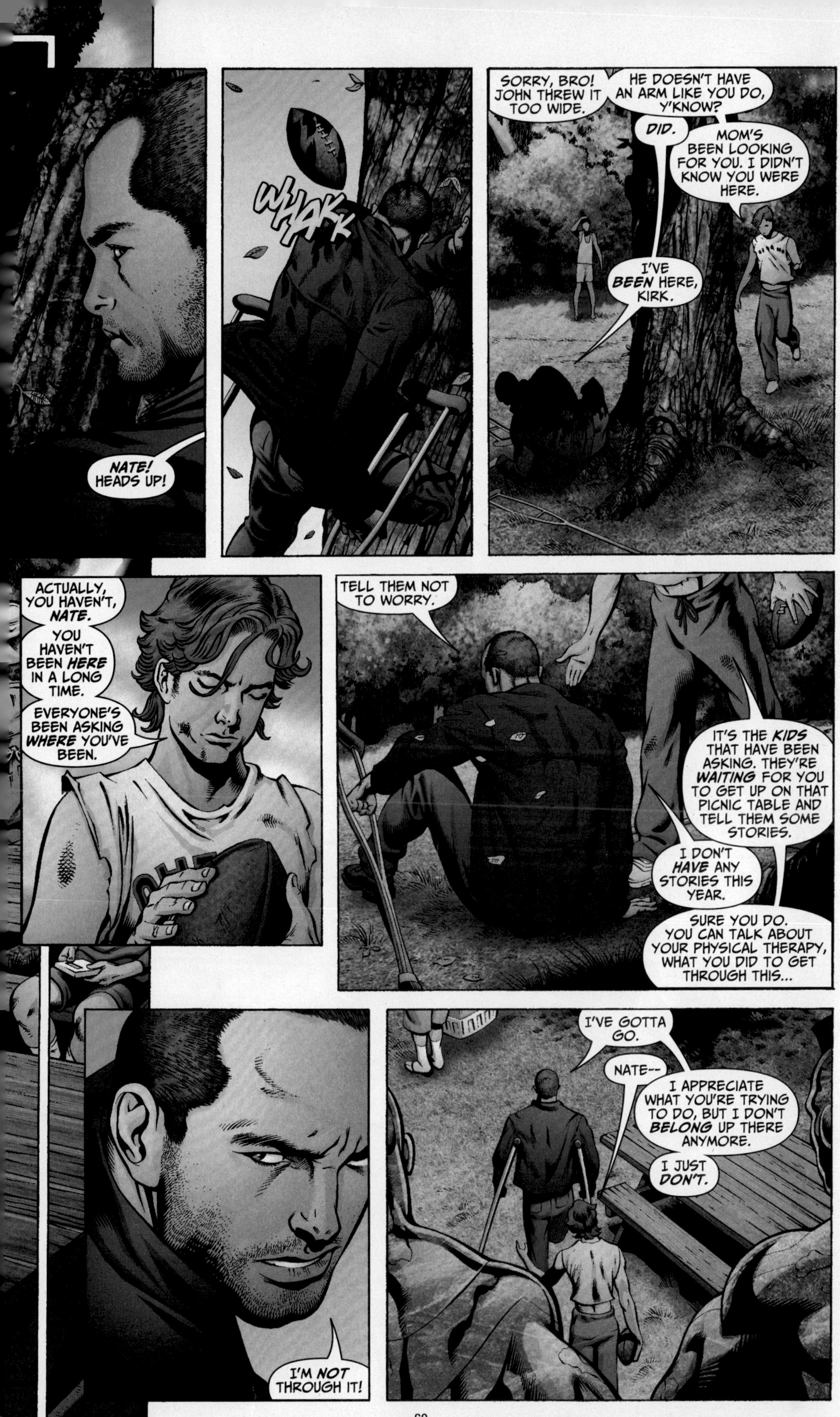
NATE! HEADS UP!
WHAKK
SORRY, BRO! JOHN THREW IT TOO WIDE.
HE DOESN'T HAVE AN ARM LIKE YOU DO, Y'KNOW?
DID.
MOM'S BEEN LOOKING FOR YOU. I DIDN'T KNOW YOU WERE HERE.
I'VE BEEN HERE, KIRK.
ACTUALLY, YOU HAVEN'T, NATE.
YOU HAVEN'T BEEN HERE IN A LONG TIME.
EVERYONE'S BEEN ASKING WHERE YOU'VE BEEN.
TELL THEM NOT TO WORRY.
IT'S THE KIDS THAT HAVE BEEN ASKING. THEY'RE WAITING FOR YOU TO GET UP ON THAT PICNIC TABLE AND TELL THEM SOME STORIES.
I DON'T HAVE ANY STORIES THIS YEAR.
SURE YOU DO. YOU CAN TALK ABOUT YOUR PHYSICAL THERAPY, WHAT YOU DID TO GET THROUGH THIS...
I'M NOT THROUGH IT!
I'VE GOTTA GO.
NATE--
I APPRECIATE WHAT YOU'RE TRYING TO DO, BUT I DON'T BELONG UP THERE ANYMORE.
I JUST DON'T.

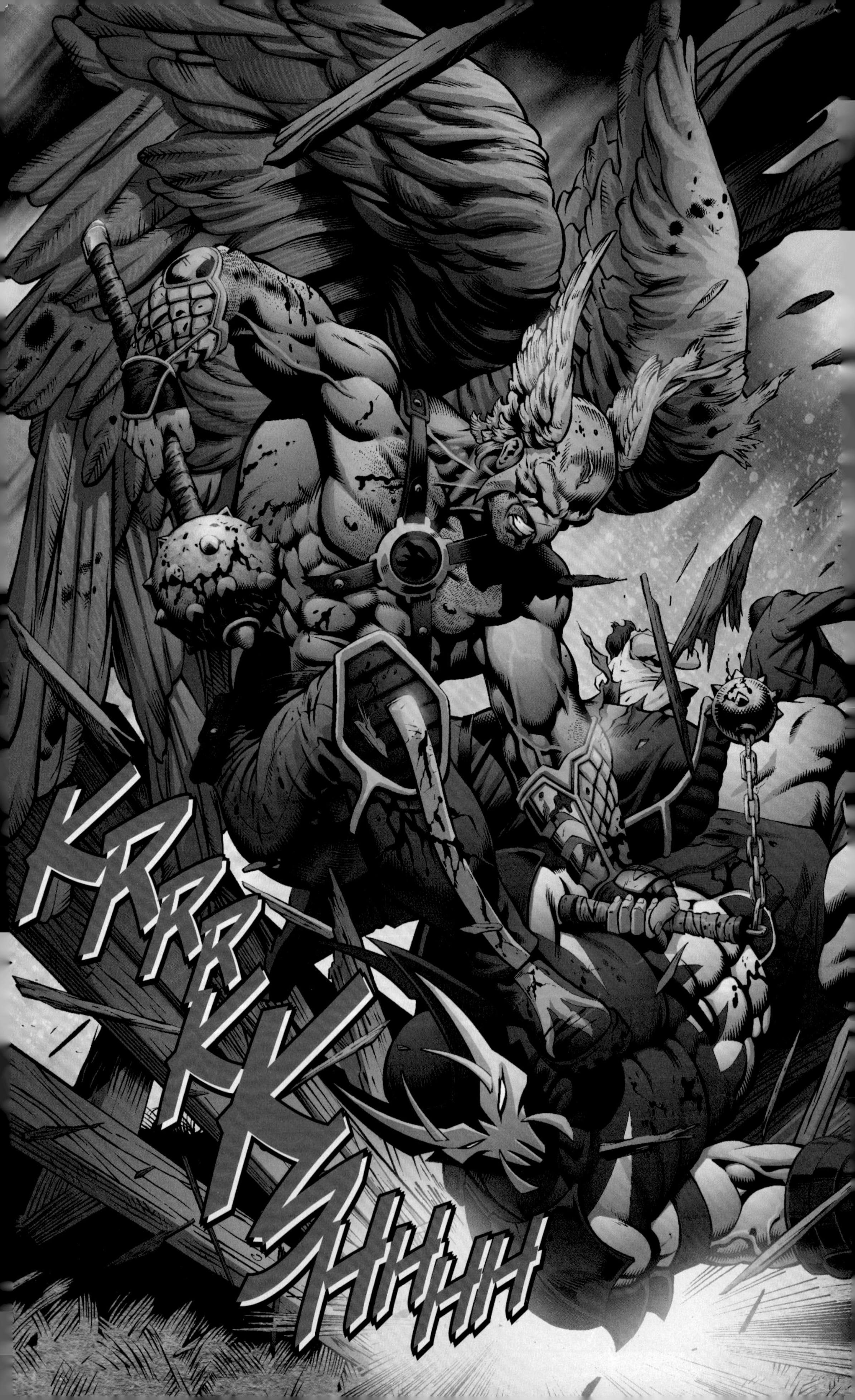
KRRRKKSHHHH

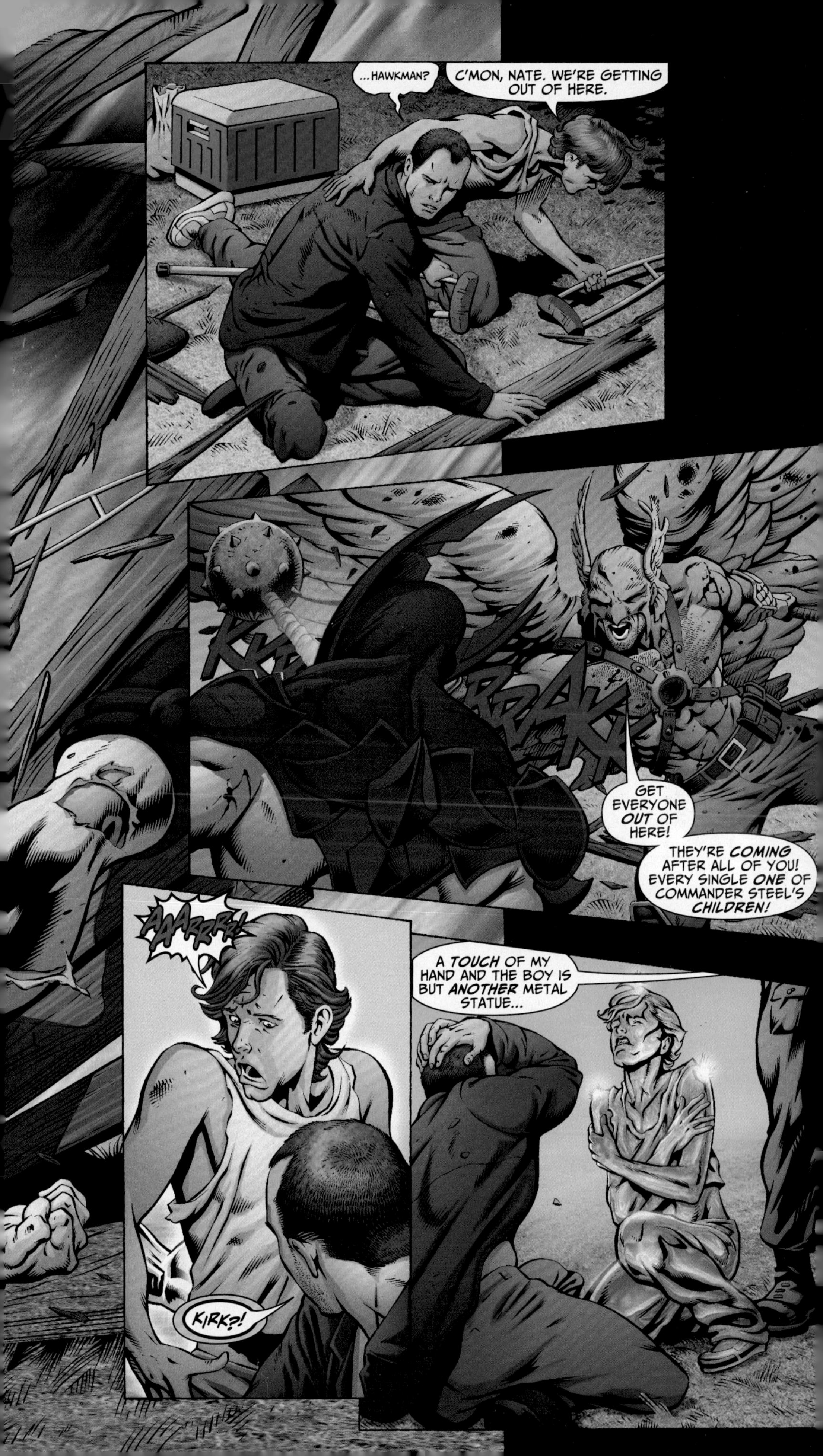
...HAWKMAN?
C'MON, NATE. WE'RE GETTING OUT OF HERE.
KRRAKK
GET EVERYONE OUT OF HERE!
THEY'RE COMING AFTER ALL OF YOU! EVERY SINGLE ONE OF COMMANDER STEEL'S CHILDREN!
AAARRR!
A TOUCH OF MY HAND AND THE BOY IS BUT ANOTHER METAL STATUE...
KIRK?!

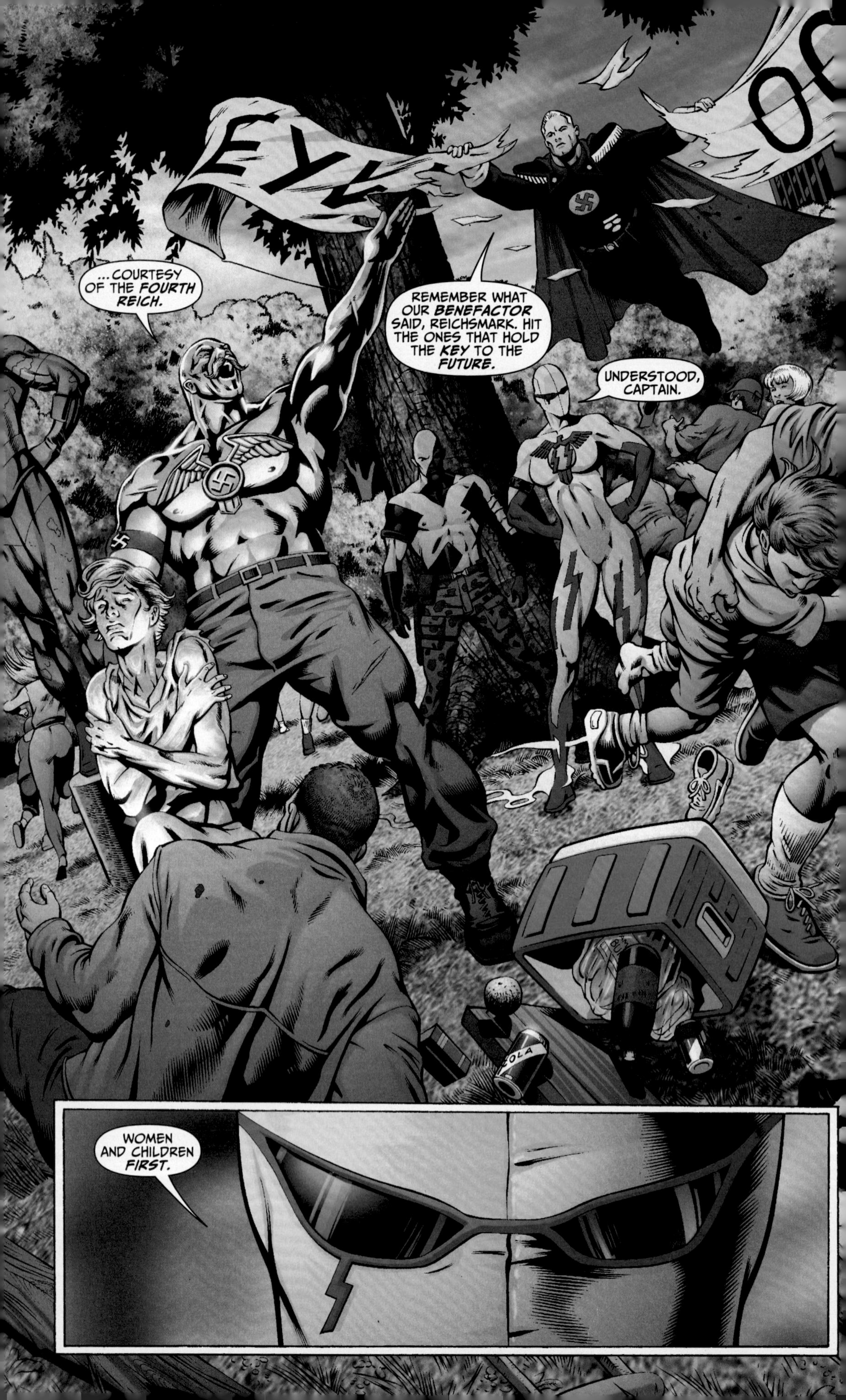
...COURTESY OF THE FOURTH REICH.
REMEMBER WHAT OUR BENEFACTOR SAID, REICHSMARK. HIT THE ONES THAT HOLD THE KEY TO THE FUTURE.
UNDERSTOOD, CAPTAIN.
WOMEN AND CHILDREN FIRST.

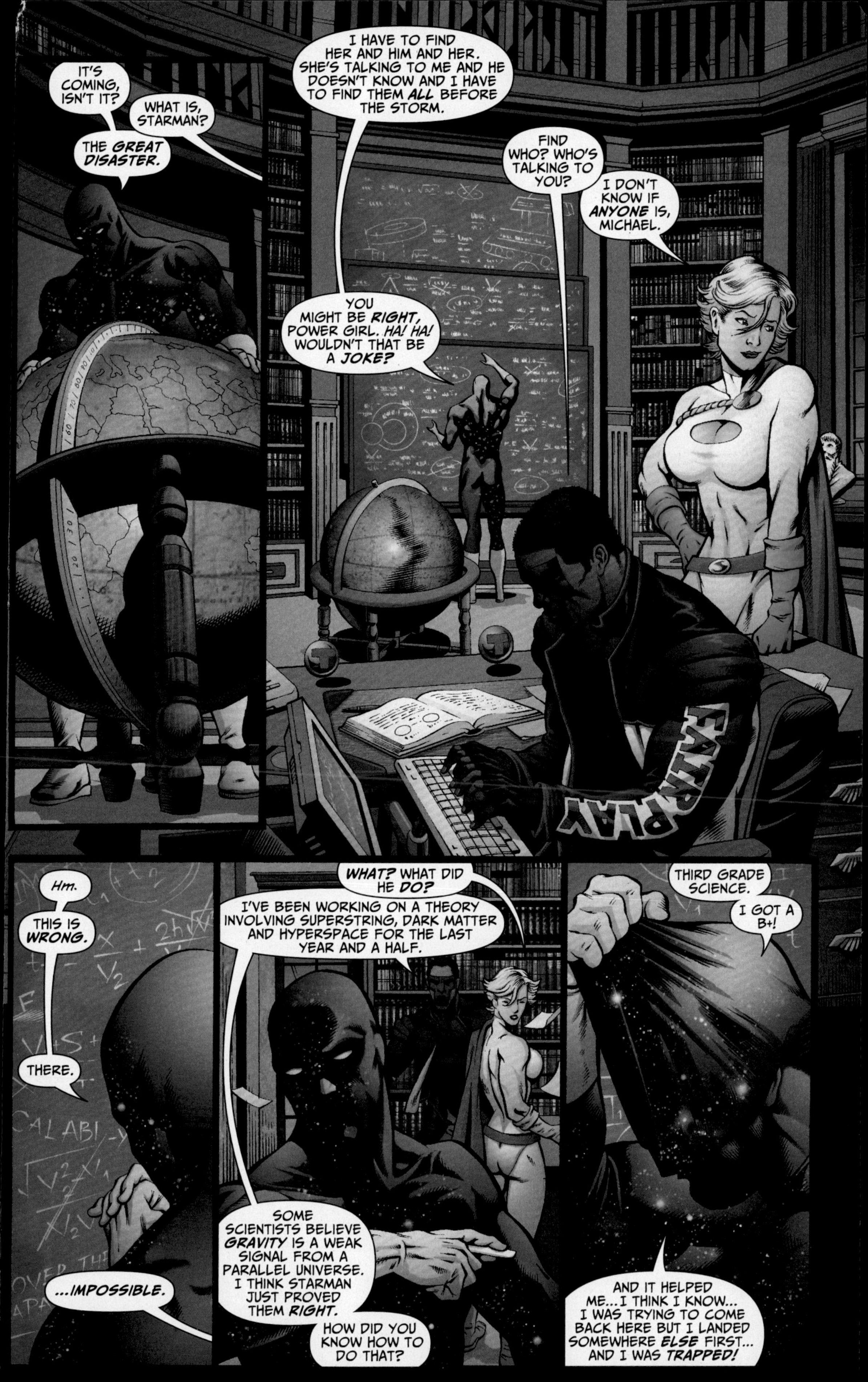

IT'S COMING, ISN'T IT?
WHAT IS, STARMAN?
THE GREAT DISASTER.
I HAVE TO FIND HER AND HIM AND HER. SHE'S TALKING TO ME AND HE DOESN'T KNOW AND I HAVE TO FIND THEM ALL BEFORE THE STORM.
FIND WHO? WHO'S TALKING TO YOU?
I DON'T KNOW IF ANYONE IS, MICHAEL.
YOU MIGHT BE RIGHT, POWER GIRL. HA! HA! WOULDN'T THAT BE A JOKE?
FAIR PLAY
Hm.
THIS IS WRONG.
THERE.
...IMPOSSIBLE.
WHAT? WHAT DID HE DO?
I'VE BEEN WORKING ON A THEORY INVOLVING SUPERSTRING, DARK MATTER AND HYPERSPACE FOR THE LAST YEAR AND A HALF.
SOME SCIENTISTS BELIEVE GRAVITY IS A WEAK SIGNAL FROM A PARALLEL UNIVERSE. I THINK STARMAN JUST PROVED THEM RIGHT.
HOW DID YOU KNOW HOW TO DO THAT?
THIRD GRADE SCIENCE.
I GOT A B+!
AND IT HELPED ME...I THINK I KNOW... I WAS TRYING TO COME BACK HERE BUT I LANDED SOMEWHERE ELSE FIRST... AND I WAS TRAPPED!

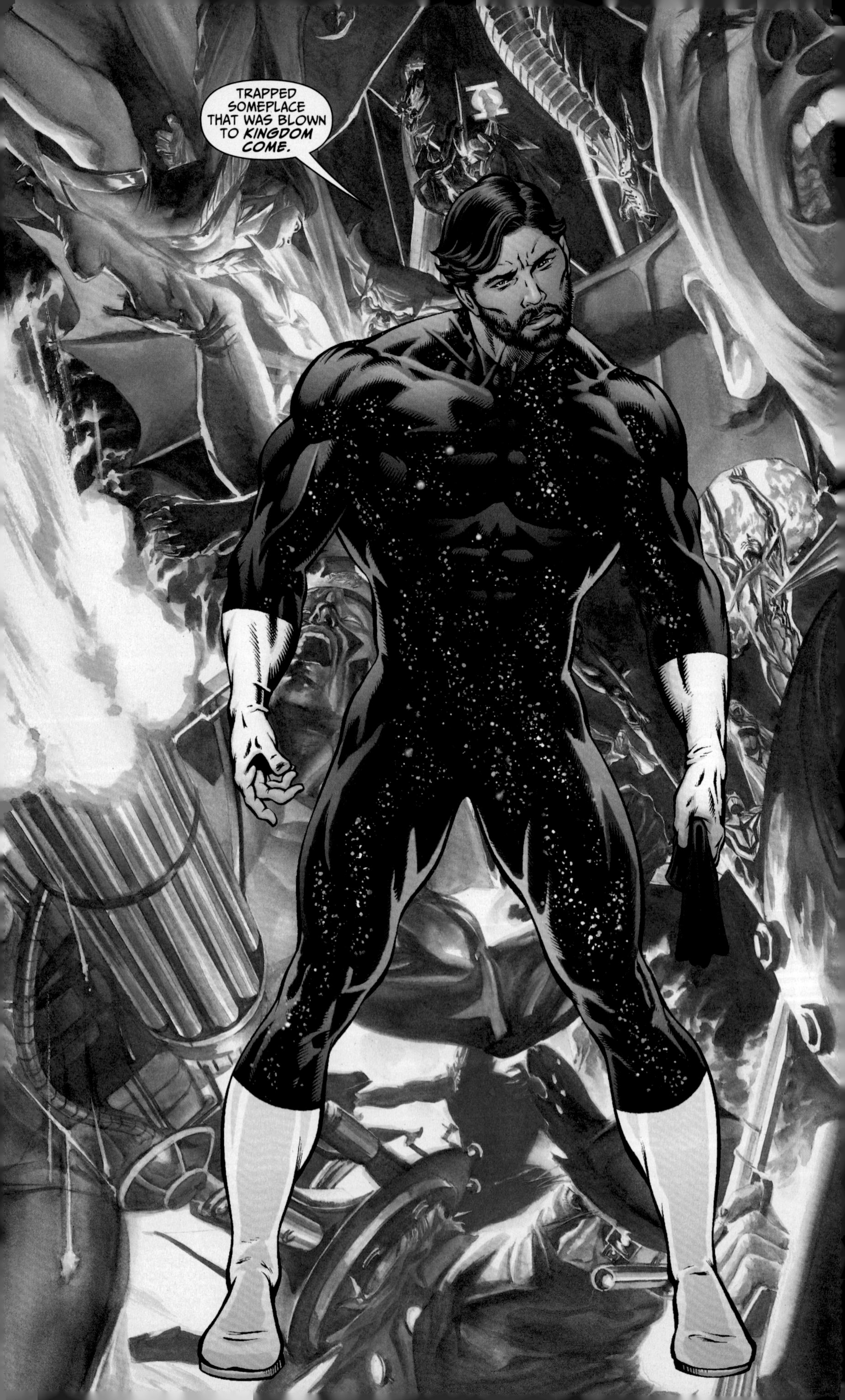
TRAPPED SOMEPLACE THAT WAS BLOWN TO *KINGDOM COME.*

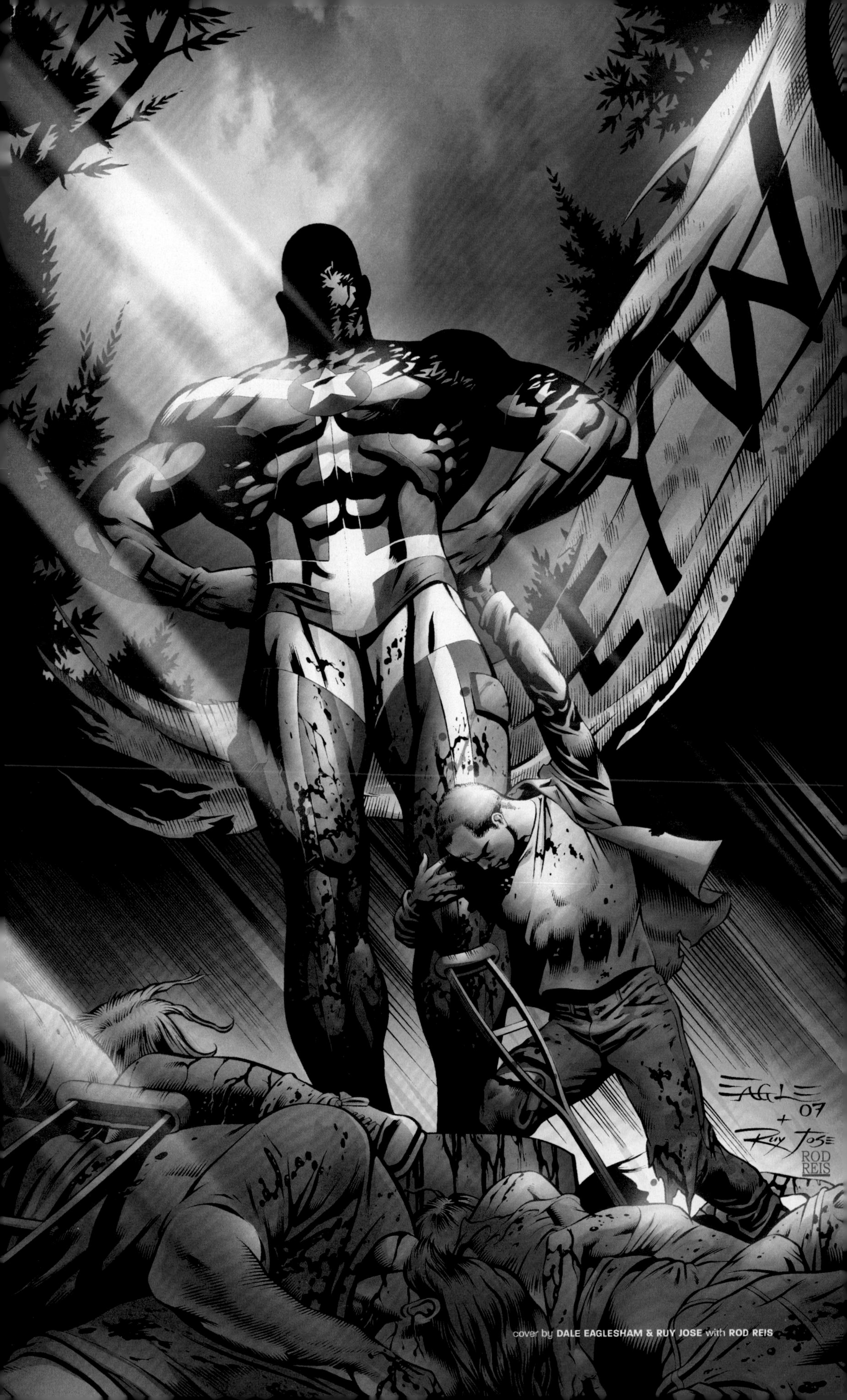
EAGLE 07
+
Ruy Jose
ROD REIS

cover by **DALE EAGLESHAM & RUY JOSE** with **ROD REIS**

THE NEXT AGE

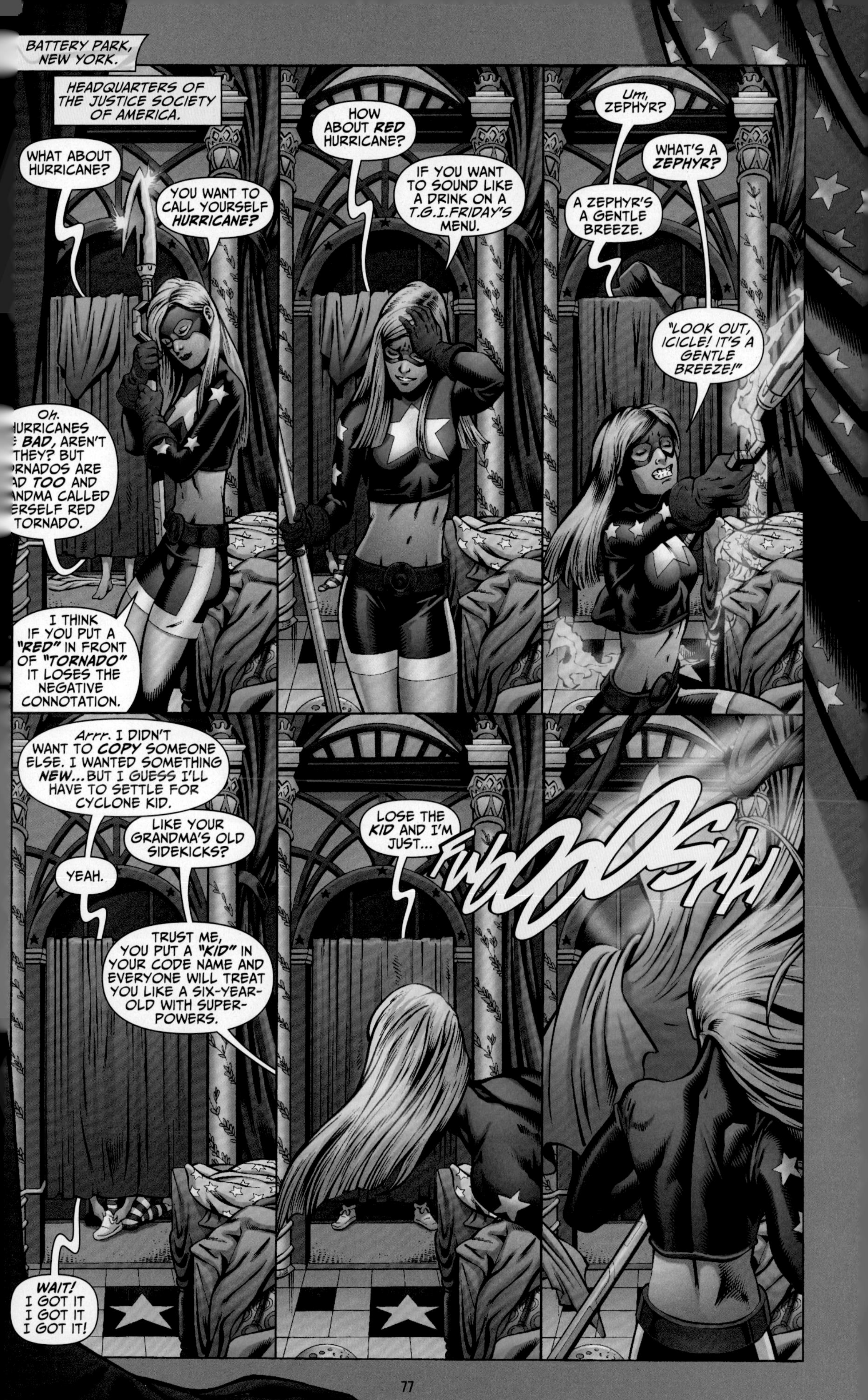
BATTERY PARK, NEW YORK.
HEADQUARTERS OF THE JUSTICE SOCIETY OF AMERICA.
WHAT ABOUT HURRICANE?
YOU WANT TO CALL YOURSELF HURRICANE?
Oh. HURRICANES
E BAD, AREN'T THEY? BUT
ORNADOS ARE
AD TOO AND
ANDMA CALLED
ERSELF RED TORNADO.
I THINK IF YOU PUT A "RED" IN FRONT OF "TORNADO" IT LOSES THE NEGATIVE CONNOTATION.
HOW ABOUT RED HURRICANE?
IF YOU WANT TO SOUND LIKE A DRINK ON A T.G.I.FRIDAY'S MENU.
Um, ZEPHYR?
WHAT'S A ZEPHYR?
A ZEPHYR'S A GENTLE BREEZE.
"LOOK OUT, ICICLE! IT'S A GENTLE BREEZE!"
Arrr. I DIDN'T WANT TO COPY SOMEONE ELSE. I WANTED SOMETHING NEW... BUT I GUESS I'LL HAVE TO SETTLE FOR CYCLONE KID.
LIKE YOUR GRANDMA'S OLD SIDEKICKS?
YEAH.
TRUST ME, YOU PUT A "KID" IN YOUR CODE NAME AND EVERYONE WILL TREAT YOU LIKE A SIX-YEAR-OLD WITH SUPER-POWERS.
WAIT! I GOT IT I GOT IT I GOT IT!
LOSE THE KID AND I'M JUST...
FWOOOSHH

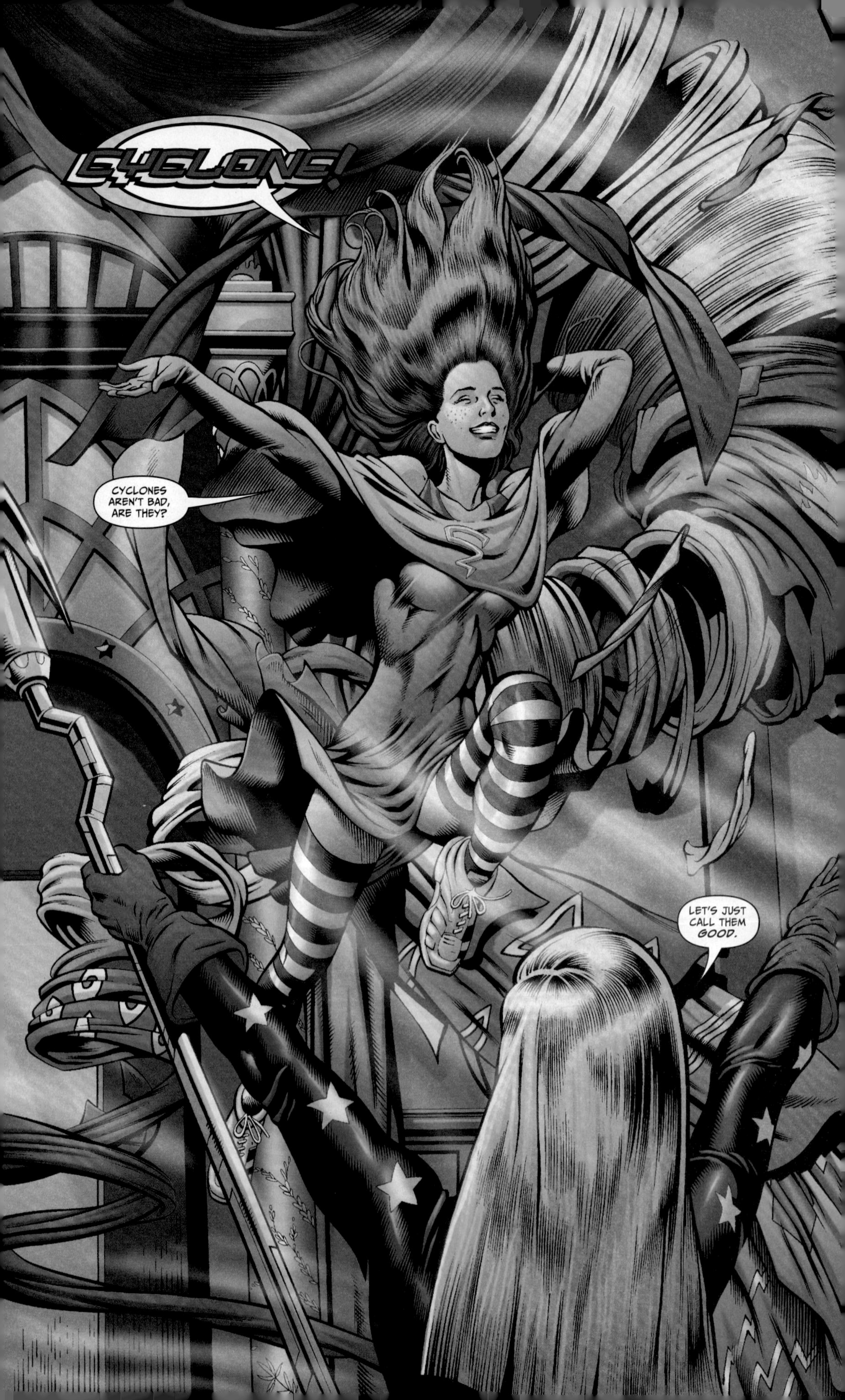
CYCLONE!
CYCLONES AREN'T BAD, ARE THEY?
LET'S JUST CALL THEM GOOD.

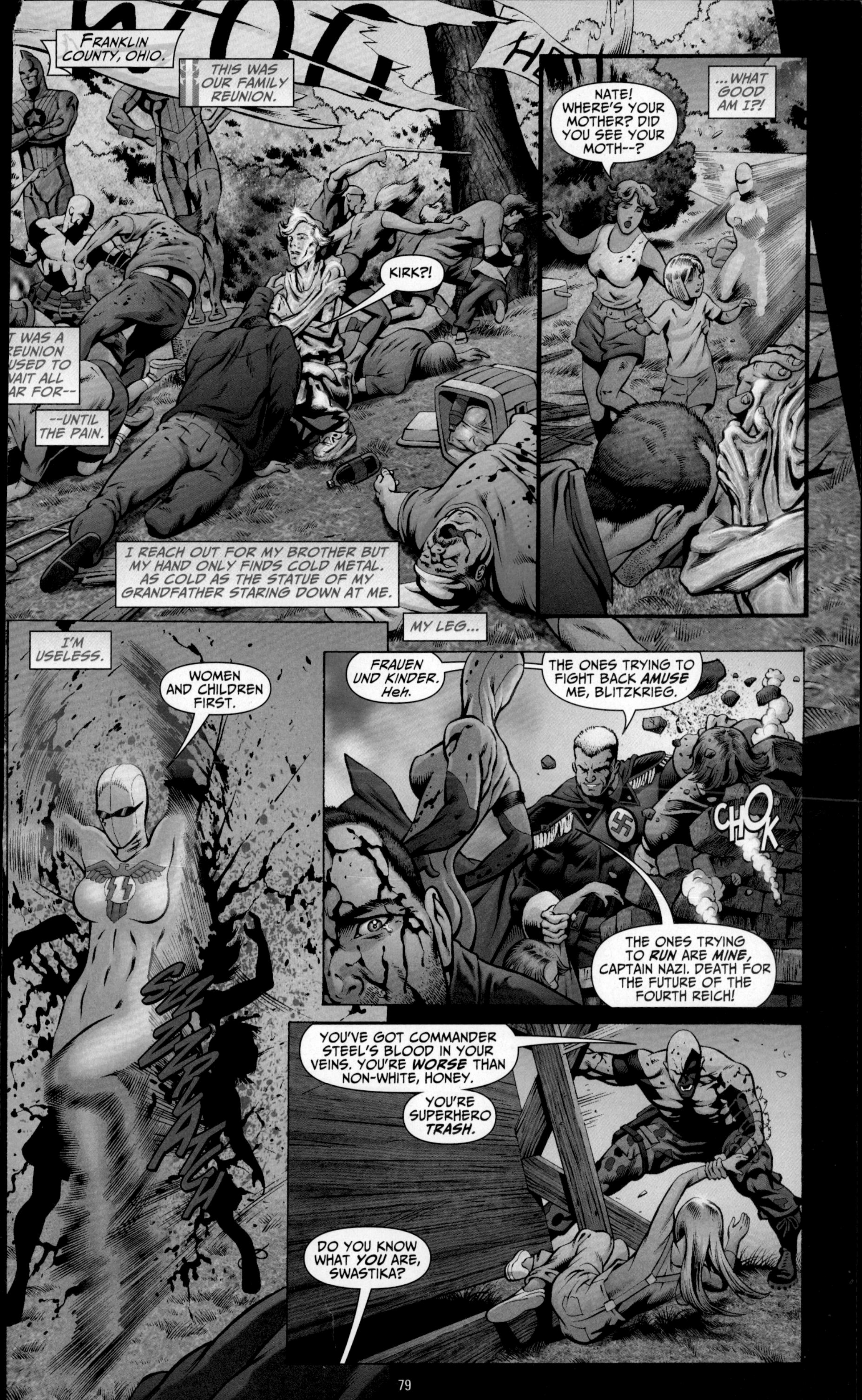
FRANKLIN COUNTY, OHIO.
THIS WAS OUR FAMILY REUNION.
KIRK?!
T WAS A REUNION USED TO WAIT ALL AR FOR--
--UNTIL THE PAIN.
I REACH OUT FOR MY BROTHER BUT MY HAND ONLY FINDS COLD METAL. AS COLD AS THE STATUE OF MY GRANDFATHER STARING DOWN AT ME.
NATE! WHERE'S YOUR MOTHER? DID YOU SEE YOUR MOTH--?
...WHAT GOOD AM I?!
MY LEG...
I'M USELESS.
WOMEN AND CHILDREN FIRST.
FRAUEN UND KINDER. Heh.
THE ONES TRYING TO FIGHT BACK AMUSE ME, BLITZKRIEG.
CHOK
THE ONES TRYING TO RUN ARE MINE, CAPTAIN NAZI. DEATH FOR THE FUTURE OF THE FOURTH REICH!
YOU'VE GOT COMMANDER STEEL'S BLOOD IN YOUR VEINS. YOU'RE WORSE THAN NON-WHITE, HONEY.
YOU'RE SUPERHERO TRASH.
DO YOU KNOW WHAT YOU ARE, SWASTIKA?

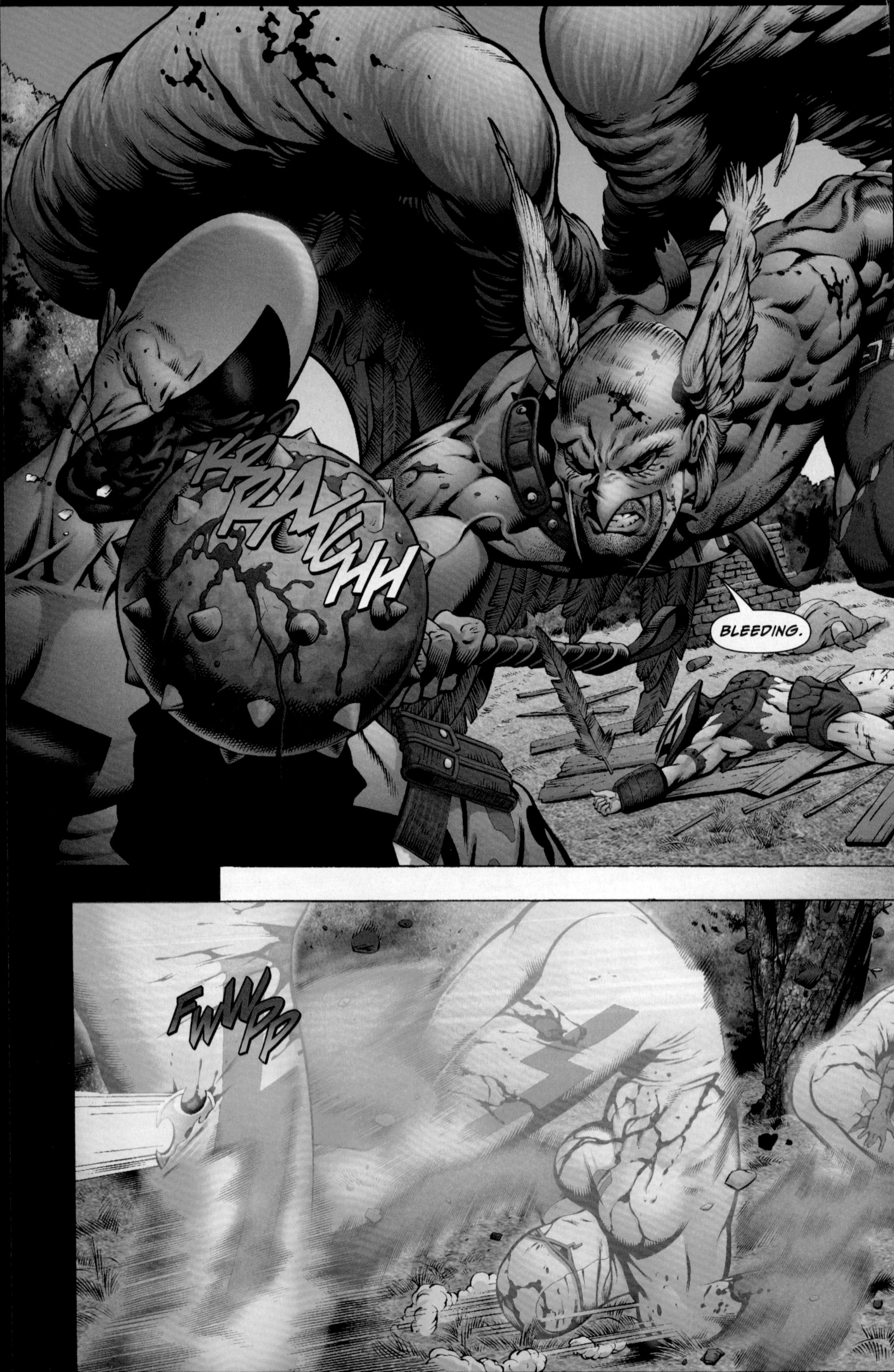
KRAKOWM
BLEEDING.
FWWDD

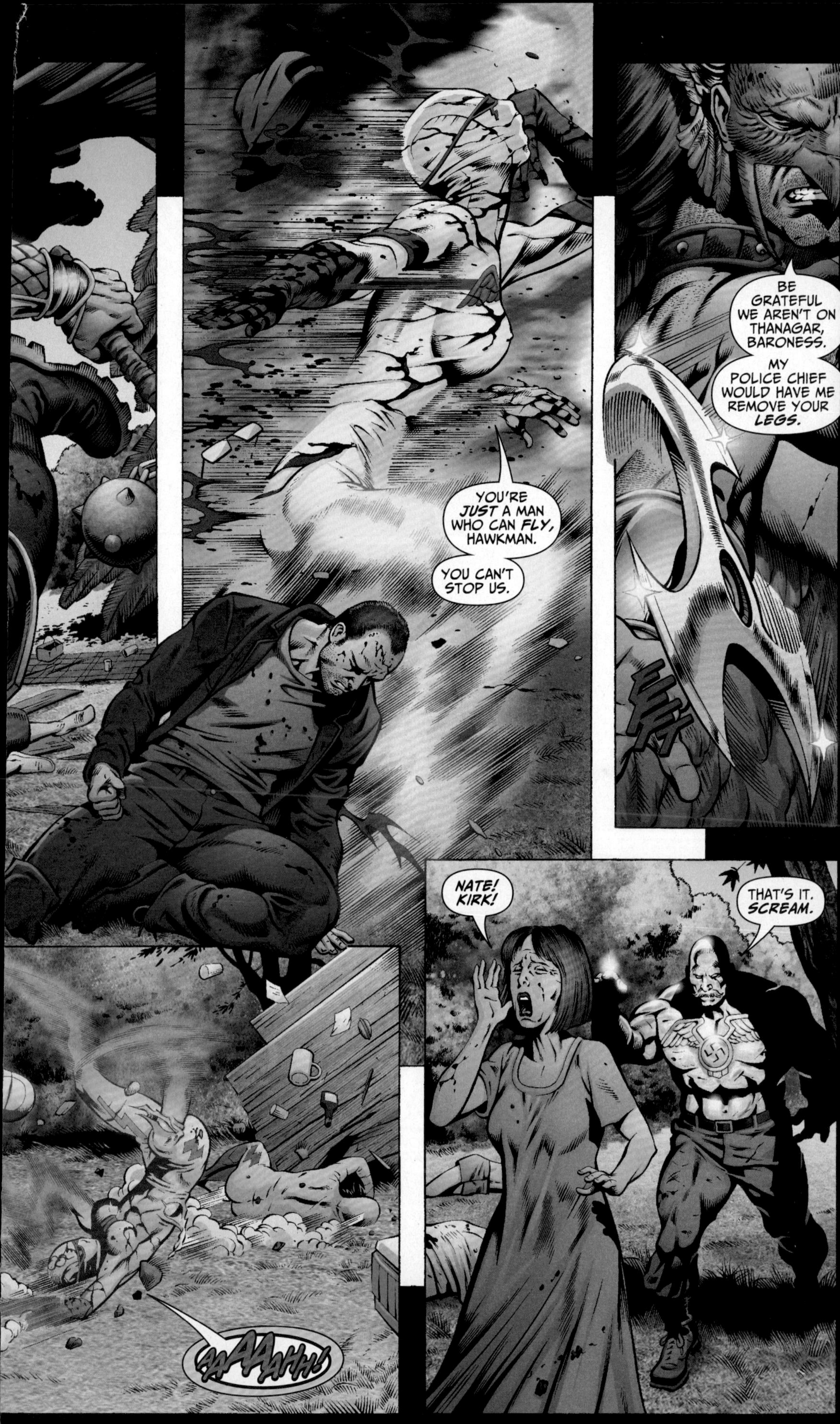
YOU'RE JUST A MAN WHO CAN FLY, HAWKMAN.
YOU CAN'T STOP US.
BE GRATEFUL WE AREN'T ON THANAGAR, BARONESS.
MY POLICE CHIEF WOULD HAVE ME REMOVE YOUR LEGS.
AAAAAHH!
NATE! KIRK!
THAT'S IT. SCREAM.

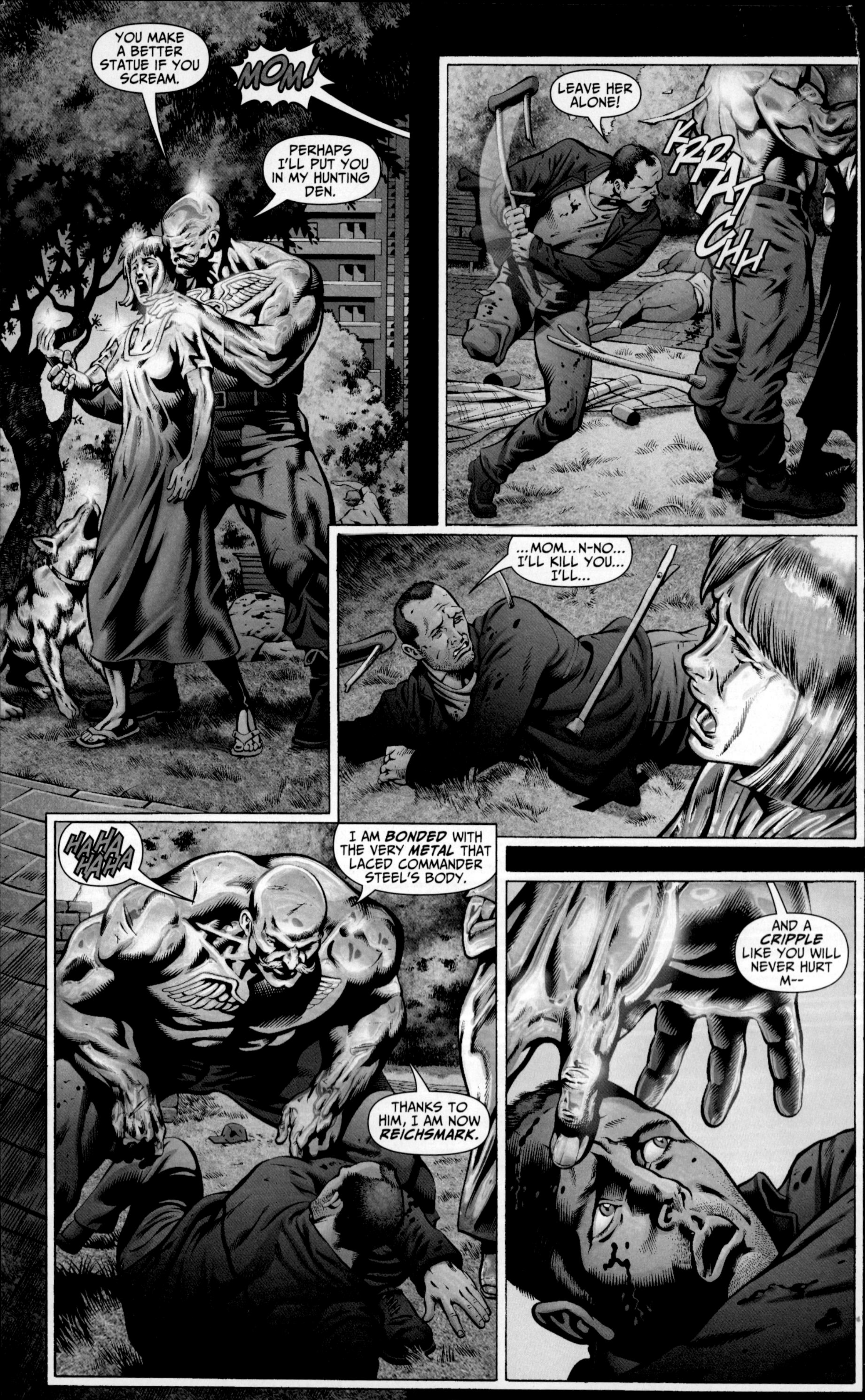

YOU MAKE A BETTER STATUE IF YOU SCREAM.
MOM!
PERHAPS I'LL PUT YOU IN MY HUNTING DEN.
LEAVE HER ALONE!
KRRAT CHH
...MOM...N-NO... I'LL KILL YOU... I'LL...
HAHA HAHA
I AM **BONDED** WITH THE VERY **METAL** THAT LACED COMMANDER STEEL'S BODY.
THANKS TO HIM, I AM NOW **REICHSMARK.**
AND A **CRIPPLE** LIKE YOU WILL NEVER HURT M--

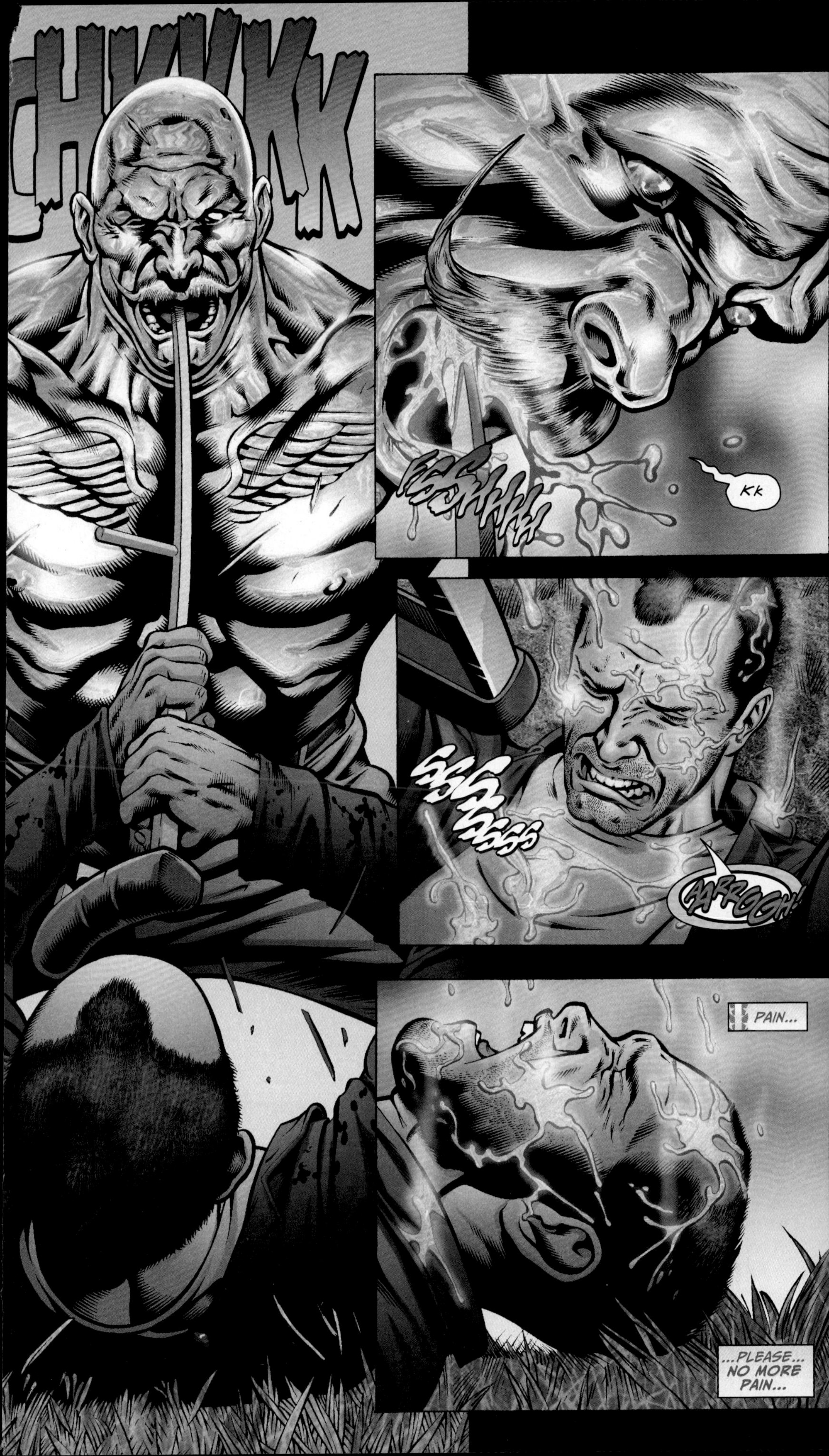

CHKKKK
FSSHHHH
KK
SSSSSSS
AARGGH!
PAIN...
...PLEASE... NO MORE PAIN...

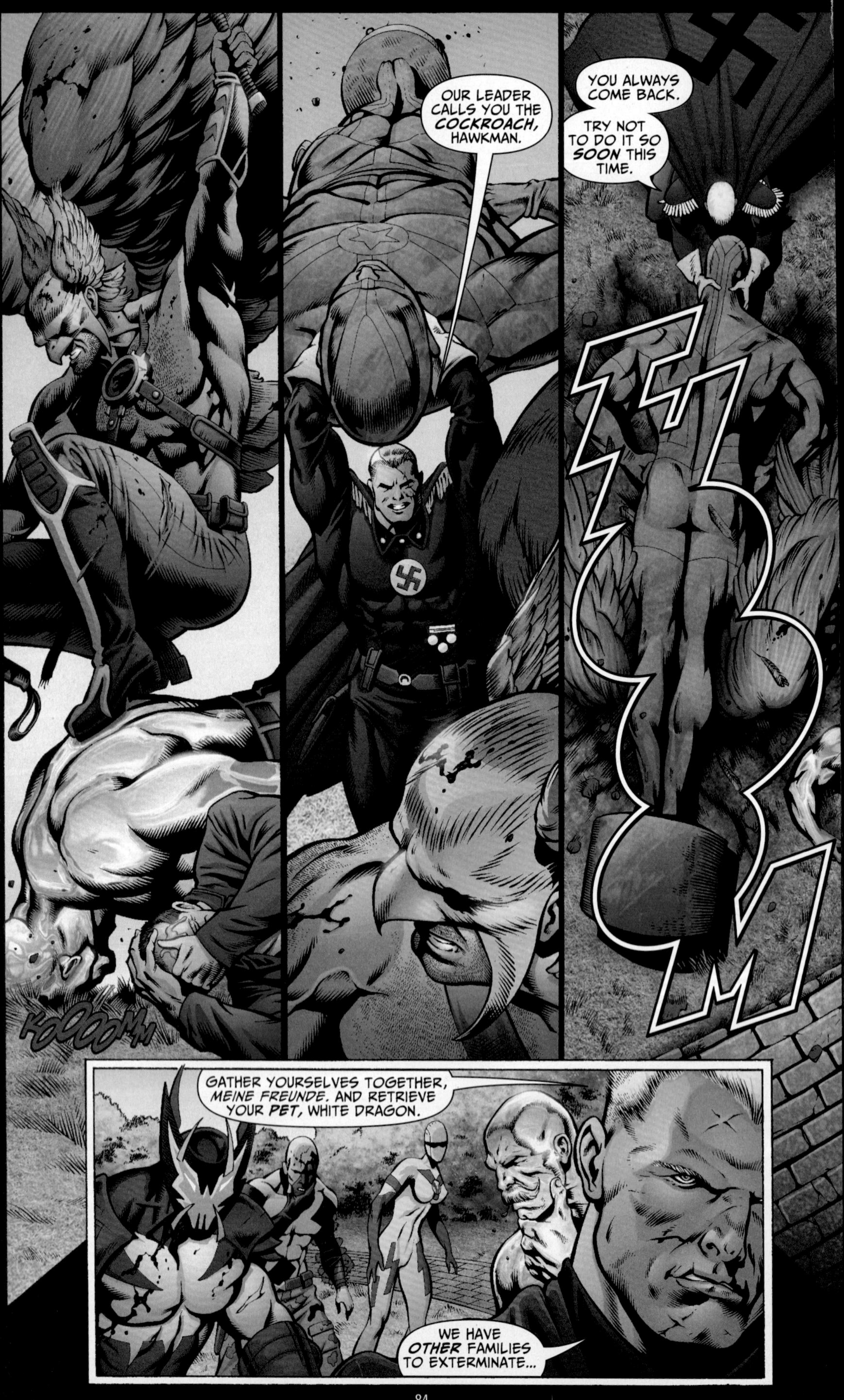
KOOOOMM
OUR LEADER CALLS YOU THE COCKROACH, HAWKMAN.
YOU ALWAYS COME BACK.
TRY NOT TO DO IT SO SOON THIS TIME.
THOOM
GATHER YOURSELVES TOGETHER, MEINE FREUNDE. AND RETRIEVE YOUR PET, WHITE DRAGON.
WE HAVE OTHER FAMILIES TO EXTERMINATE...

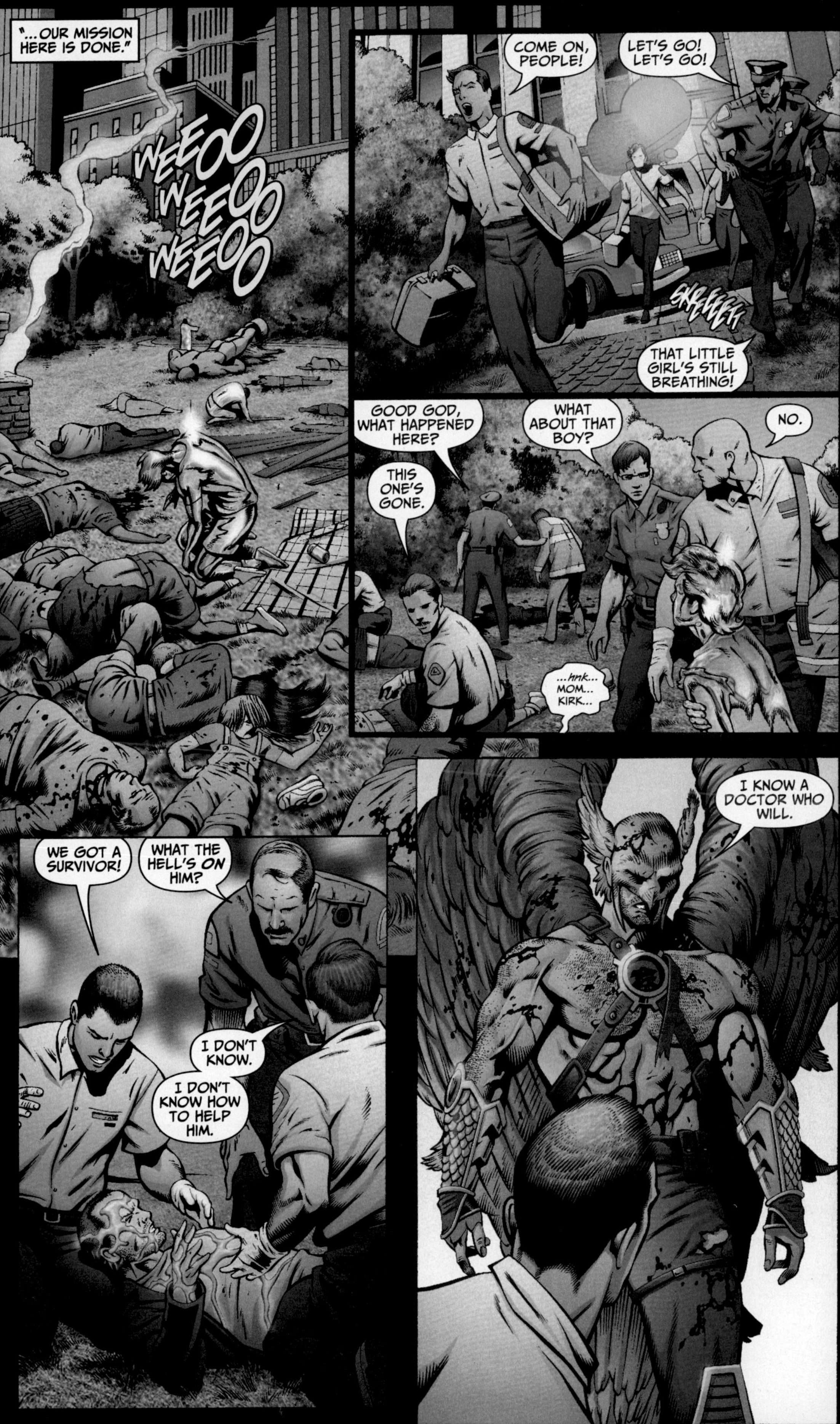
"...OUR MISSION HERE IS DONE."
WEEOO WEEOO WEEOO
COME ON, PEOPLE!
LET'S GO! LET'S GO!
SKREEEEK
THAT LITTLE GIRL'S STILL BREATHING!
GOOD GOD, WHAT HAPPENED HERE?
THIS ONE'S GONE.
WHAT ABOUT THAT BOY?
NO.
...hnk... MOM... KIRK...
WE GOT A SURVIVOR!
WHAT THE HELL'S ON HIM?
I DON'T KNOW.
I DON'T KNOW HOW TO HELP HIM.
I KNOW A DOCTOR WHO WILL.

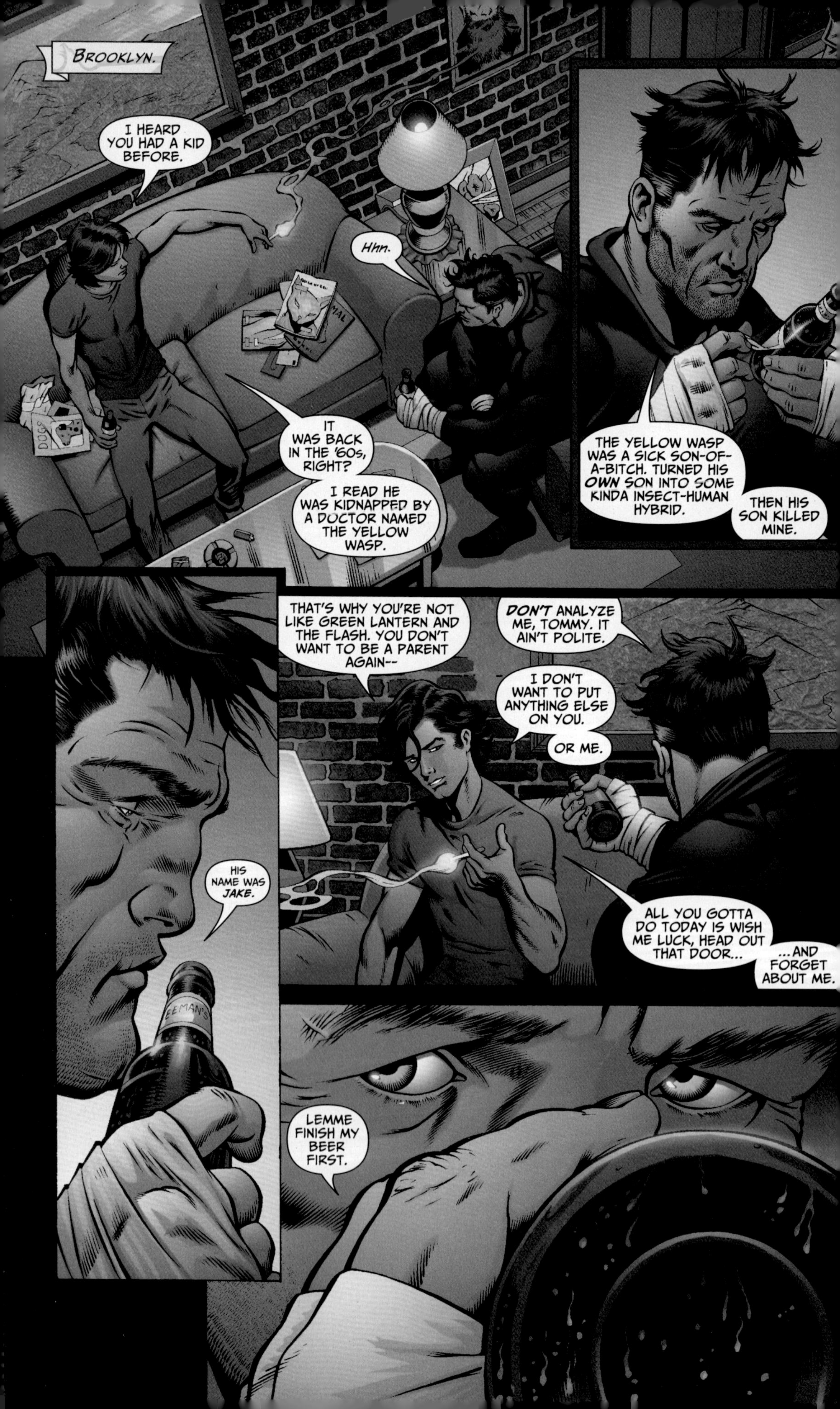
BROOKLYN.
I HEARD YOU HAD A KID BEFORE.
Hhn.
IT WAS BACK IN THE '60s, RIGHT?
I READ HE WAS KIDNAPPED BY A DOCTOR NAMED THE YELLOW WASP.
THE YELLOW WASP WAS A SICK SON-OF-A-BITCH. TURNED HIS OWN SON INTO SOME KINDA INSECT-HUMAN HYBRID.
THEN HIS SON KILLED MINE.
HIS NAME WAS JAKE.
THAT'S WHY YOU'RE NOT LIKE GREEN LANTERN AND THE FLASH. YOU DON'T WANT TO BE A PARENT AGAIN--
DON'T ANALYZE ME, TOMMY. IT AIN'T POLITE.
I DON'T WANT TO PUT ANYTHING ELSE ON YOU.
OR ME.
ALL YOU GOTTA DO TODAY IS WISH ME LUCK, HEAD OUT THAT DOOR...
...AND FORGET ABOUT ME.
LEMME FINISH MY BEER FIRST.

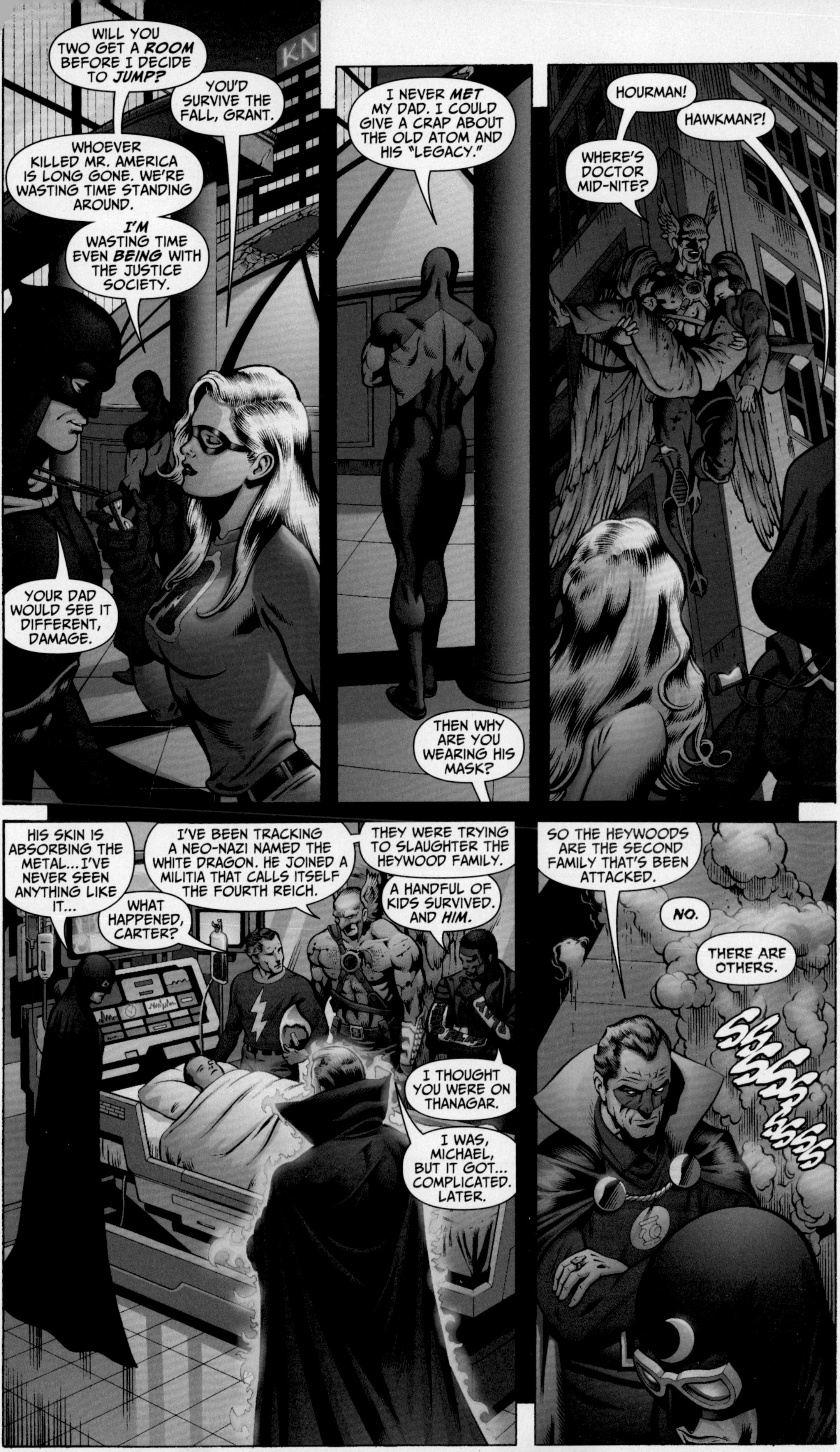
WILL YOU TWO GET A ROOM BEFORE I DECIDE TO JUMP?
YOU'D SURVIVE THE FALL, GRANT.
WHOEVER KILLED MR. AMERICA IS LONG GONE. WE'RE WASTING TIME STANDING AROUND.
I'M WASTING TIME EVEN BEING WITH THE JUSTICE SOCIETY.
YOUR DAD WOULD SEE IT DIFFERENT, DAMAGE.
I NEVER MET MY DAD. I COULD GIVE A CRAP ABOUT THE OLD ATOM AND HIS "LEGACY."
THEN WHY ARE YOU WEARING HIS MASK?
HOURMAN!
HAWKMAN?!
WHERE'S DOCTOR MID-NITE?
HIS SKIN IS ABSORBING THE METAL...I'VE NEVER SEEN ANYTHING LIKE IT...
WHAT HAPPENED, CARTER?
I'VE BEEN TRACKING A NEO-NAZI NAMED THE WHITE DRAGON. HE JOINED A MILITIA THAT CALLS ITSELF THE FOURTH REICH.
THEY WERE TRYING TO SLAUGHTER THE HEYWOOD FAMILY.
A HANDFUL OF KIDS SURVIVED. AND HIM.
I THOUGHT YOU WERE ON THANAGAR.
I WAS, MICHAEL, BUT IT GOT... COMPLICATED. LATER.
SO THE HEYWOODS ARE THE SECOND FAMILY THAT'S BEEN ATTACKED.
NO.
THERE ARE OTHERS.
SSSSSSSSSSS

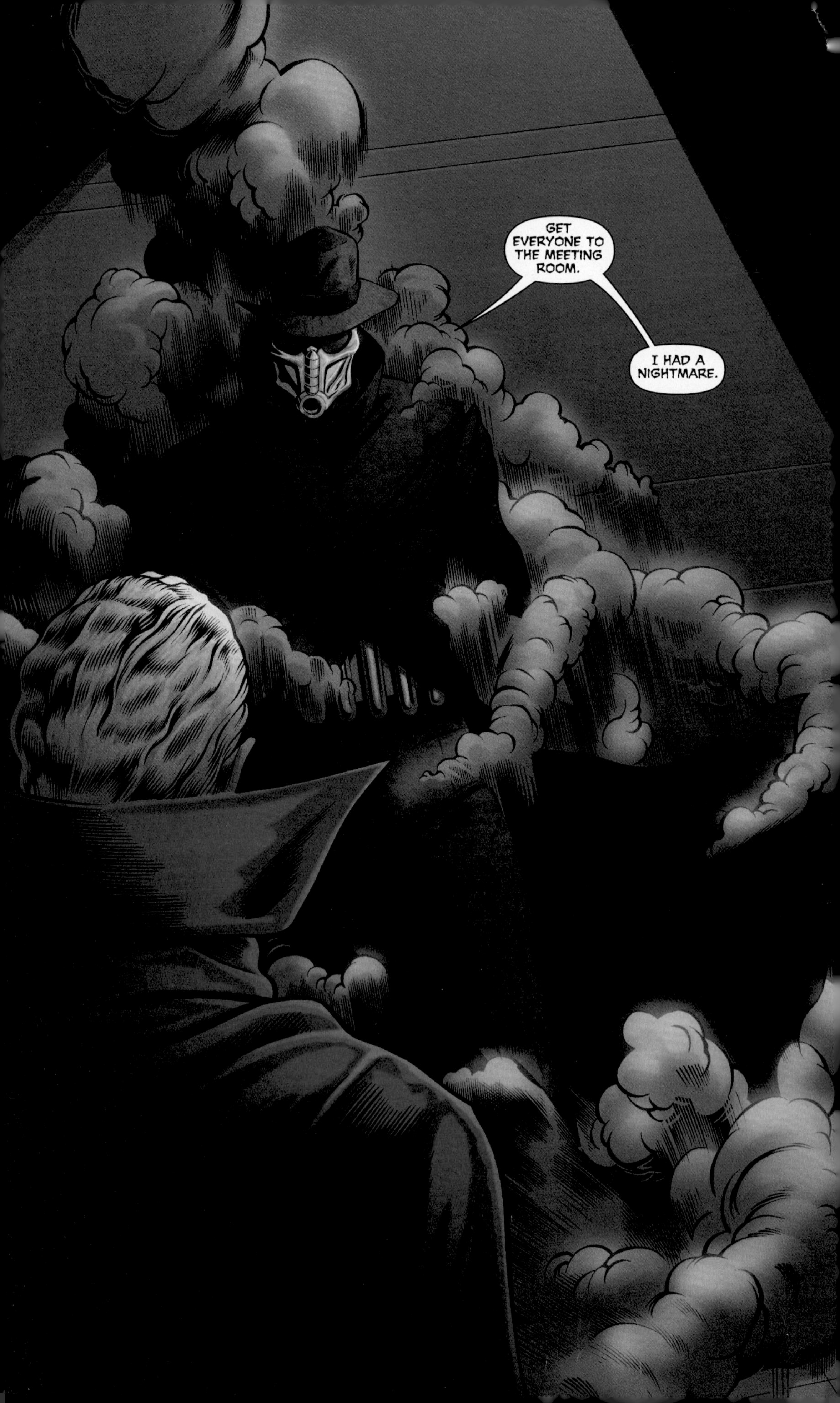
GET EVERYONE TO THE MEETING ROOM.
I HAD A NIGHTMARE.

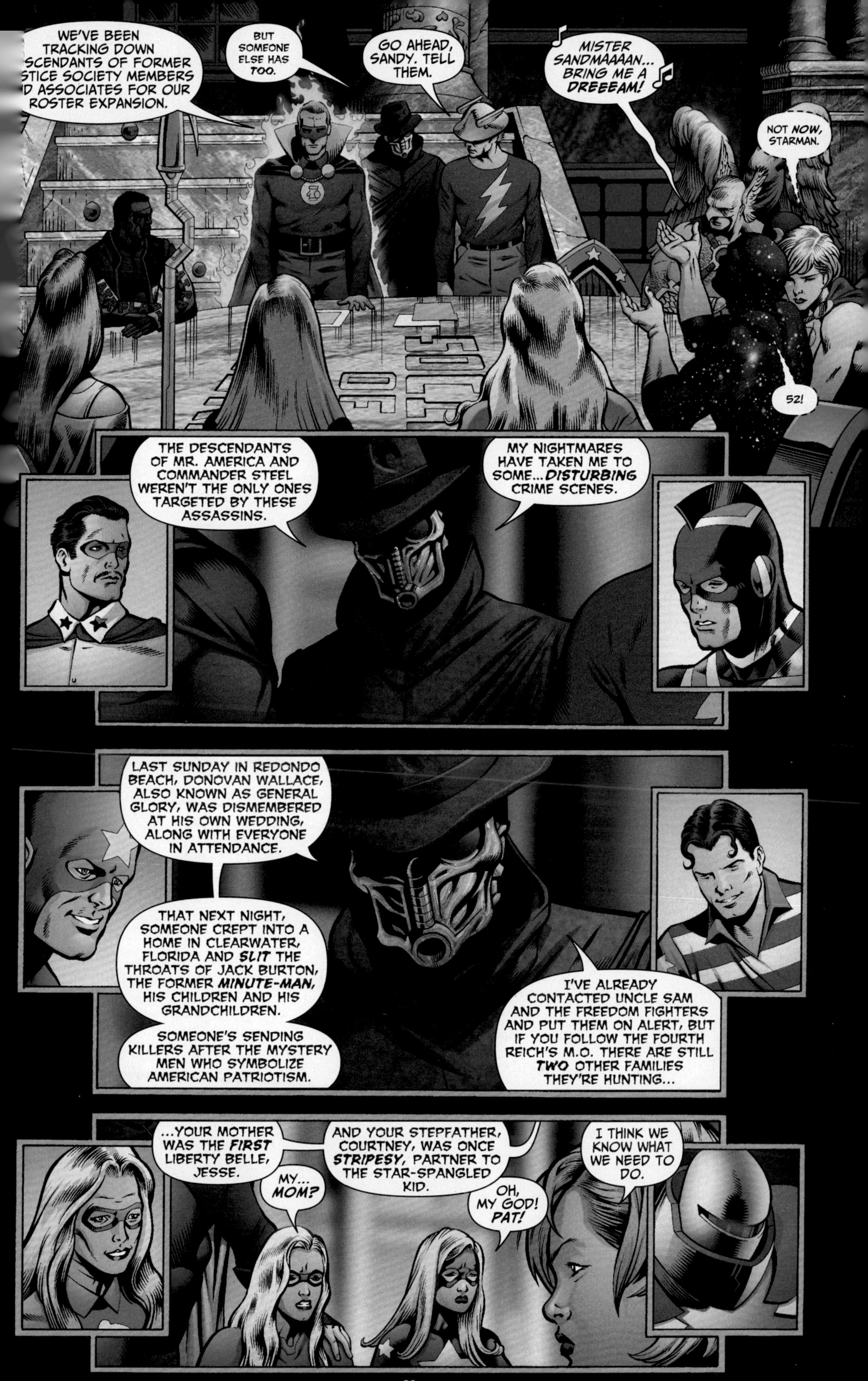
WE'VE BEEN TRACKING DOWN SCENDANTS OF FORMER STICE SOCIETY MEMBERS D ASSOCIATES FOR OUR ROSTER EXPANSION.
BUT SOMEONE ELSE HAS TOO.
GO AHEAD, SANDY. TELL THEM.
MISTER SANDMAAAAN... BRING ME A DREEEAM!
NOT NOW, STARMAN.
52!
THE DESCENDANTS OF MR. AMERICA AND COMMANDER STEEL WEREN'T THE ONLY ONES TARGETED BY THESE ASSASSINS.
MY NIGHTMARES HAVE TAKEN ME TO SOME...DISTURBING CRIME SCENES.
LAST SUNDAY IN REDONDO BEACH, DONOVAN WALLACE, ALSO KNOWN AS GENERAL GLORY, WAS DISMEMBERED AT HIS OWN WEDDING, ALONG WITH EVERYONE IN ATTENDANCE.
THAT NEXT NIGHT, SOMEONE CREPT INTO A HOME IN CLEARWATER, FLORIDA AND SLIT THE THROATS OF JACK BURTON, THE FORMER MINUTE-MAN, HIS CHILDREN AND HIS GRANDCHILDREN.
SOMEONE'S SENDING KILLERS AFTER THE MYSTERY MEN WHO SYMBOLIZE AMERICAN PATRIOTISM.
I'VE ALREADY CONTACTED UNCLE SAM AND THE FREEDOM FIGHTERS AND PUT THEM ON ALERT, BUT IF YOU FOLLOW THE FOURTH REICH'S M.O. THERE ARE STILL TWO OTHER FAMILIES THEY'RE HUNTING...
...YOUR MOTHER WAS THE FIRST LIBERTY BELLE, JESSE.
MY... MOM?
AND YOUR STEPFATHER, COURTNEY, WAS ONCE STRIPESY, PARTNER TO THE STAR-SPANGLED KID.
OH, MY GOD! PAT!
I THINK WE KNOW WHAT WE NEED TO DO.

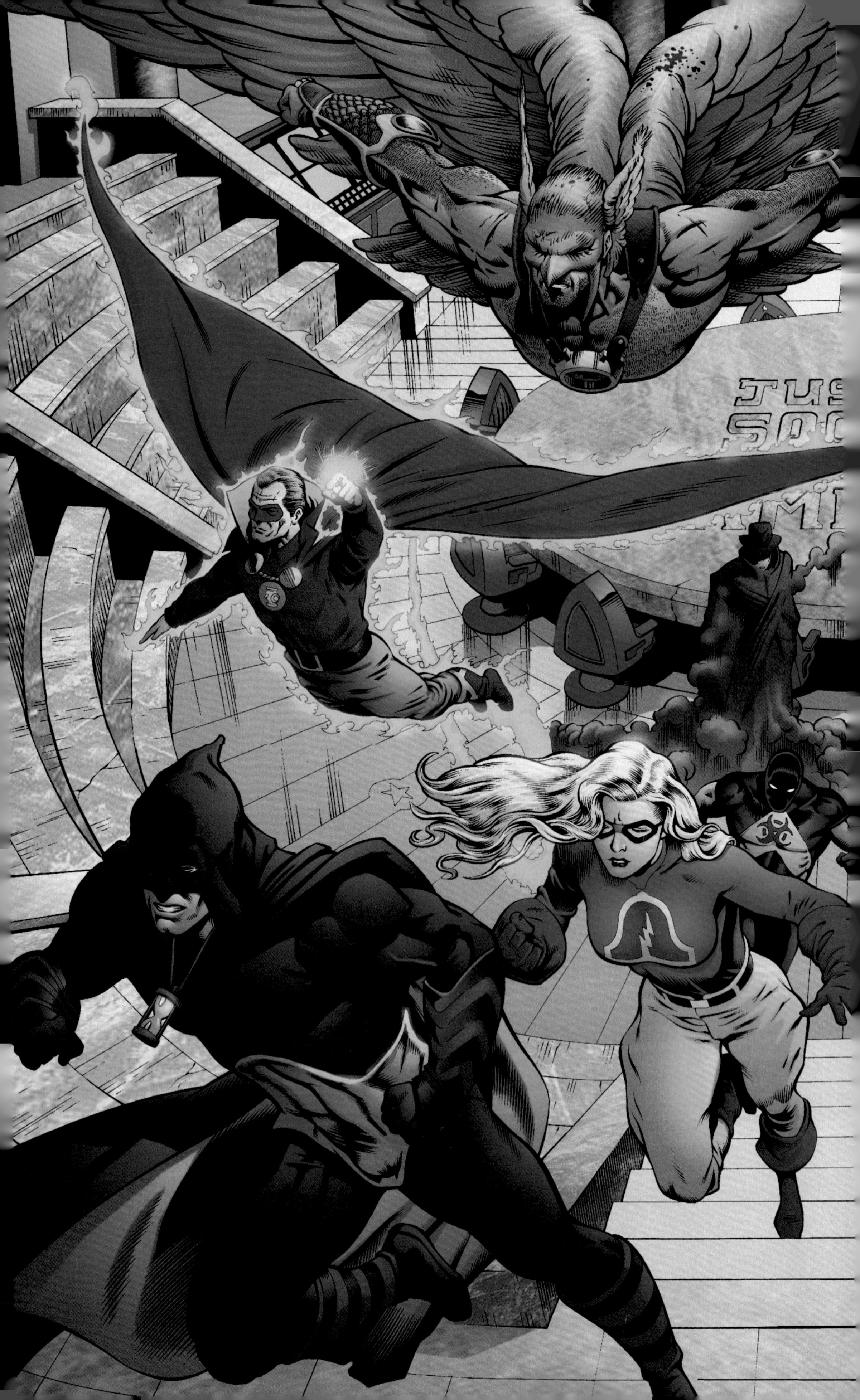

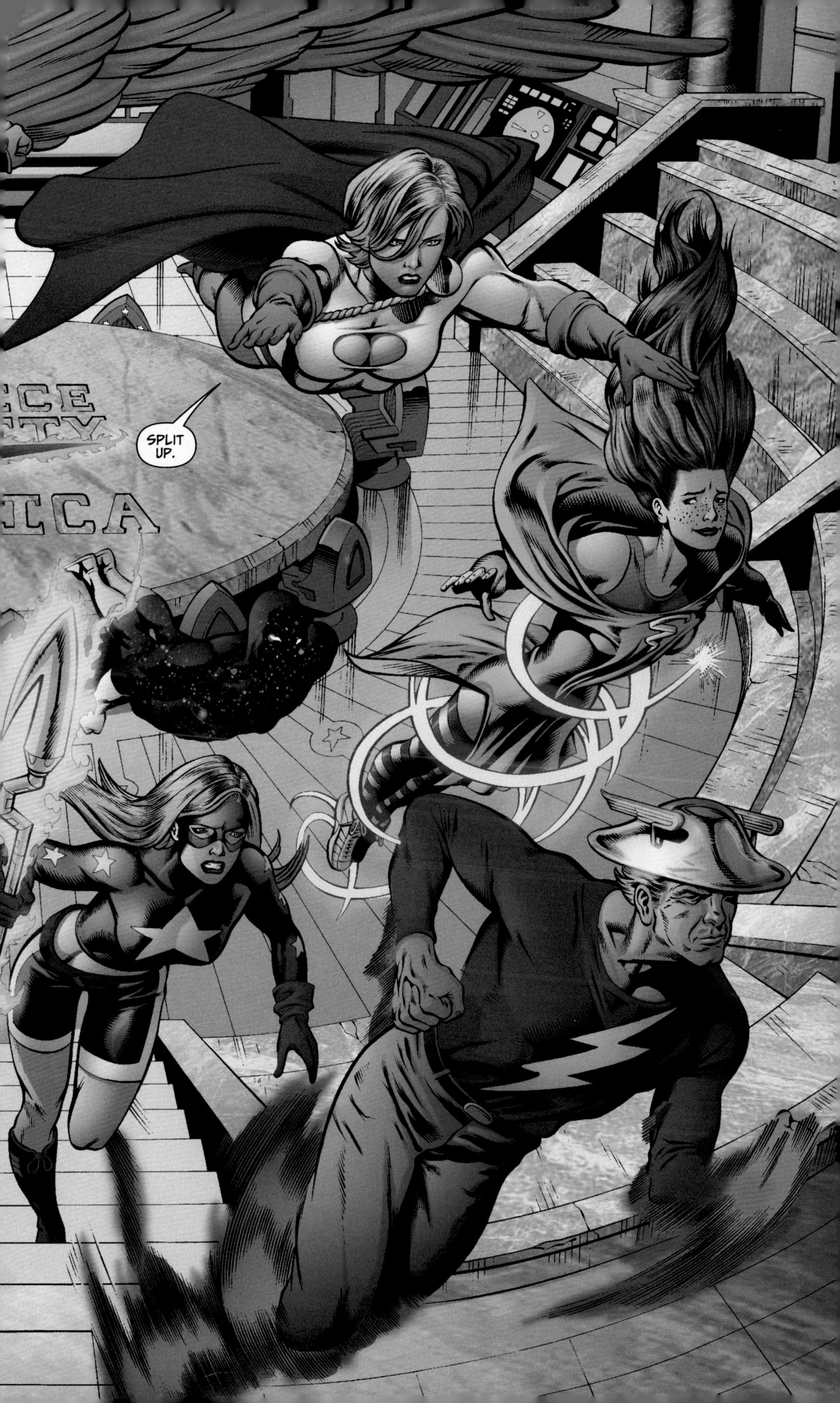
SPLIT UP.

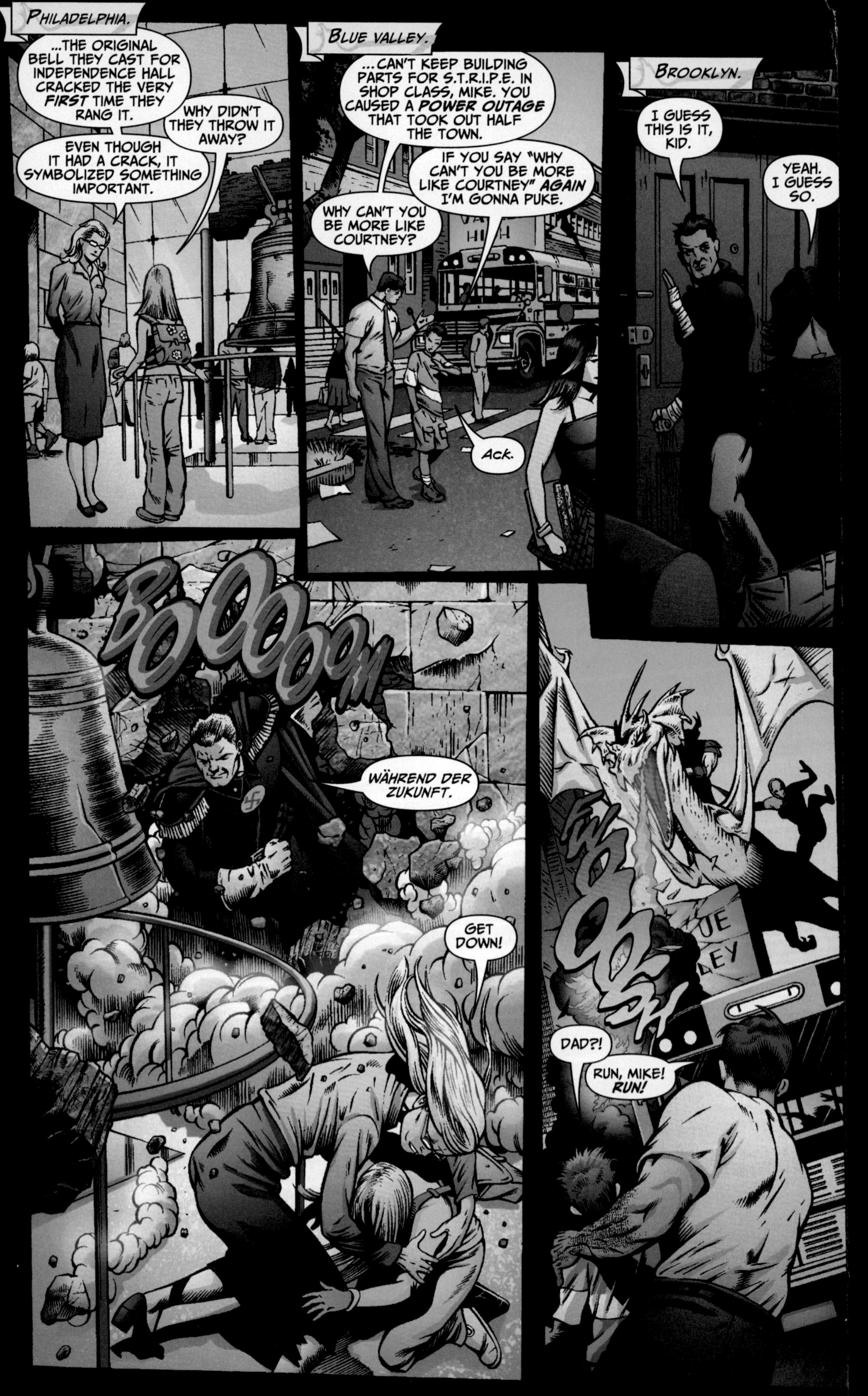

Philadelphia.
...THE ORIGINAL BELL THEY CAST FOR INDEPENDENCE HALL CRACKED THE VERY FIRST TIME THEY RANG IT.
WHY DIDN'T THEY THROW IT AWAY?
EVEN THOUGH IT HAD A CRACK, IT SYMBOLIZED SOMETHING IMPORTANT.
Blue valley.
...CAN'T KEEP BUILDING PARTS FOR S.T.R.I.P.E. IN SHOP CLASS, MIKE. YOU CAUSED A POWER OUTAGE THAT TOOK OUT HALF THE TOWN.
WHY CAN'T YOU BE MORE LIKE COURTNEY?
IF YOU SAY "WHY CAN'T YOU BE MORE LIKE COURTNEY" AGAIN I'M GONNA PUKE.
Ack.
Brooklyn.
I GUESS THIS IS IT, KID.
YEAH. I GUESS SO.
BOOOOOM
WÄHREND DER ZUKUNFT.
GET DOWN!
DAD?!
RUN, MIKE! RUN!

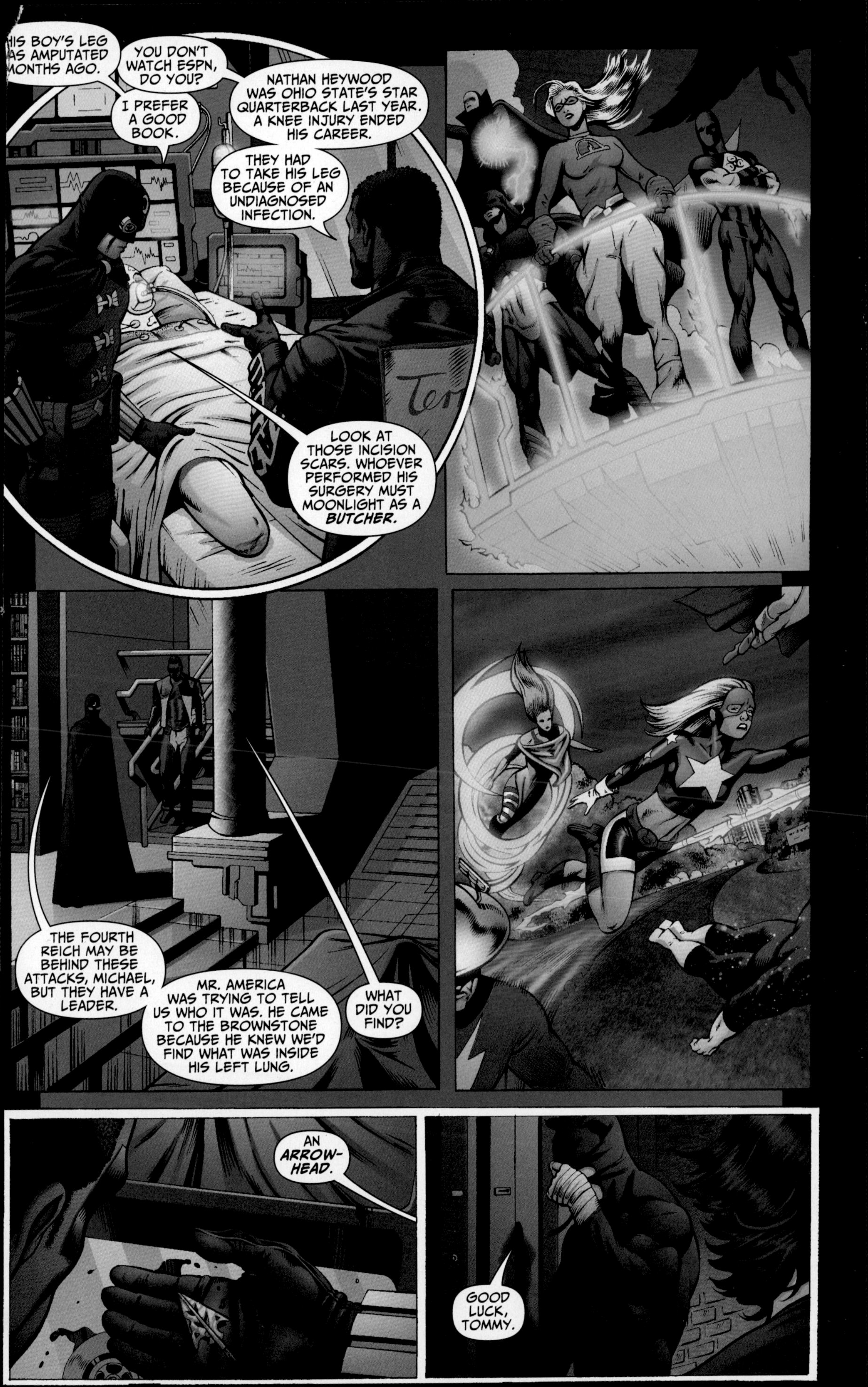

HIS BOY'S LEG WAS AMPUTATED MONTHS AGO.
YOU DON'T WATCH ESPN, DO YOU?
I PREFER A GOOD BOOK.
NATHAN HEYWOOD WAS OHIO STATE'S STAR QUARTERBACK LAST YEAR. A KNEE INJURY ENDED HIS CAREER.
THEY HAD TO TAKE HIS LEG BECAUSE OF AN UNDIAGNOSED INFECTION.
LOOK AT THOSE INCISION SCARS. WHOEVER PERFORMED HIS SURGERY MUST MOONLIGHT AS A BUTCHER.
THE FOURTH REICH MAY BE BEHIND THESE ATTACKS, MICHAEL, BUT THEY HAVE A LEADER.
MR. AMERICA WAS TRYING TO TELL US WHO IT WAS. HE CAME TO THE BROWNSTONE BECAUSE HE KNEW WE'D FIND WHAT WAS INSIDE HIS LEFT LUNG.
WHAT DID YOU FIND?
AN ARROW-HEAD.
GOOD LUCK, TOMMY.

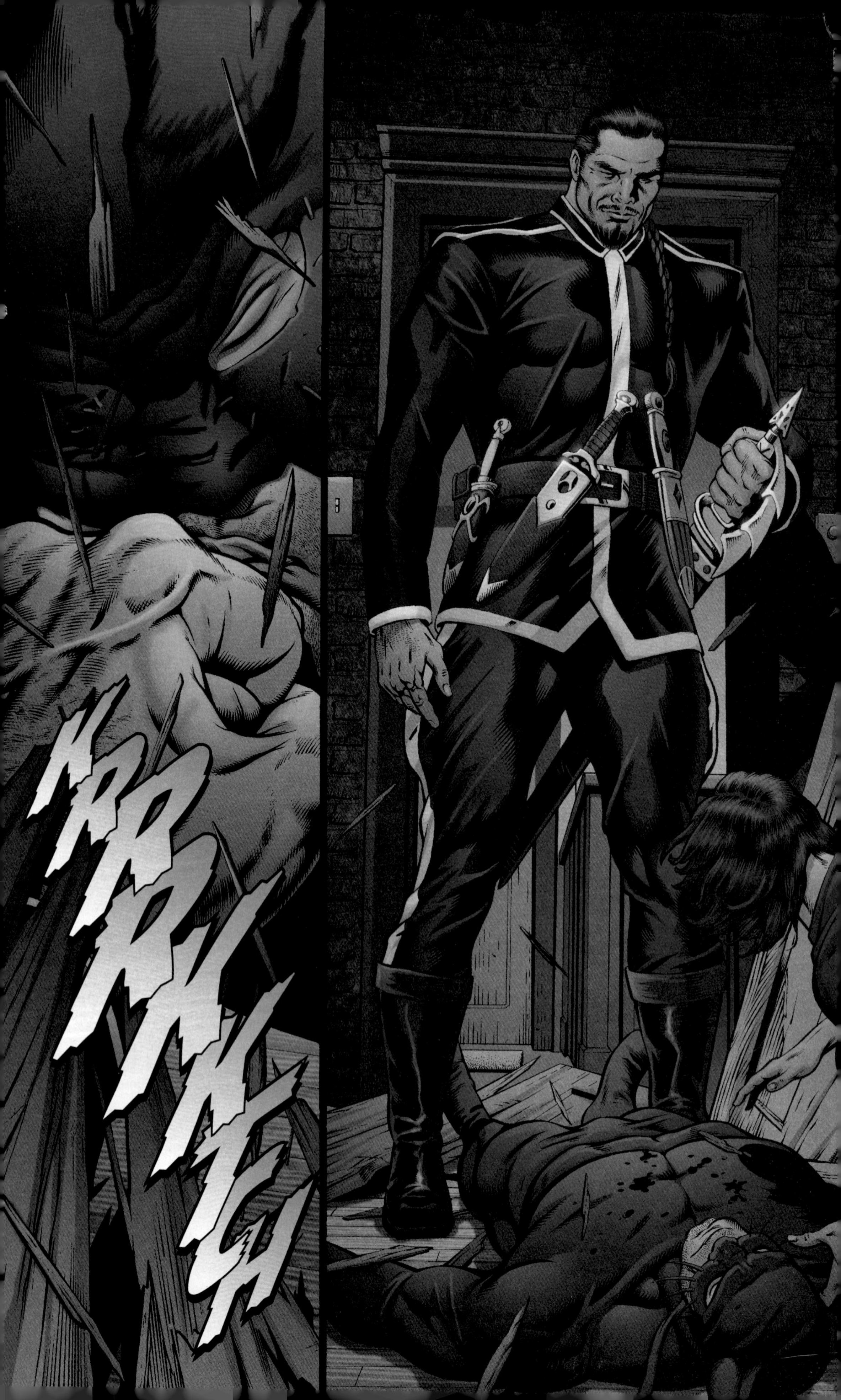
KRRANCH

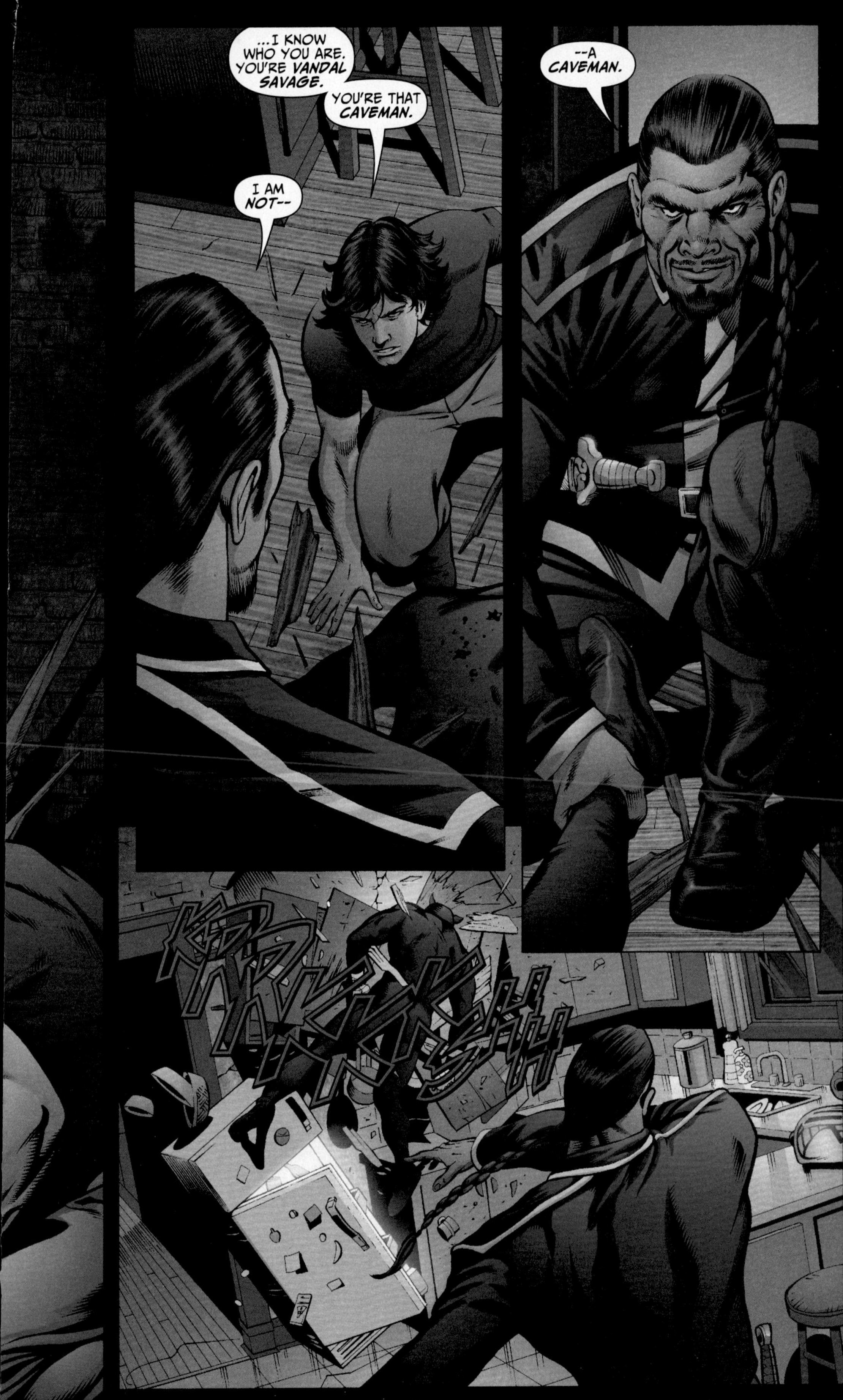
...I KNOW WHO YOU ARE. YOU'RE VANDAL SAVAGE.
YOU'RE THAT CAVEMAN.
I AM NOT--
--A CAVEMAN.
KRRNNKKSHH

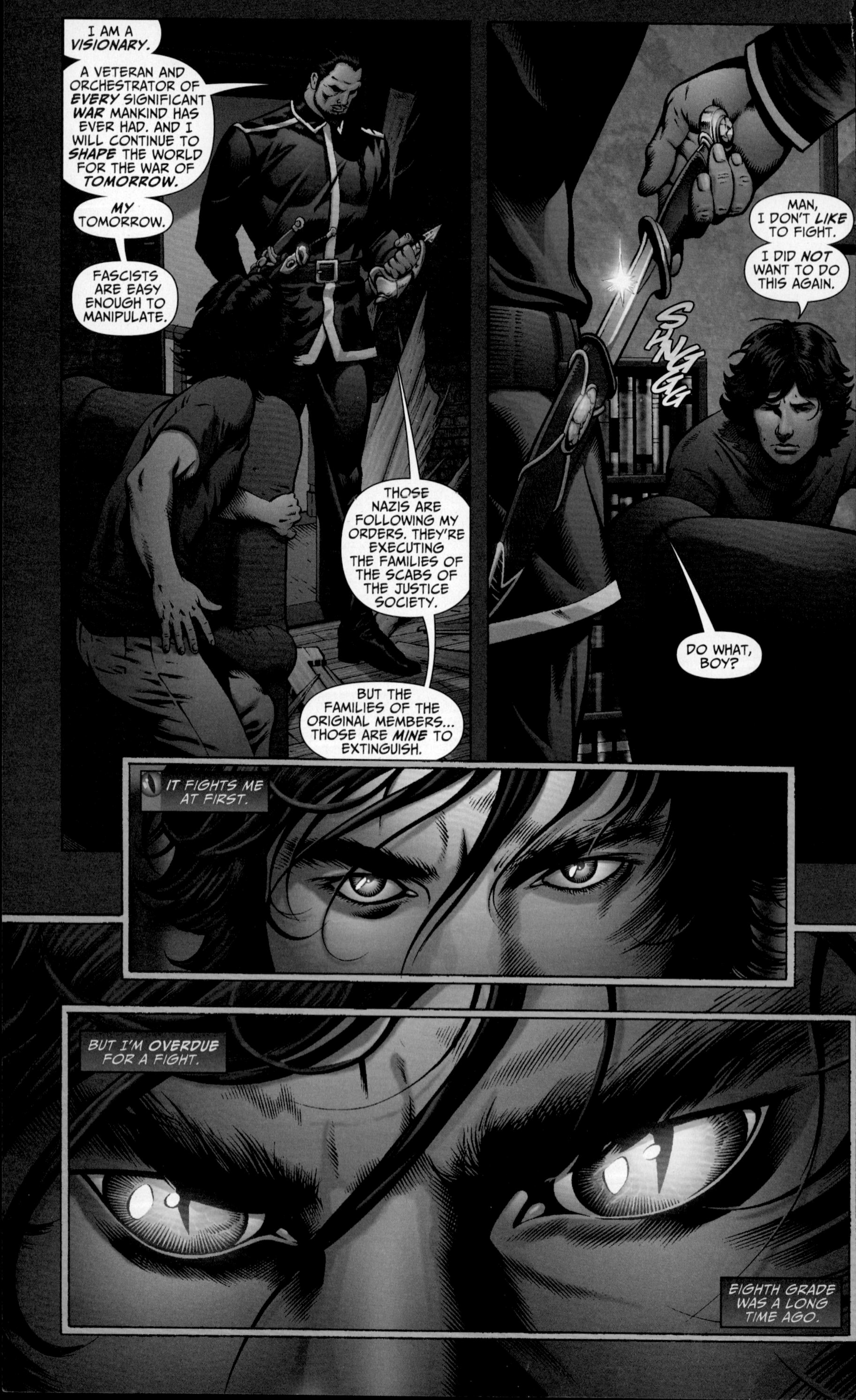

I AM A VISIONARY.
A VETERAN AND ORCHESTRATOR OF EVERY SIGNIFICANT WAR MANKIND HAS EVER HAD. AND I WILL CONTINUE TO SHAPE THE WORLD FOR THE WAR OF TOMORROW.
MY TOMORROW.
FASCISTS ARE EASY ENOUGH TO MANIPULATE.
THOSE NAZIS ARE FOLLOWING MY ORDERS. THEY'RE EXECUTING THE FAMILIES OF THE SCABS OF THE JUSTICE SOCIETY.
BUT THE FAMILIES OF THE ORIGINAL MEMBERS... THOSE ARE MINE TO EXTINGUISH.
MAN, I DON'T LIKE TO FIGHT.
I DID NOT WANT TO DO THIS AGAIN.
SHNGGG
DO WHAT, BOY?
IT FIGHTS ME AT FIRST.
BUT I'M OVERDUE FOR A FIGHT.
EIGHTH GRADE WAS A LONG TIME AGO.

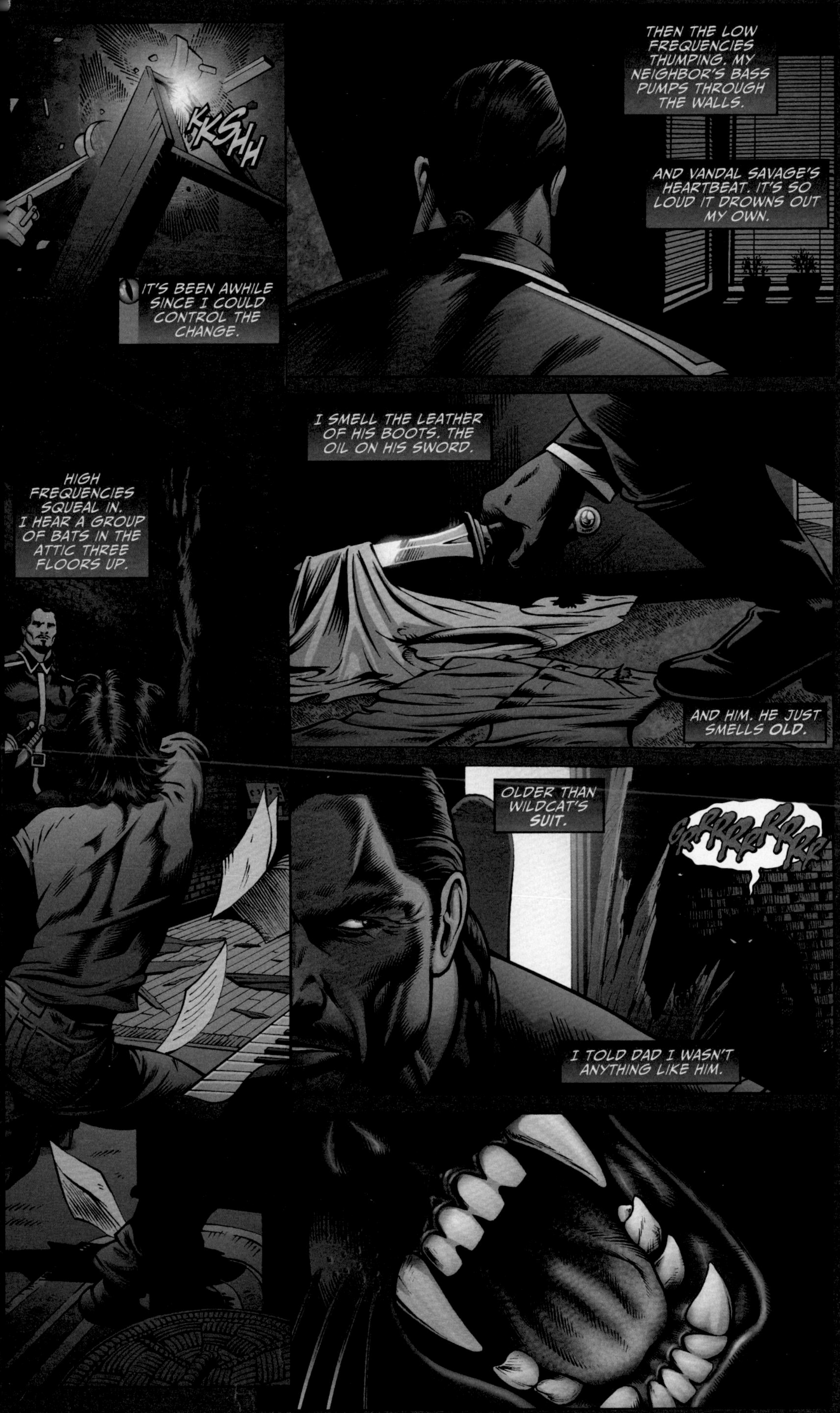
KKSHH
IT'S BEEN AWHILE SINCE I COULD CONTROL THE CHANGE.
THEN THE LOW FREQUENCIES THUMPING. MY NEIGHBOR'S BASS PUMPS THROUGH THE WALLS.
AND VANDAL SAVAGE'S HEARTBEAT. IT'S SO LOUD IT DROWNS OUT MY OWN.
HIGH FREQUENCIES SQUEAL IN. I HEAR A GROUP OF BATS IN THE ATTIC THREE FLOORS UP.
I SMELL THE LEATHER OF HIS BOOTS. THE OIL ON HIS SWORD.
AND HIM. HE JUST SMELLS OLD.
OLDER THAN WILDCAT'S SUIT.
GRRRRRRRRR
I TOLD DAD I WASN'T ANYTHING LIKE HIM.

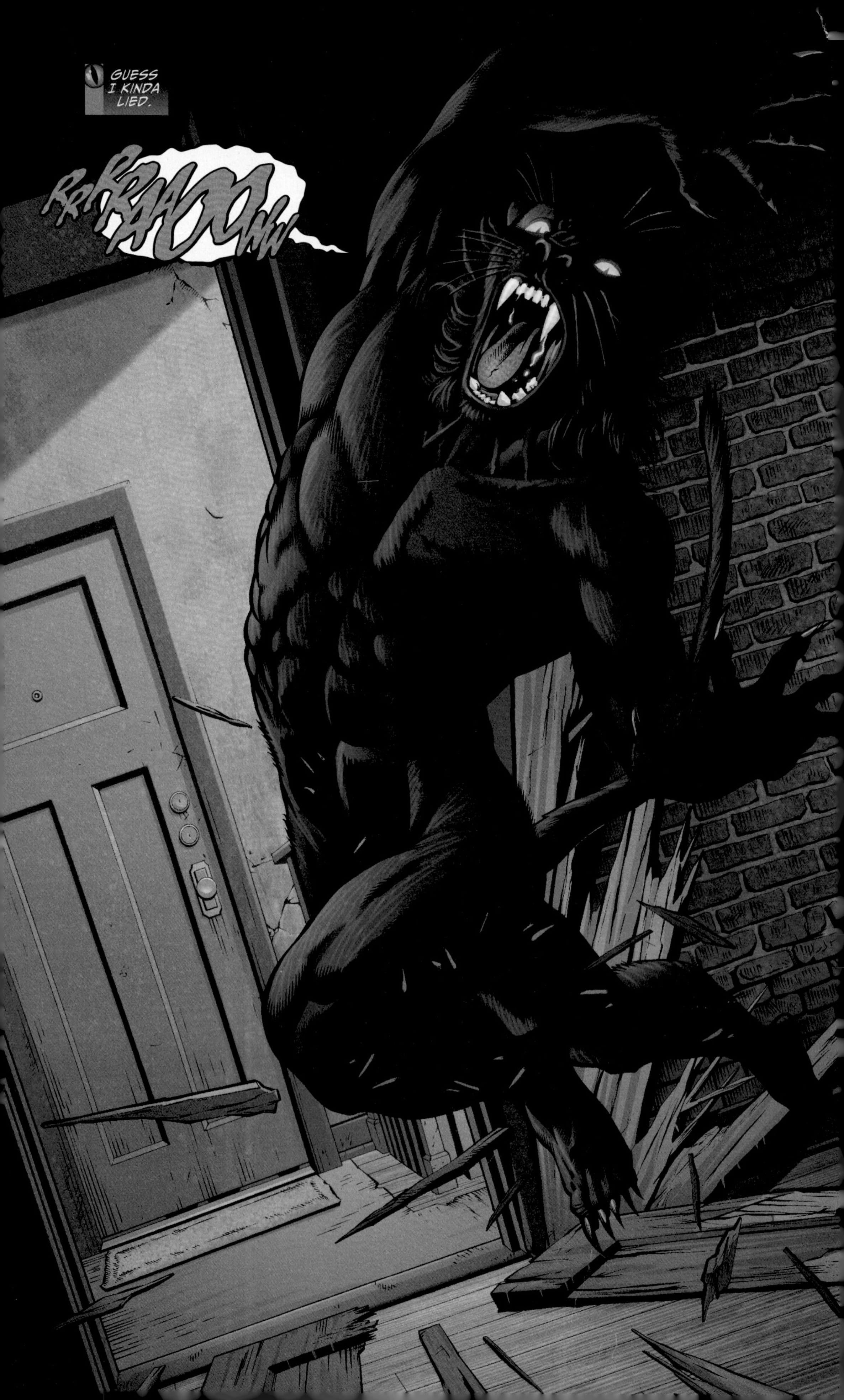
GUESS I KINDA LIED.
RRRRAAOOWW

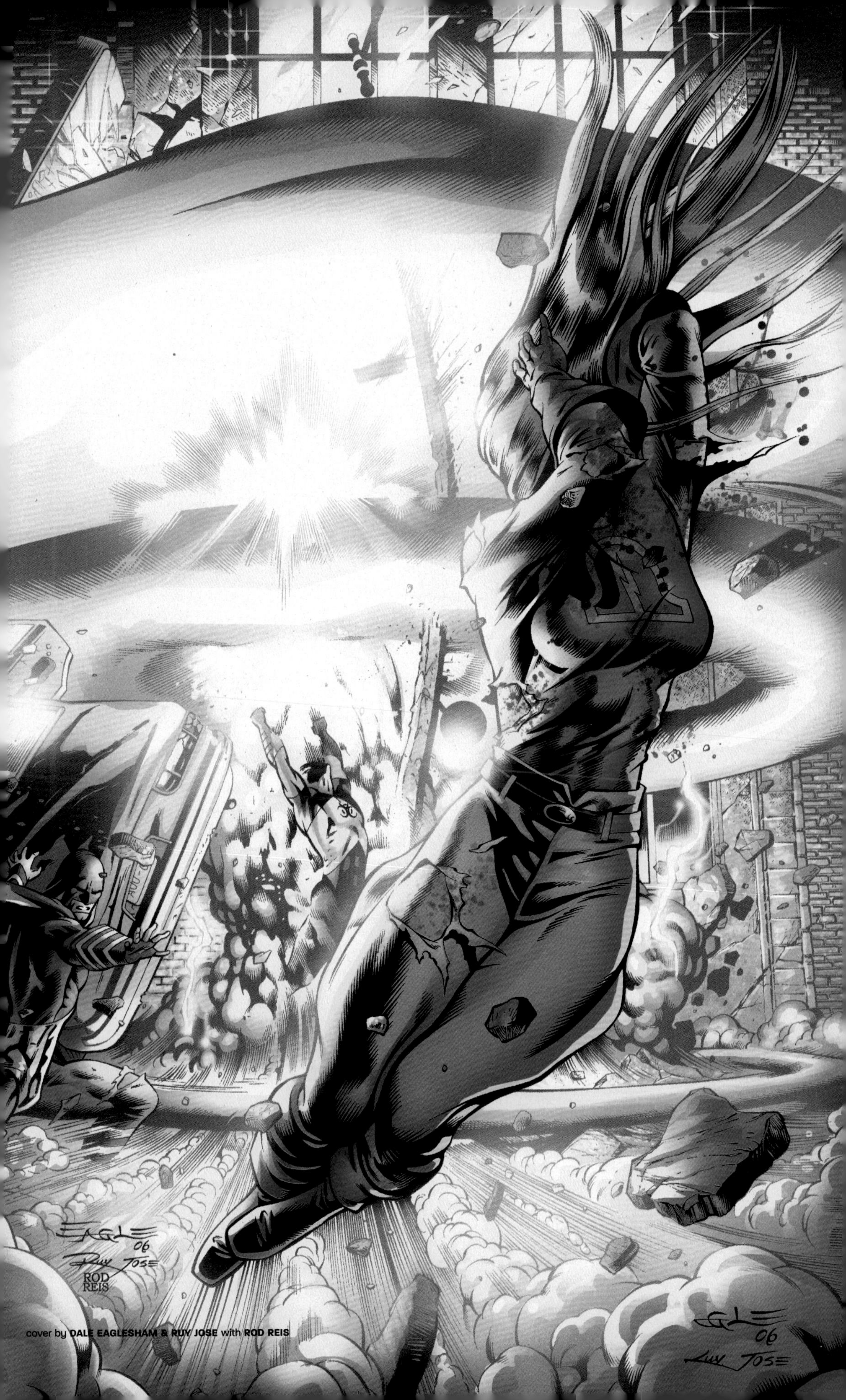
EAGLE 06
RUY JOSE
ROD REIS
EGLE 06
RUY JOSE

cover by **DALE EAGLESHAM & RUY JOSE** with **ROD REIS**

THE NEXT AGE

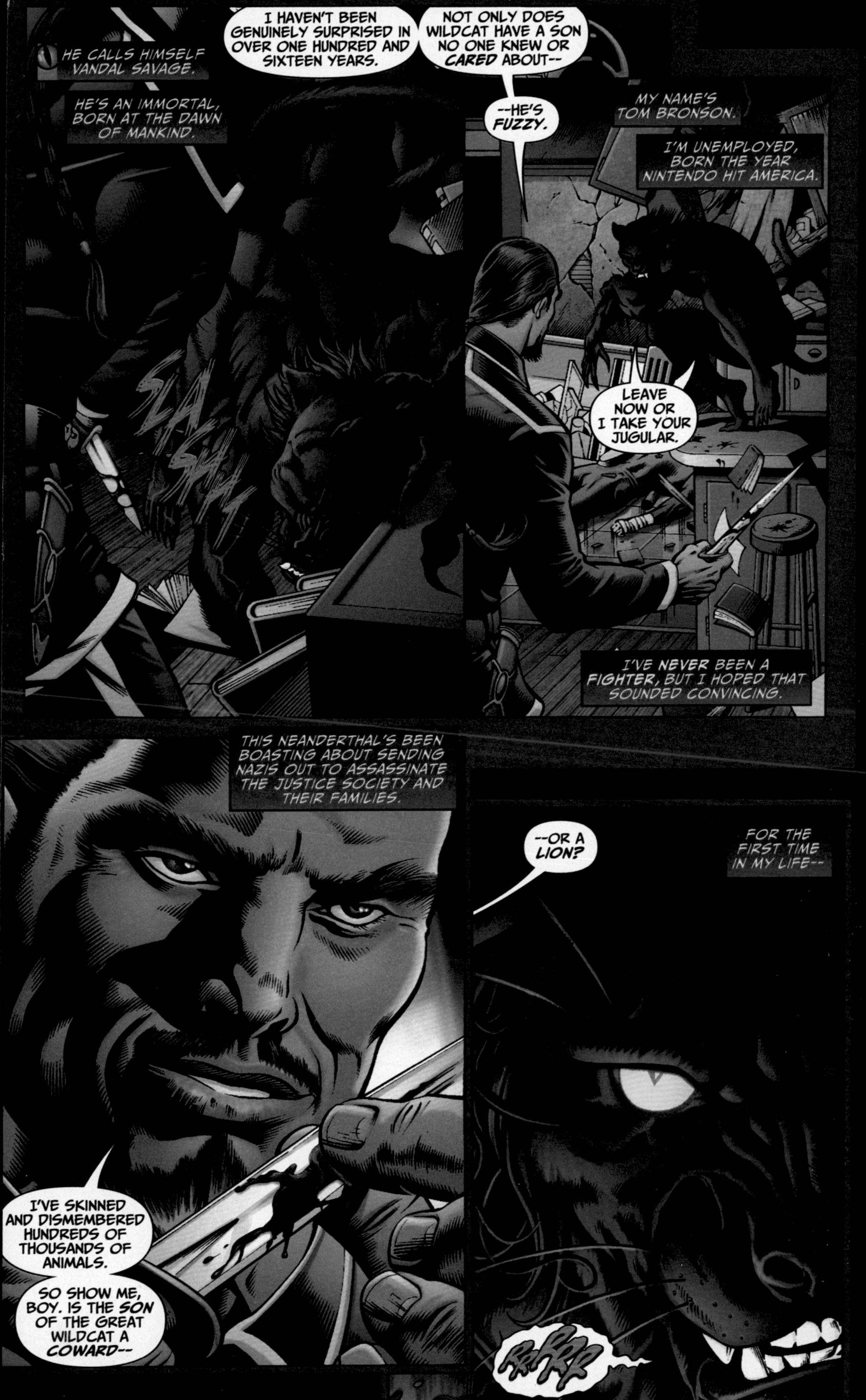
HE CALLS HIMSELF VANDAL SAVAGE.
HE'S AN IMMORTAL, BORN AT THE DAWN OF MANKIND.
I HAVEN'T BEEN GENUINELY SURPRISED IN OVER ONE HUNDRED AND SIXTEEN YEARS.
NOT ONLY DOES WILDCAT HAVE A SON NO ONE KNEW OR CARED ABOUT--
--HE'S FUZZY.
MY NAME'S TOM BRONSON.
I'M UNEMPLOYED, BORN THE YEAR NINTENDO HIT AMERICA.
LEAVE NOW OR I TAKE YOUR JUGULAR.
I'VE NEVER BEEN A FIGHTER, BUT I HOPED THAT SOUNDED CONVINCING.
THIS NEANDERTHAL'S BEEN BOASTING ABOUT SENDING NAZIS OUT TO ASSASSINATE THE JUSTICE SOCIETY AND THEIR FAMILIES.
I'VE SKINNED AND DISMEMBERED HUNDREDS OF THOUSANDS OF ANIMALS.
SO SHOW ME, BOY. IS THE SON OF THE GREAT WILDCAT A COWARD--
--OR A LION?
FOR THE FIRST TIME IN MY LIFE--

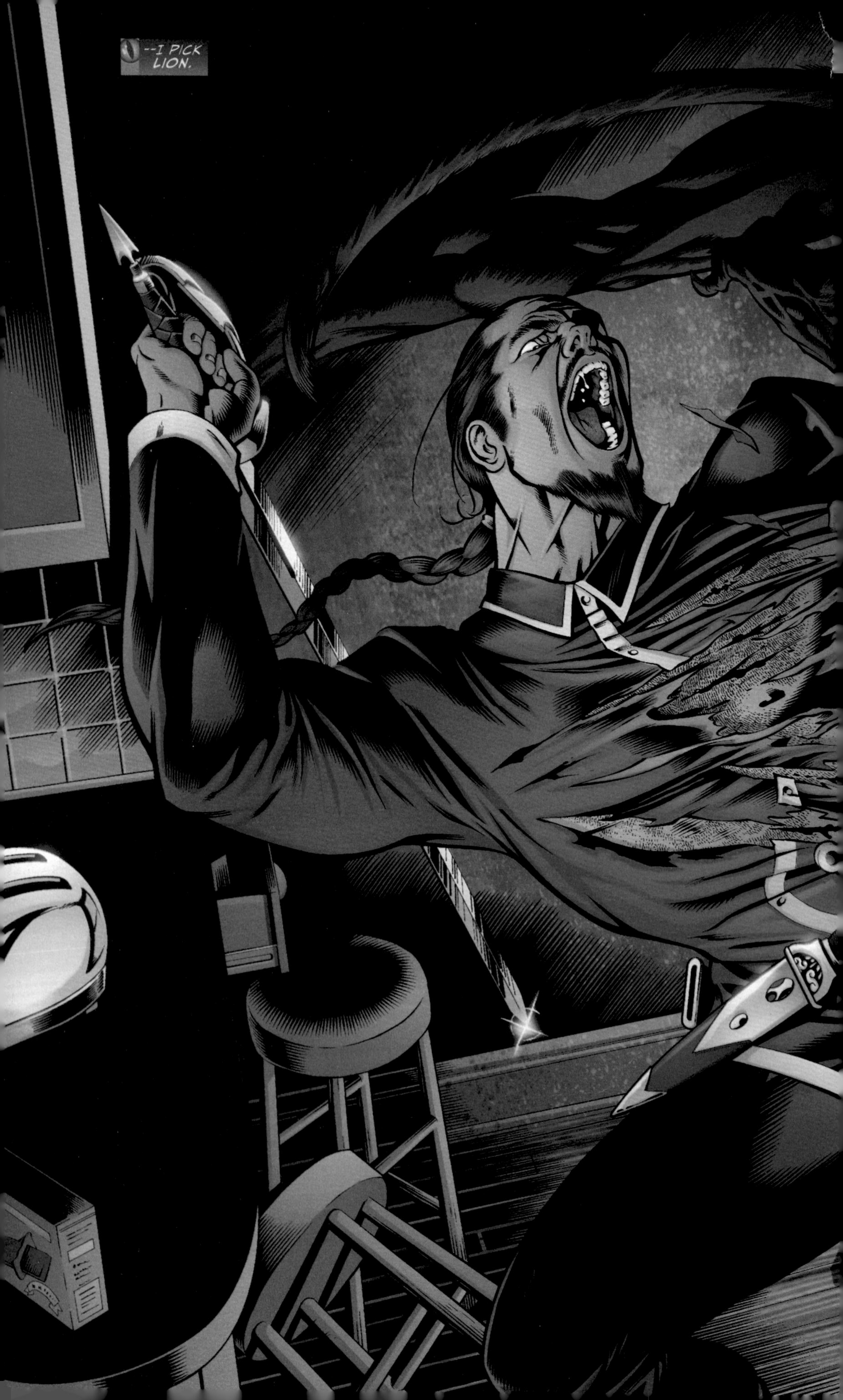
--I PICK LION.

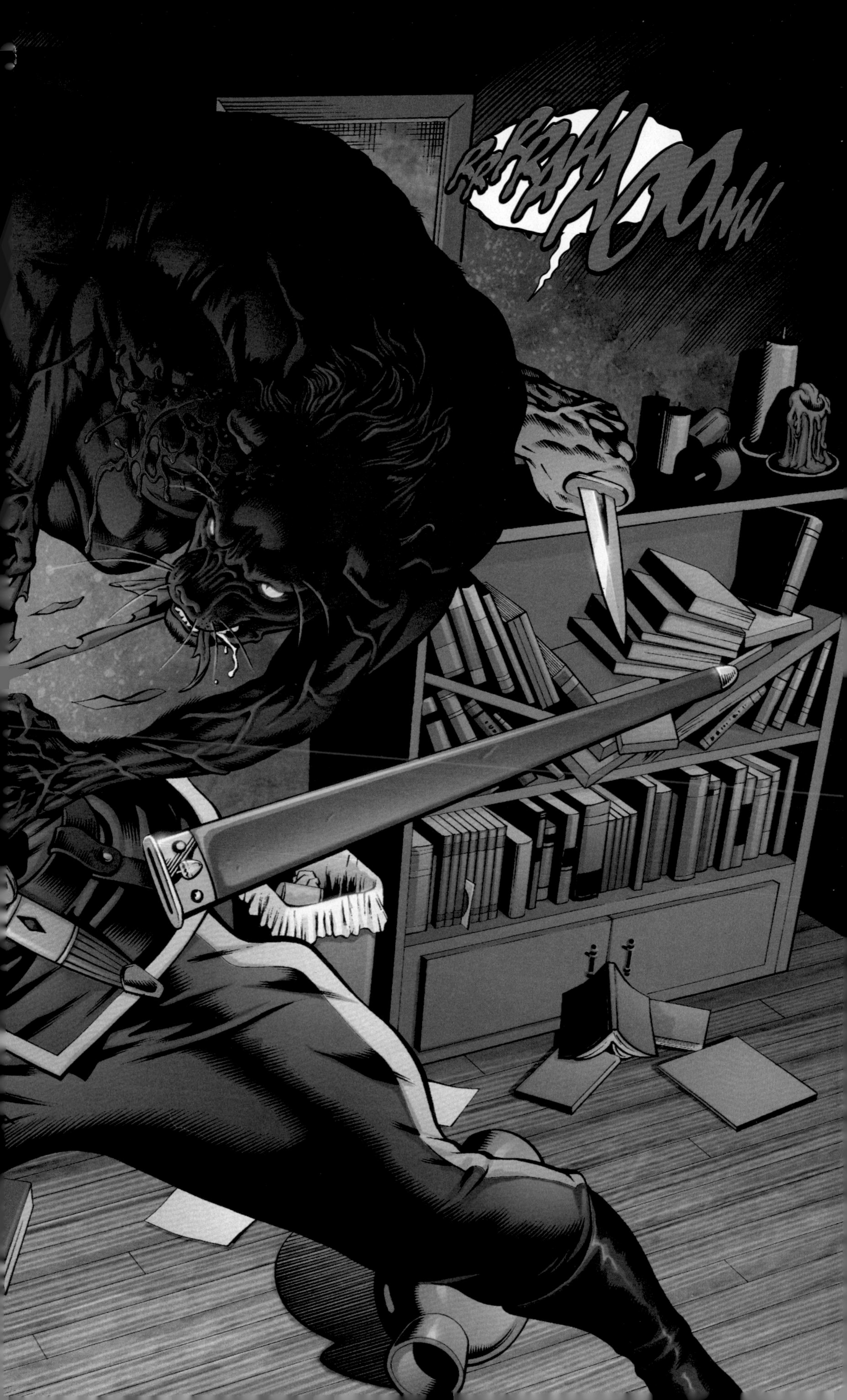
RRRRAAAOOww

BLUE VALLEY.

BO@OM

YOUR BOY DIES FIRST, STRIPESY.

I THOUGHT I KNEW ALL THE SPEEDSTERS.

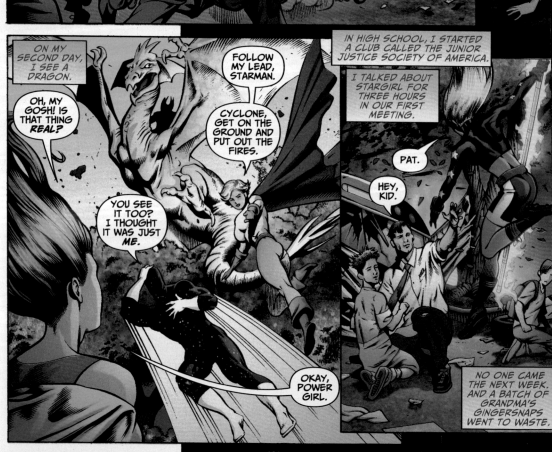

ON MY SECOND DAY, I SEE A DRAGON.

OH, MY GOSH! IS THAT THING REAL?

FOLLOW MY LEAD, STARMAN.

CYCLONE, GET ON THE GROUND AND PUT OUT THE FIRES.

YOU SEE IT TOO? I THOUGHT IT WAS JUST ME.

OKAY, POWER GIRL.

IN HIGH SCHOOL, I STARTED A CLUB CALLED THE JUNIOR JUSTICE SOCIETY OF AMERICA.

I TALKED ABOUT STARGIRL FOR THREE HOURS IN OUR FIRST MEETING.

PAT.

HEY, KID.

NO ONE CAME THE NEXT WEEK. AND A BATCH OF GRANDMA'S GINGERSNAPS WENT TO WASTE.

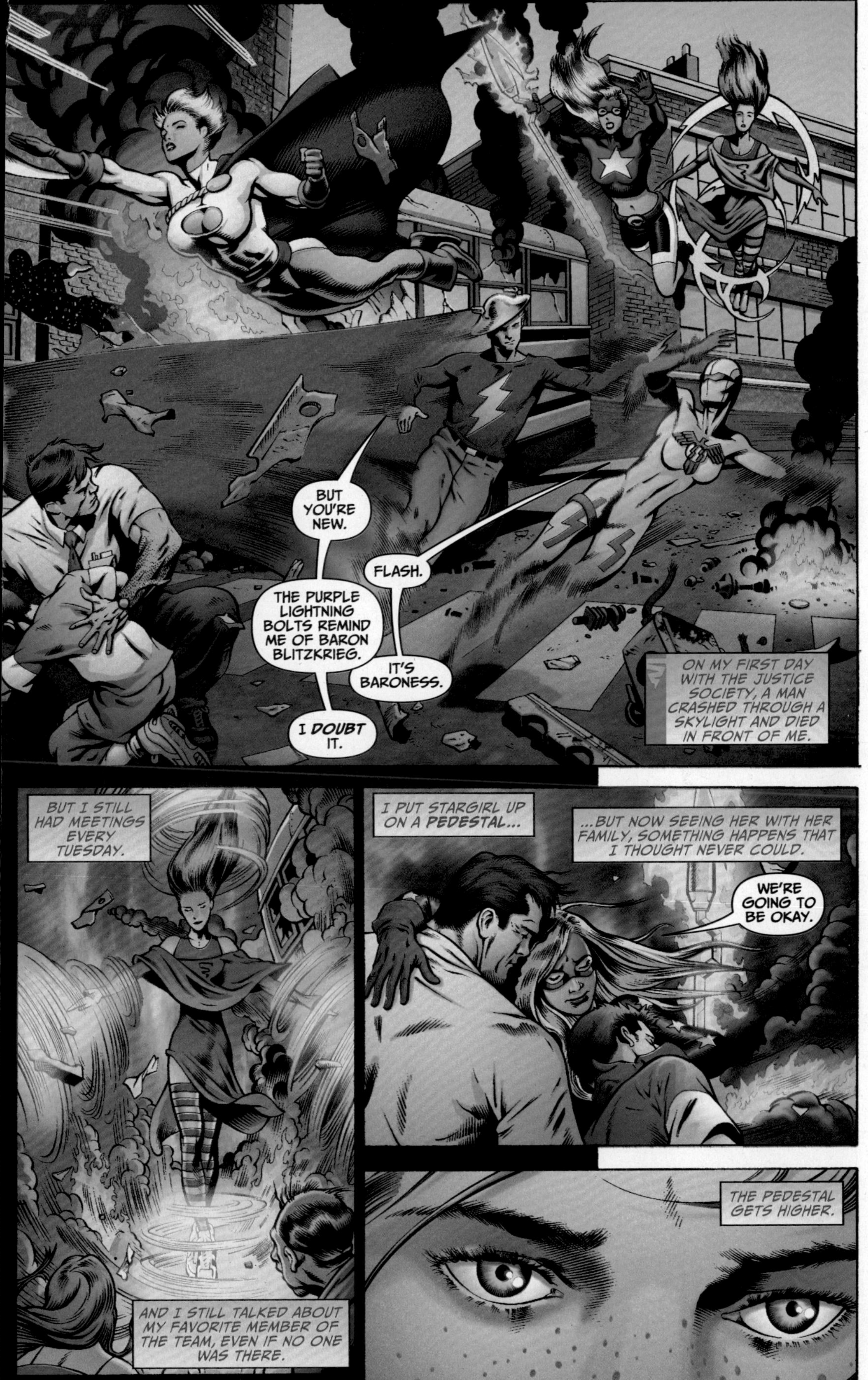
BUT YOU'RE NEW.
FLASH.
THE PURPLE LIGHTNING BOLTS REMIND ME OF BARON BLITZKRIEG.
IT'S BARONESS.
I DOUBT IT.
ON MY FIRST DAY WITH THE JUSTICE SOCIETY, A MAN CRASHED THROUGH A SKYLIGHT AND DIED IN FRONT OF ME.
BUT I STILL HAD MEETINGS EVERY TUESDAY.
AND I STILL TALKED ABOUT MY FAVORITE MEMBER OF THE TEAM, EVEN IF NO ONE WAS THERE.
I PUT STARGIRL UP ON A PEDESTAL...
...BUT NOW SEEING HER WITH HER FAMILY, SOMETHING HAPPENS THAT I THOUGHT NEVER COULD.
WE'RE GOING TO BE OKAY.
THE PEDESTAL GETS HIGHER.

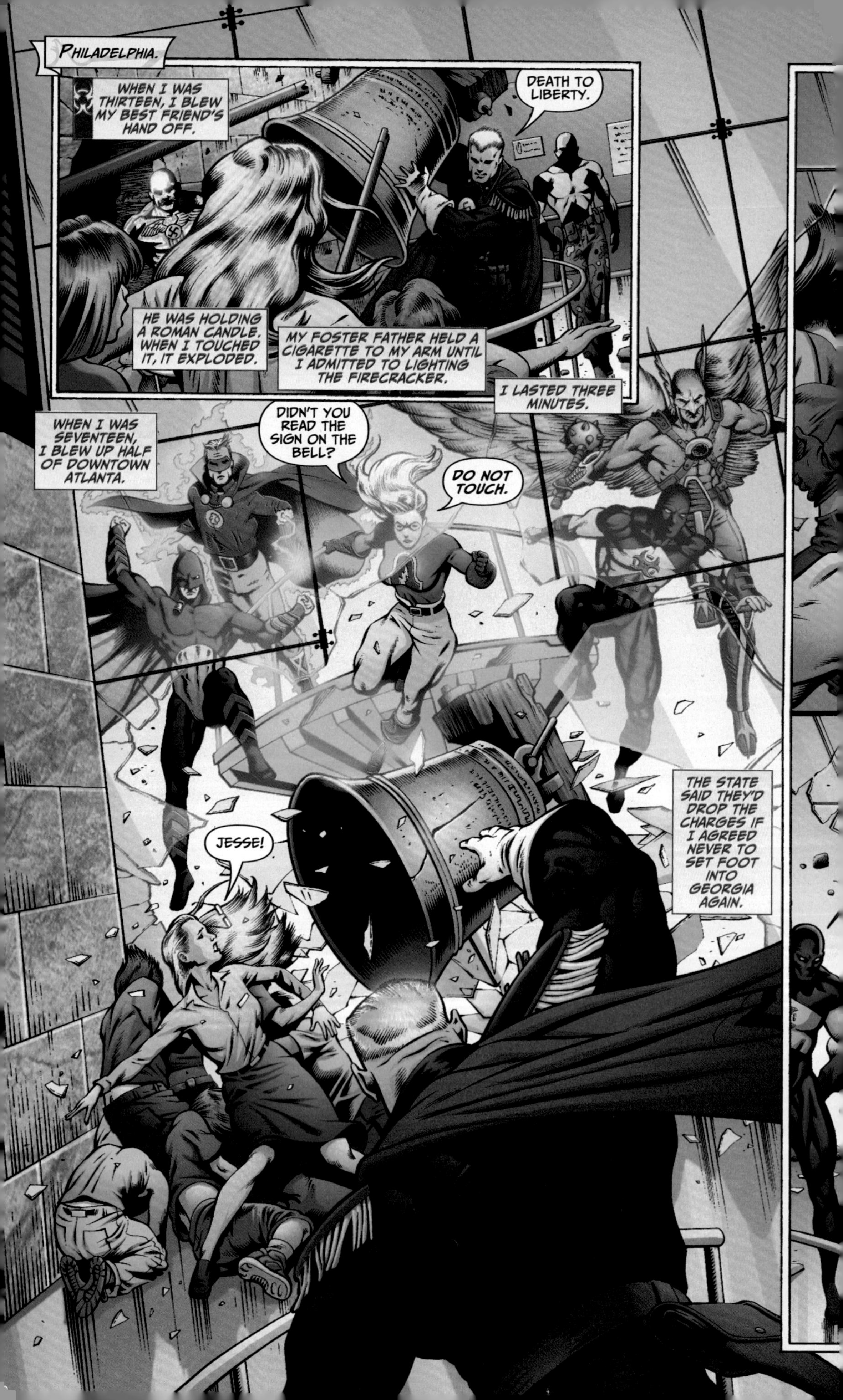

Philadelphia.
WHEN I WAS THIRTEEN, I BLEW MY BEST FRIEND'S HAND OFF.
DEATH TO LIBERTY.
HE WAS HOLDING A ROMAN CANDLE. WHEN I TOUCHED IT, IT EXPLODED.
MY FOSTER FATHER HELD A CIGARETTE TO MY ARM UNTIL I ADMITTED TO LIGHTING THE FIRECRACKER.
I LASTED THREE MINUTES.
WHEN I WAS SEVENTEEN, I BLEW UP HALF OF DOWNTOWN ATLANTA.
DIDN'T YOU READ THE SIGN ON THE BELL?
DO NOT TOUCH.
THE STATE SAID THEY'D DROP THE CHARGES IF I AGREED NEVER TO SET FOOT INTO GEORGIA AGAIN.
JESSE!

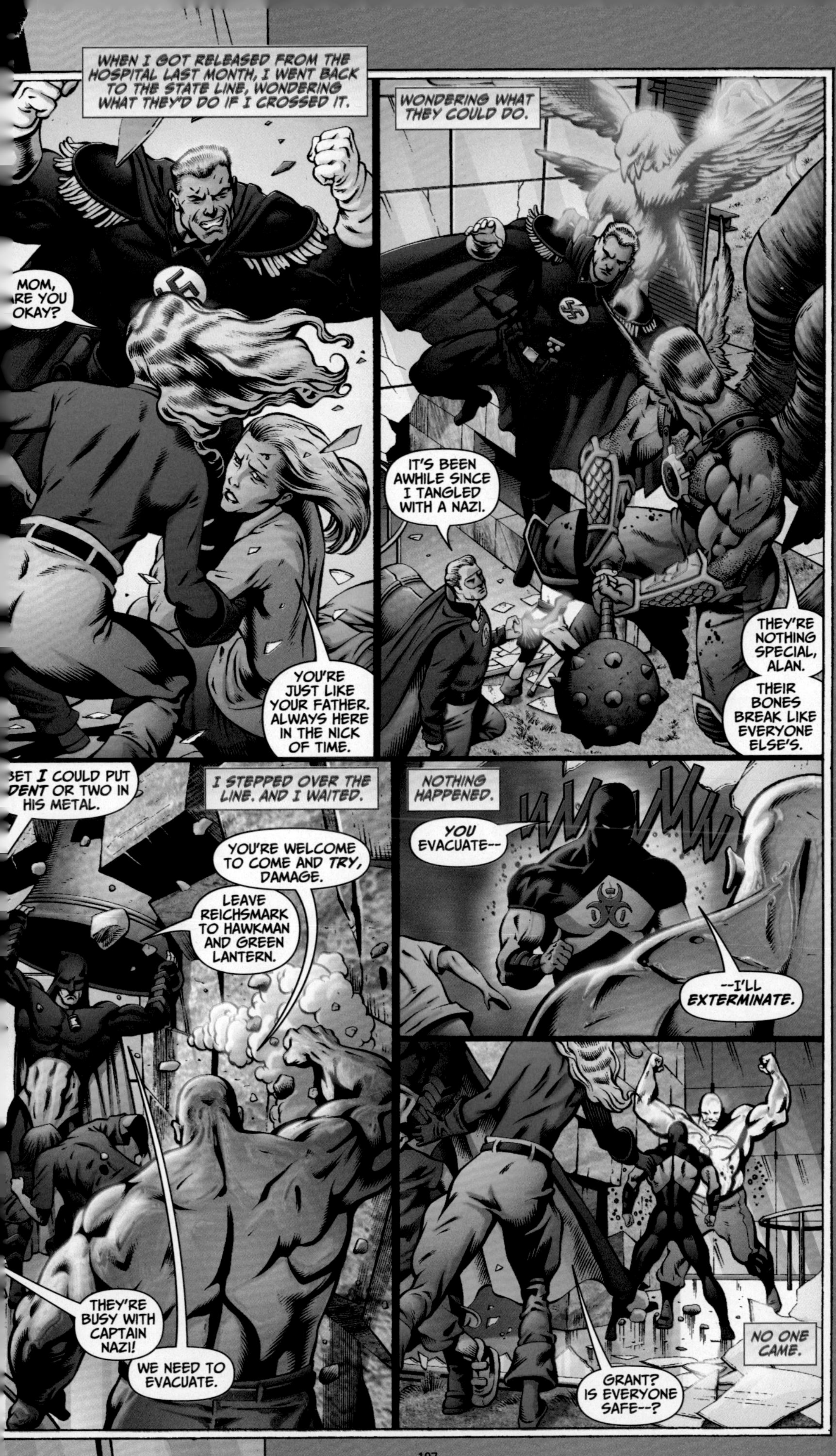
WHEN I GOT RELEASED FROM THE HOSPITAL LAST MONTH, I WENT BACK TO THE STATE LINE, WONDERING WHAT THEY'D DO IF I CROSSED IT.
MOM, ARE YOU OKAY?
YOU'RE JUST LIKE YOUR FATHER. ALWAYS HERE IN THE NICK OF TIME.
WONDERING WHAT THEY COULD DO.
IT'S BEEN AWHILE SINCE I TANGLED WITH A NAZI.
THEY'RE NOTHING SPECIAL, ALAN.
THEIR BONES BREAK LIKE EVERYONE ELSE'S.
BET I COULD PUT DENT OR TWO IN HIS METAL.
I STEPPED OVER THE LINE. AND I WAITED.
YOU'RE WELCOME TO COME AND TRY, DAMAGE.
LEAVE REICHSMARK TO HAWKMAN AND GREEN LANTERN.
THEY'RE BUSY WITH CAPTAIN NAZI!
WE NEED TO EVACUATE.
NOTHING HAPPENED.
YOU EVACUATE--
--I'LL EXTERMINATE.
NO ONE CAME.
GRANT? IS EVERYONE SAFE--?

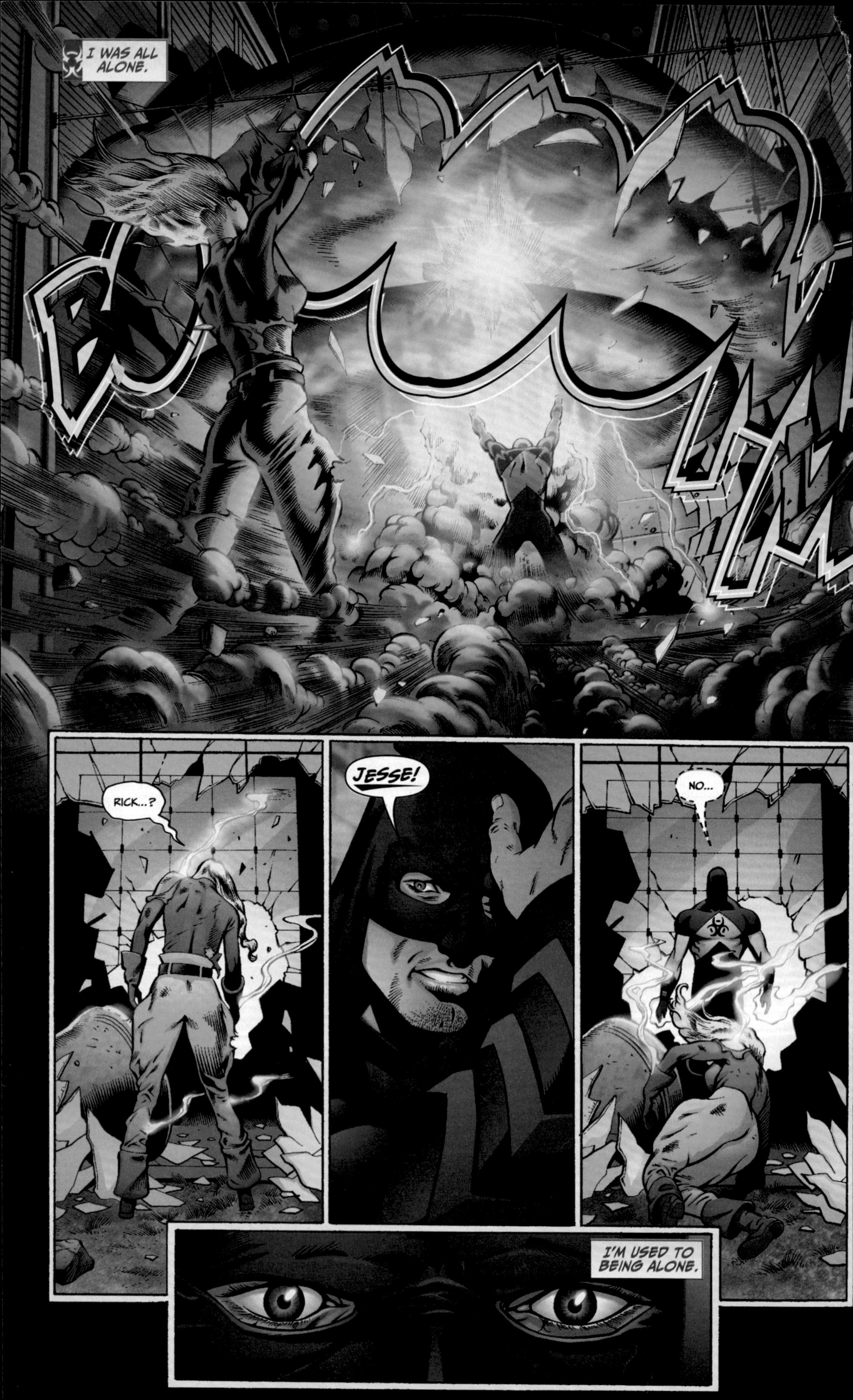
I WAS ALL ALONE.
RICK...?
JESSE!
NO...
I'M USED TO BEING ALONE.

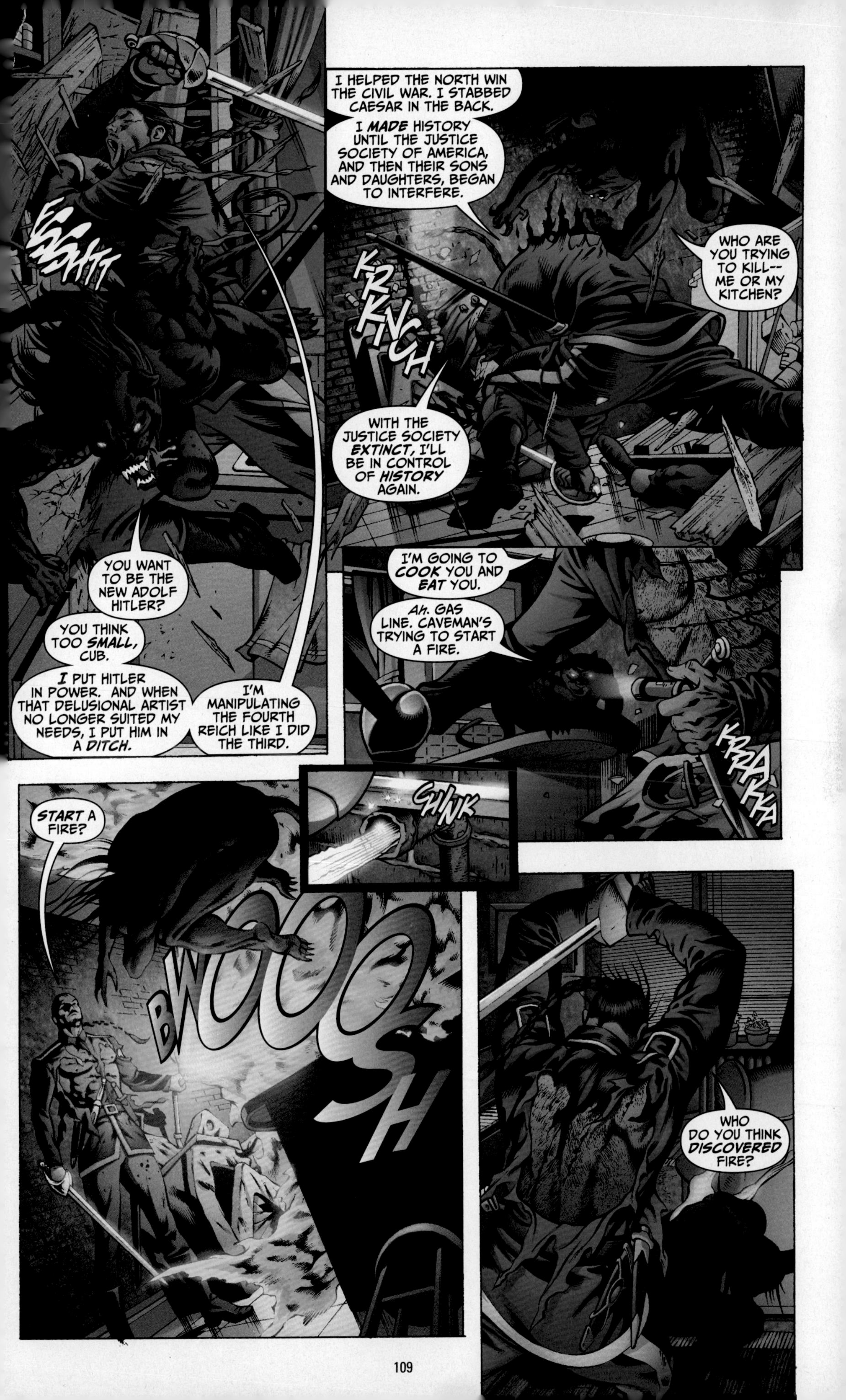
I HELPED THE NORTH WIN THE CIVIL WAR. I STABBED CAESAR IN THE BACK.
I *MADE* HISTORY UNTIL THE JUSTICE SOCIETY OF AMERICA, AND THEN THEIR SONS AND DAUGHTERS, BEGAN TO INTERFERE.
WHO ARE YOU TRYING TO KILL-- ME OR MY KITCHEN?
KRKNCH
WITH THE JUSTICE SOCIETY *EXTINCT*, I'LL BE IN CONTROL OF *HISTORY* AGAIN.
YOU WANT TO BE THE NEW ADOLF HITLER?
YOU THINK TOO *SMALL*, CUB.
I PUT HITLER IN POWER. AND WHEN THAT DELUSIONAL ARTIST NO LONGER SUITED MY NEEDS, I PUT HIM IN A *DITCH.*
I'M MANIPULATING THE FOURTH REICH LIKE I DID THE THIRD.
I'M GOING TO *COOK* YOU AND *EAT* YOU.
Ah. GAS LINE. CAVEMAN'S TRYING TO START A FIRE.
KRAKKA
CHINK
START A FIRE?
BWOOOSH
WHO DO YOU THINK *DISCOVERED* FIRE?

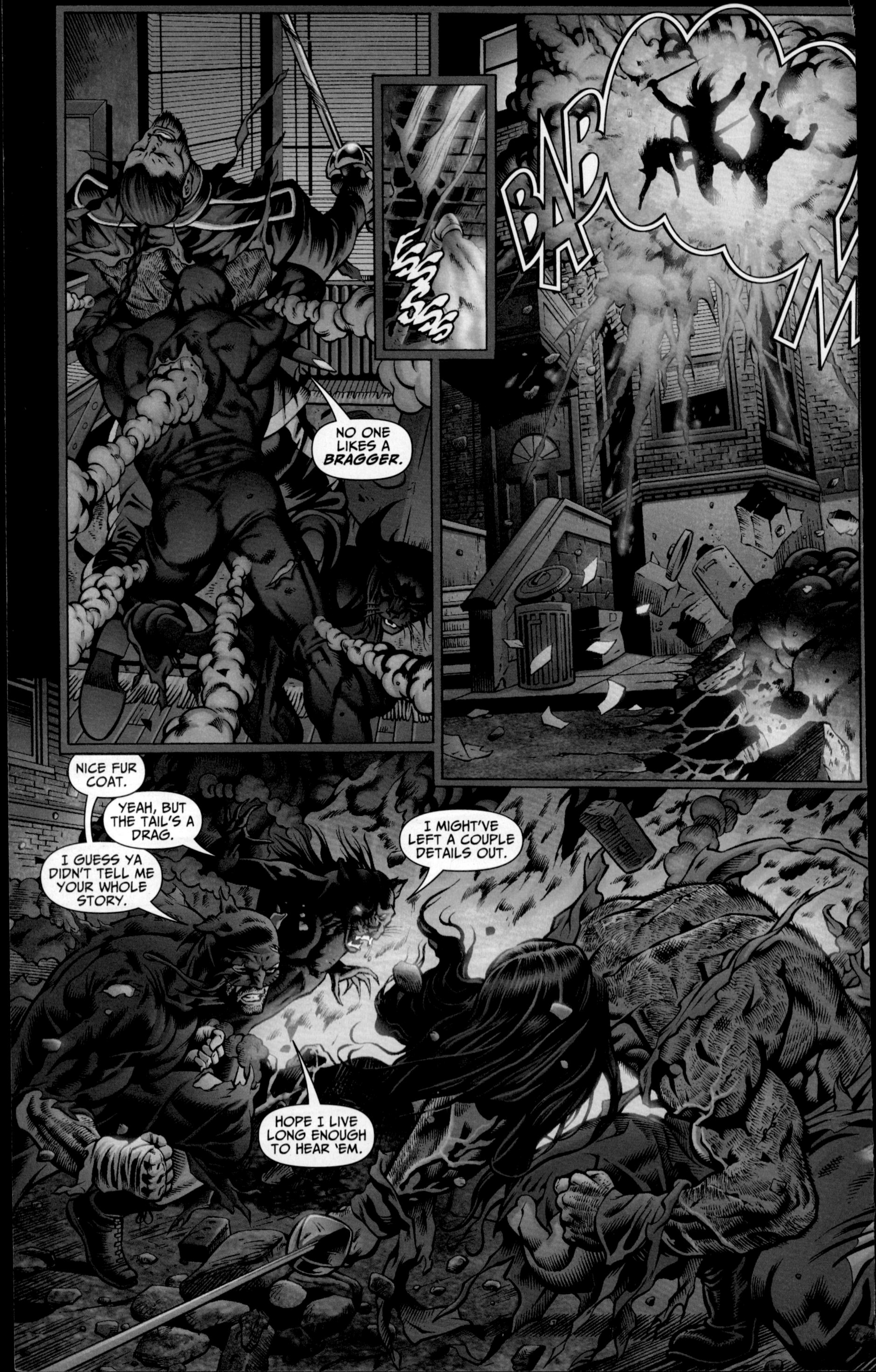
NO ONE LIKES A BRAGGER.
ESSSSSS
BABA
NICE FUR COAT.
YEAH, BUT THE TAIL'S A DRAG.
I GUESS YA DIDN'T TELL ME YOUR WHOLE STORY.
I MIGHT'VE LEFT A COUPLE DETAILS OUT.
HOPE I LIVE LONG ENOUGH TO HEAR 'EM.

I DIDN'T KNOW SHE WAS BEHIND ME.

YOU DIDN'T *LOOK.*

I'VE SEEN A LOT OF EVIL IN MY LIFE, YOUNG LADY, BUT I'LL *NEVER* UNDERSTAND MONSTERS LIKE YOU.

AND I'LL *NEVER* TOLERATE THEM.

...RICK...

I'M HERE, BABY.

...IT WAS... AN ACCIDENT...

I'LL BURN THIS ENTIRE TOWN DOWN!

Pfft! NOW WHEN HAS *THAT* HELPED ANYONE?

BAD DRAGON! *BAD!*

YOU HEARD HIM.

BAD.

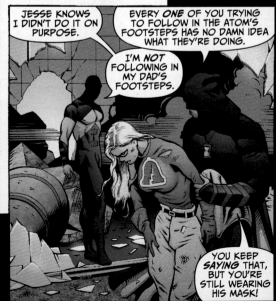

JESSE KNOWS I DIDN'T DO IT ON PURPOSE.

EVERY *ONE* OF YOU TRYING TO FOLLOW IN THE ATOM'S FOOTSTEPS HAS NO DAMN IDEA WHAT THEY'RE DOING.

I'M *NOT* FOLLOWING IN MY DAD'S FOOTSTEPS.

YOU KEEP *SAYING* THAT, BUT YOU'RE STILL WEARING HIS MASK!

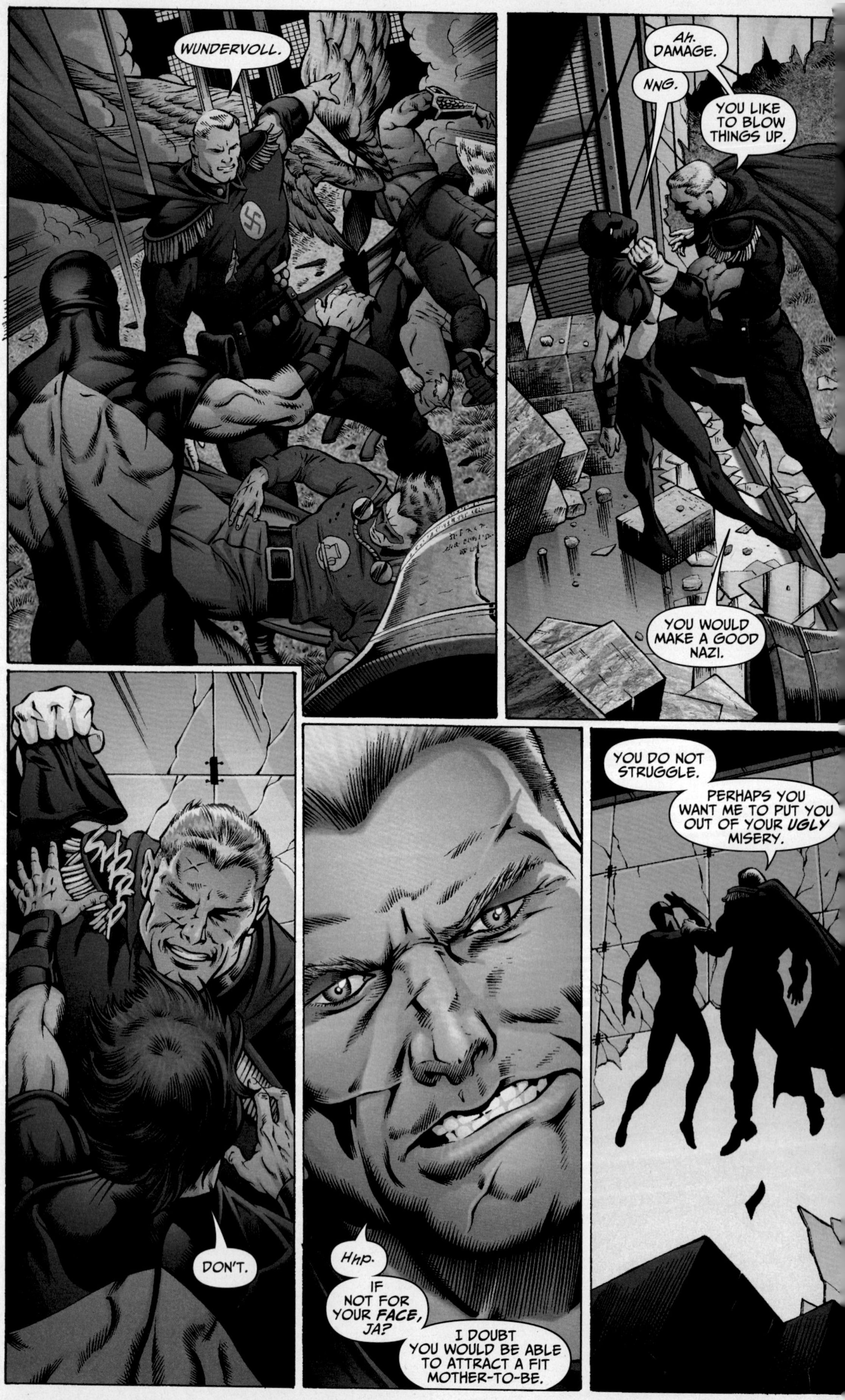
WUNDERVOLL.
Ah. DAMAGE.
NNG.
YOU LIKE TO BLOW THINGS UP.
YOU WOULD MAKE A GOOD NAZI.
DON'T.
Hnp.
IF NOT FOR YOUR FACE, JA?
I DOUBT YOU WOULD BE ABLE TO ATTRACT A FIT MOTHER-TO-BE.
YOU DO NOT STRUGGLE.
PERHAPS YOU WANT ME TO PUT YOU OUT OF YOUR UGLY MISERY.

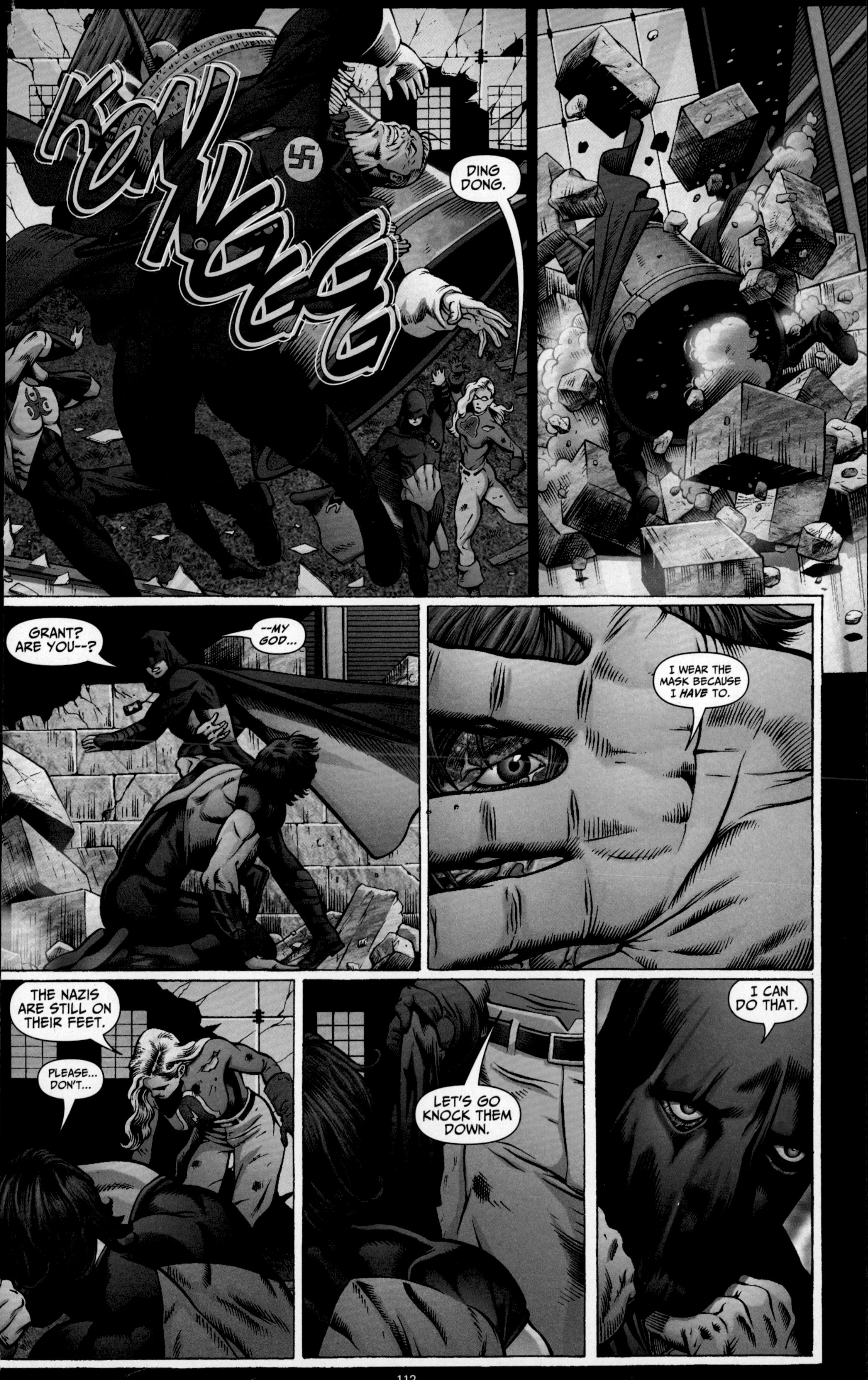
DING DONG.
GRANT? ARE YOU--?
--MY GOD...
I WEAR THE MASK BECAUSE I *HAVE* TO.
THE NAZIS ARE STILL ON THEIR FEET.
PLEASE... DON'T...
LET'S GO KNOCK THEM DOWN.
I CAN DO THAT.

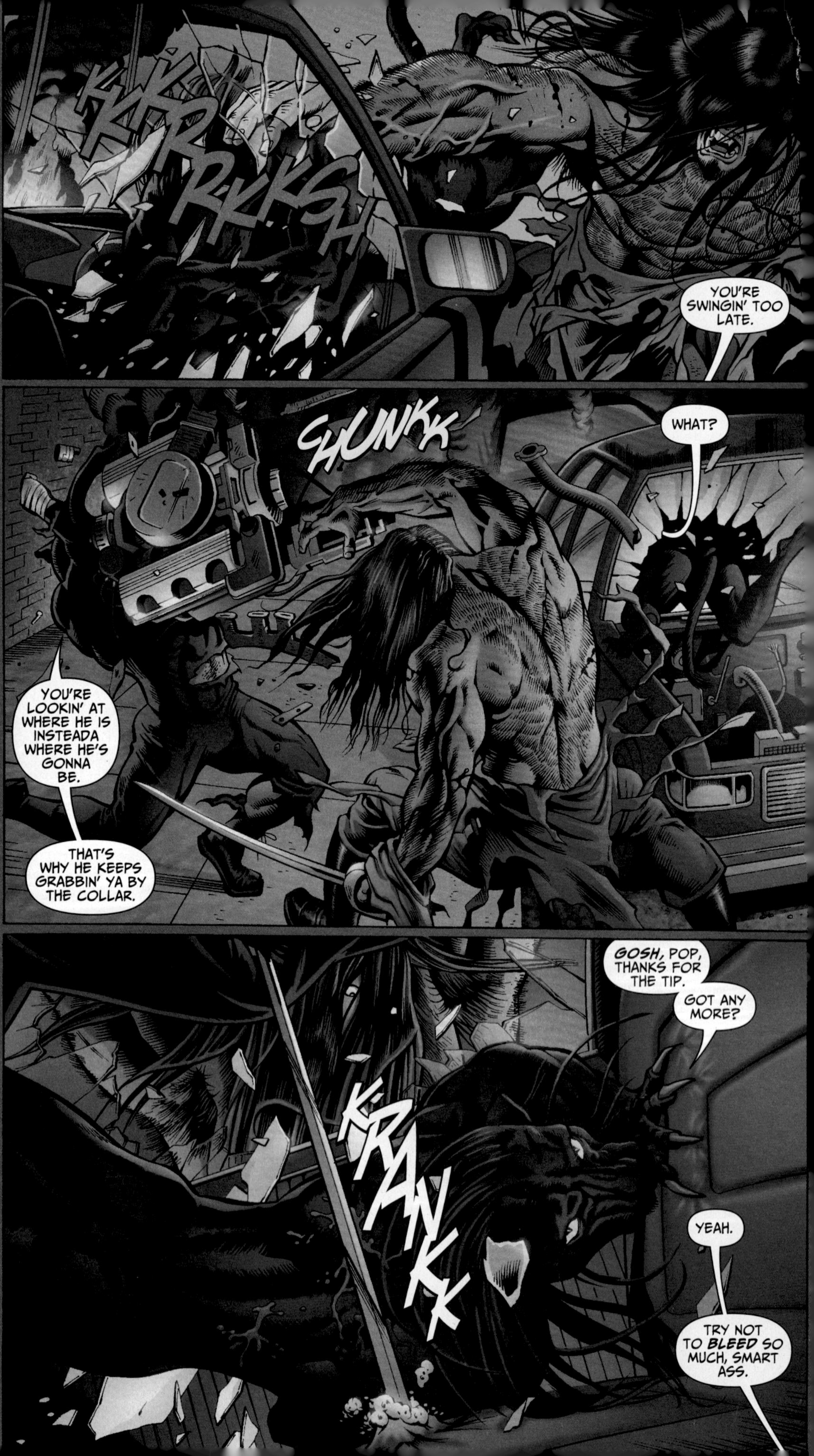
KKKR
RKKSH
YOU'RE SWINGIN' TOO LATE.
CHUNKK
WHAT?
YOU'RE LOOKIN' AT WHERE HE IS INSTEADA WHERE HE'S GONNA BE.
THAT'S WHY HE KEEPS GRABBIN' YA BY THE COLLAR.
GOSH, POP, THANKS FOR THE TIP.
GOT ANY MORE?
K-RANKK
YEAH.
TRY NOT TO BLEED SO MUCH, SMART ASS.

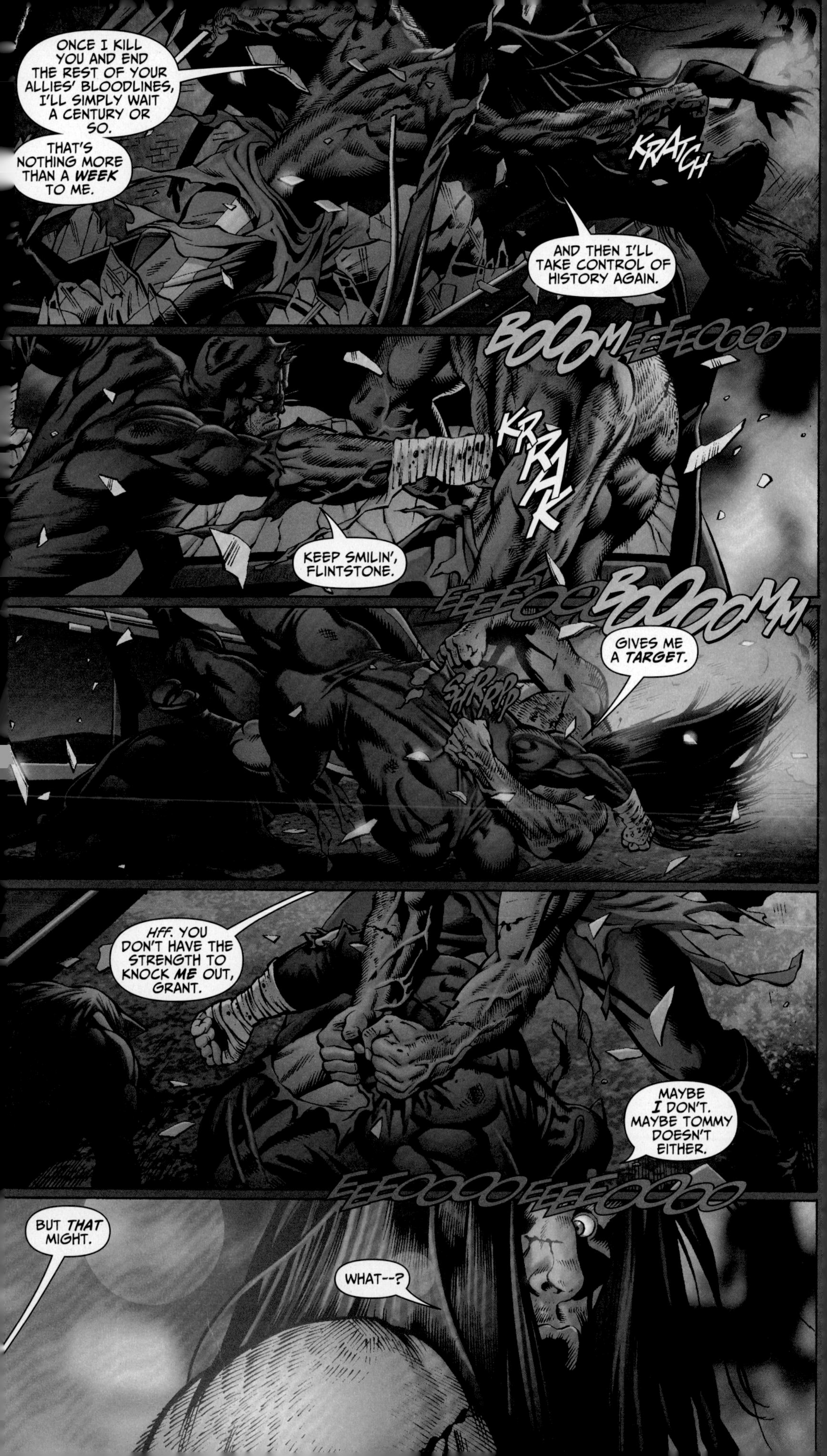
ONCE I KILL YOU AND END THE REST OF YOUR ALLIES' BLOODLINES, I'LL SIMPLY WAIT A CENTURY OR SO.
THAT'S NOTHING MORE THAN A *WEEK* TO ME.
KRATCH
AND THEN I'LL TAKE CONTROL OF HISTORY AGAIN.
BOOOMEEEEOooo
KRRAKK
KEEP SMILIN', FLINTSTONE.
EEEEOOOBOOOOOMM
GIVES ME A *TARGET*.
SHRRP
HFF. YOU DON'T HAVE THE STRENGTH TO KNOCK *ME* OUT, GRANT.
MAYBE *I* DON'T. MAYBE TOMMY DOESN'T EITHER.
EEEOOOOOEEEEOOOoo
BUT *THAT* MIGHT.
WHAT--?

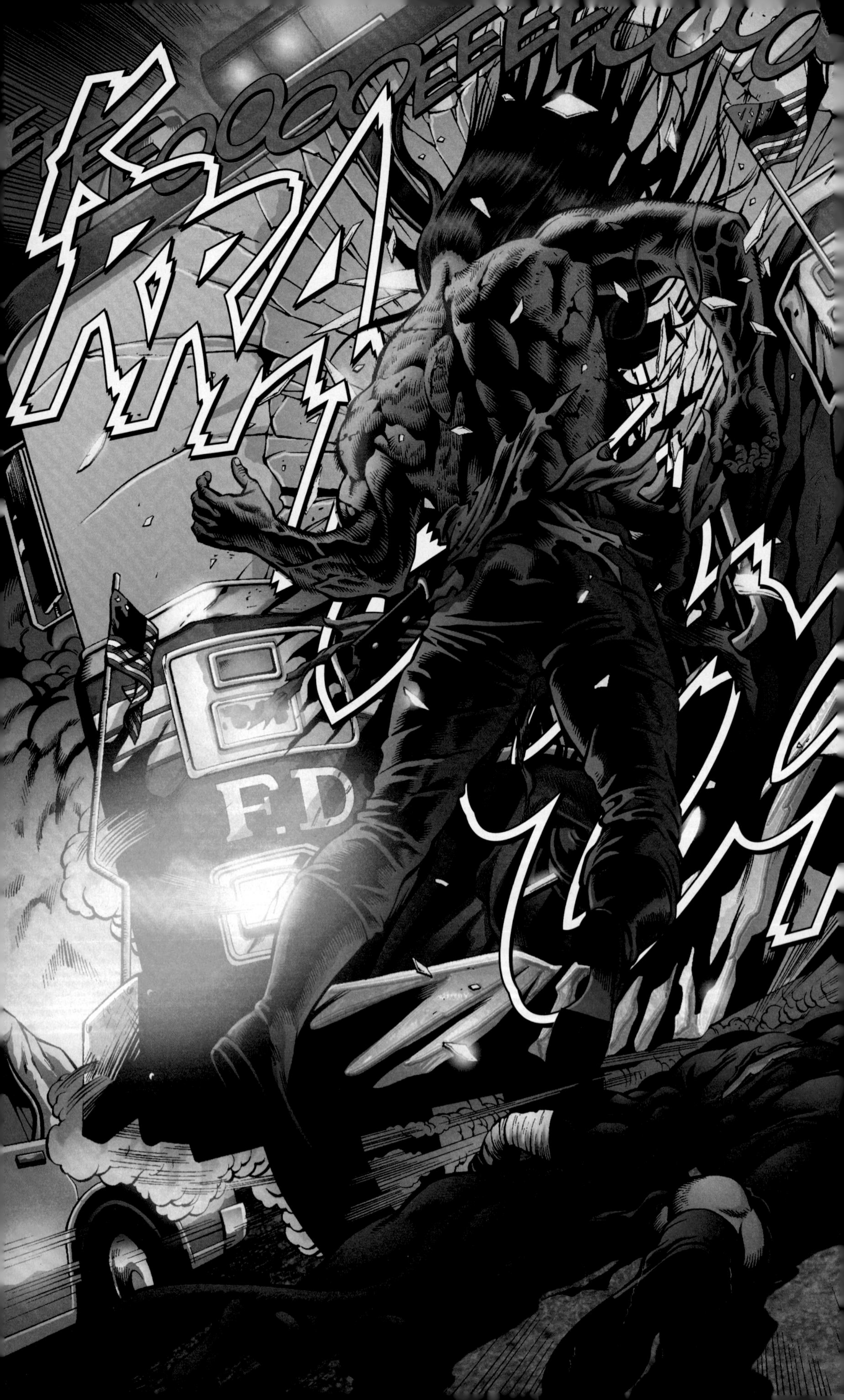
F.D

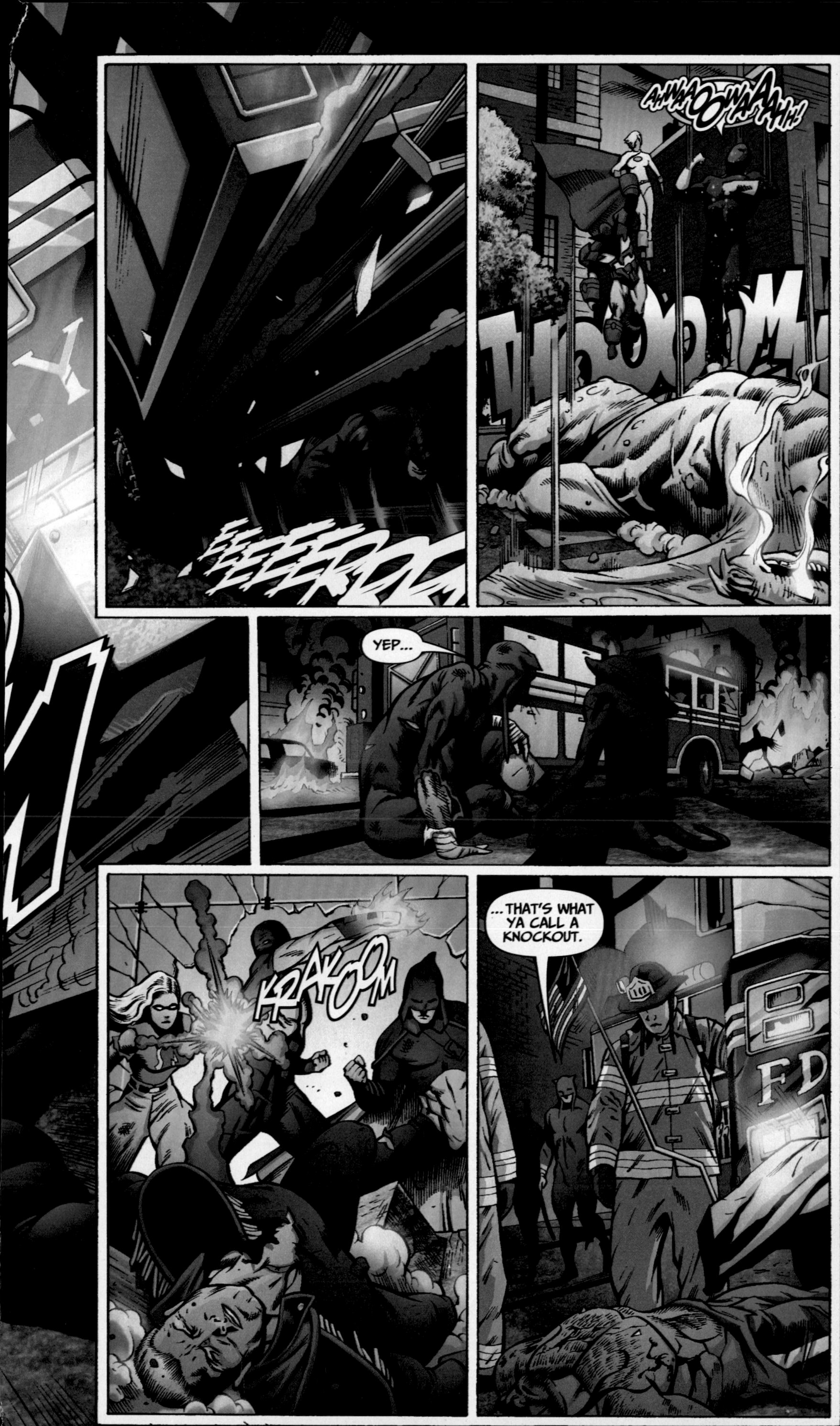
EEEERROOM
AHWAOOWAAAHH!
THOOOM!
YEP...
KRAKOOM
...THAT'S WHAT YA CALL A KNOCKOUT.
FD

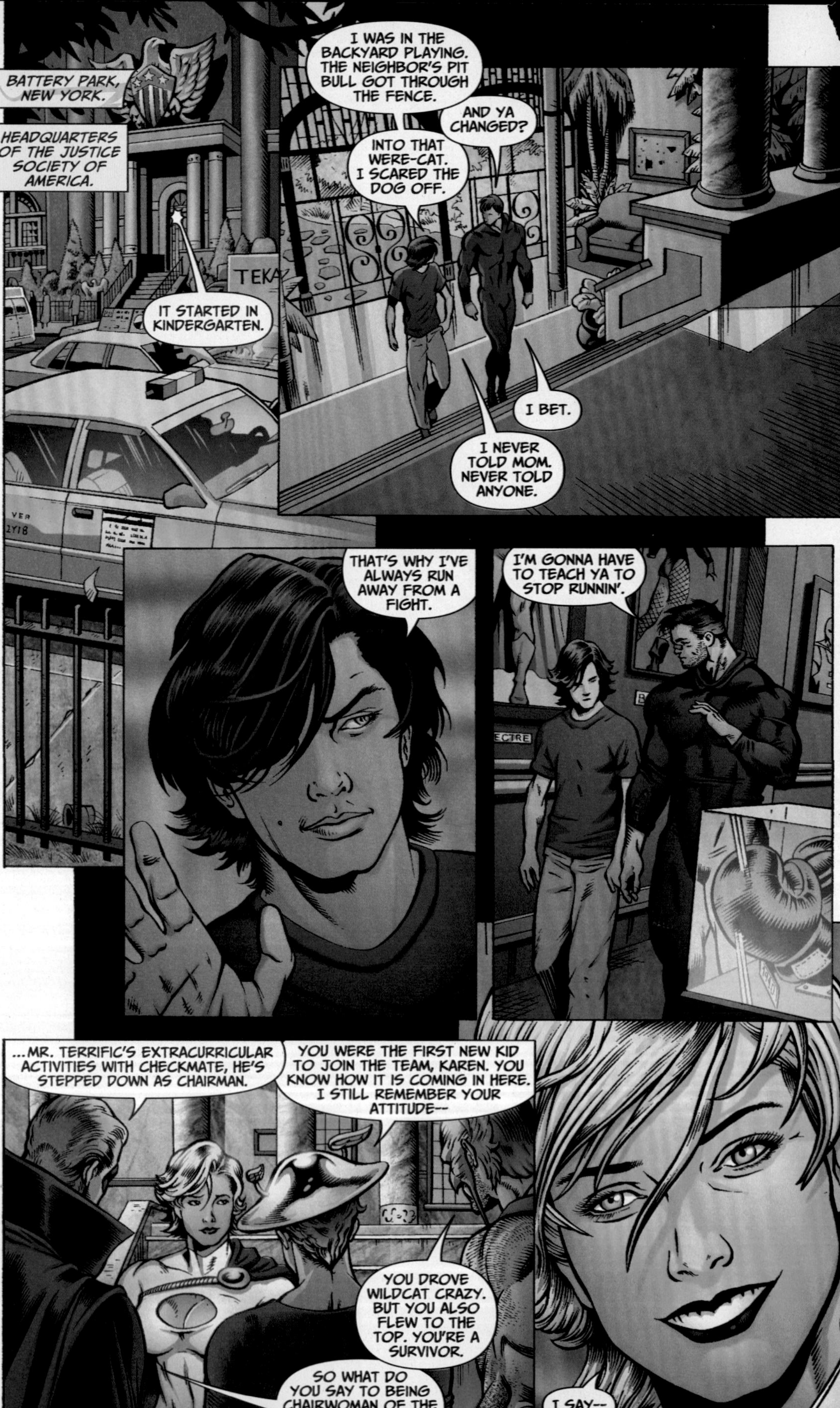

BATTERY PARK, NEW YORK.
HEADQUARTERS OF THE JUSTICE SOCIETY OF AMERICA.
IT STARTED IN KINDERGARTEN.
TEKA
I WAS IN THE BACKYARD PLAYING. THE NEIGHBOR'S PIT BULL GOT THROUGH THE FENCE.
AND YA CHANGED?
INTO THAT WERE-CAT. I SCARED THE DOG OFF.
I BET.
I NEVER TOLD MOM. NEVER TOLD ANYONE.
THAT'S WHY I'VE ALWAYS RUN AWAY FROM A FIGHT.
I'M GONNA HAVE TO TEACH YA TO STOP RUNNIN'.
...MR. TERRIFIC'S EXTRACURRICULAR ACTIVITIES WITH CHECKMATE, HE'S STEPPED DOWN AS CHAIRMAN.
YOU WERE THE FIRST NEW KID TO JOIN THE TEAM, KAREN. YOU KNOW HOW IT IS COMING IN HERE. I STILL REMEMBER YOUR ATTITUDE--
YOU DROVE WILDCAT CRAZY. BUT YOU ALSO FLEW TO THE TOP. YOU'RE A SURVIVOR.
SO WHAT DO YOU SAY TO BEING CHAIRWOMAN OF THE JUSTICE SOCIETY OF AMERICA?
I SAY--
--HELL, YES.

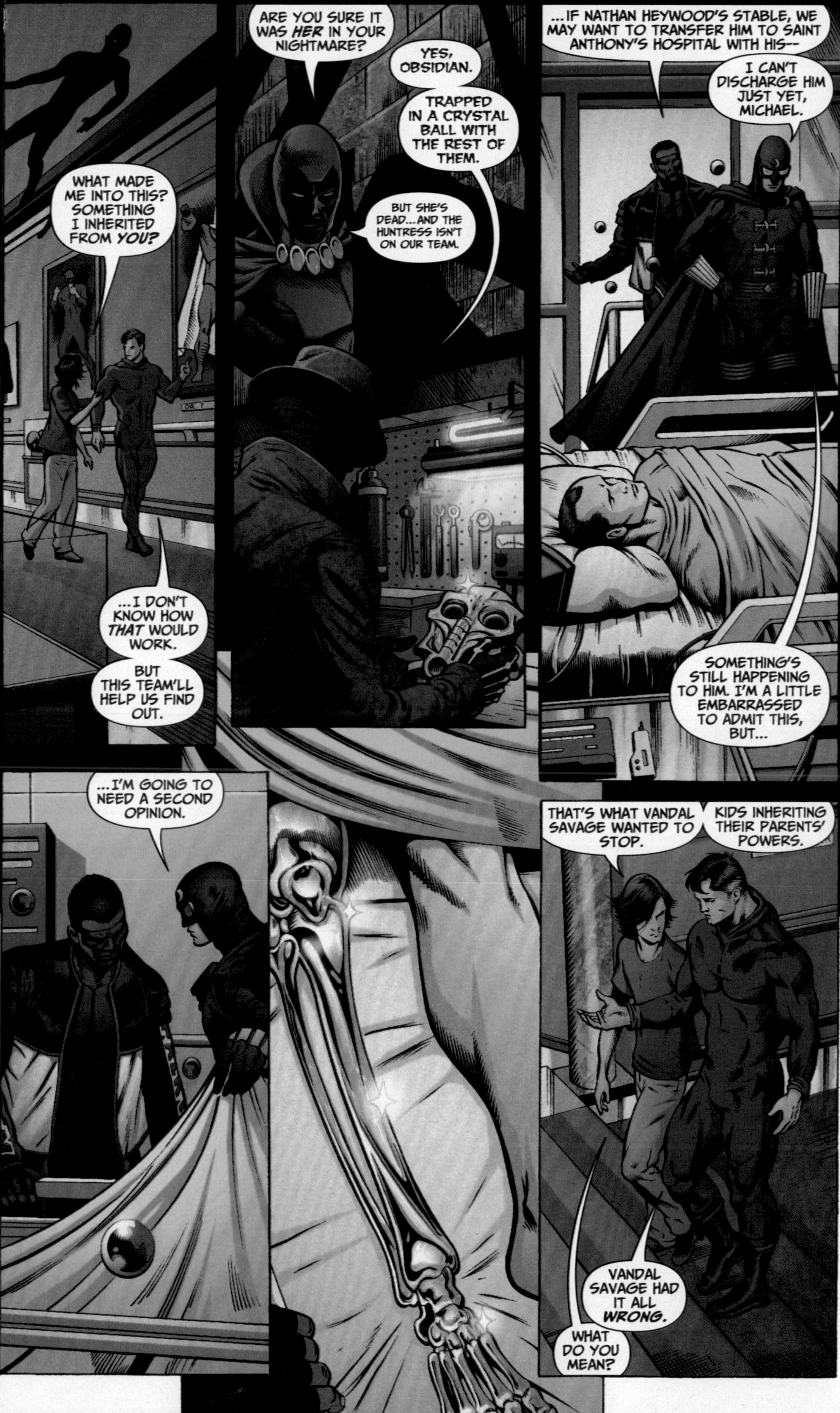
WHAT MADE ME INTO THIS? SOMETHING I INHERITED FROM *YOU?*
...I DON'T KNOW HOW *THAT* WOULD WORK.
BUT THIS TEAM'LL HELP US FIND OUT.
ARE YOU SURE IT WAS *HER* IN YOUR NIGHTMARE?
YES, OBSIDIAN.
TRAPPED IN A CRYSTAL BALL WITH THE REST OF THEM.
BUT SHE'S DEAD...AND THE HUNTRESS ISN'T ON OUR TEAM.
...IF NATHAN HEYWOOD'S STABLE, WE MAY WANT TO TRANSFER HIM TO SAINT ANTHONY'S HOSPITAL WITH HIS--
I CAN'T DISCHARGE HIM JUST YET, MICHAEL.
SOMETHING'S STILL HAPPENING TO HIM. I'M A LITTLE EMBARRASSED TO ADMIT THIS, BUT...
...I'M GOING TO NEED A SECOND OPINION.
THAT'S WHAT VANDAL SAVAGE WANTED TO STOP.
KIDS INHERITING THEIR PARENTS' POWERS.
VANDAL SAVAGE HAD IT ALL *WRONG.*
WHAT DO YOU MEAN?

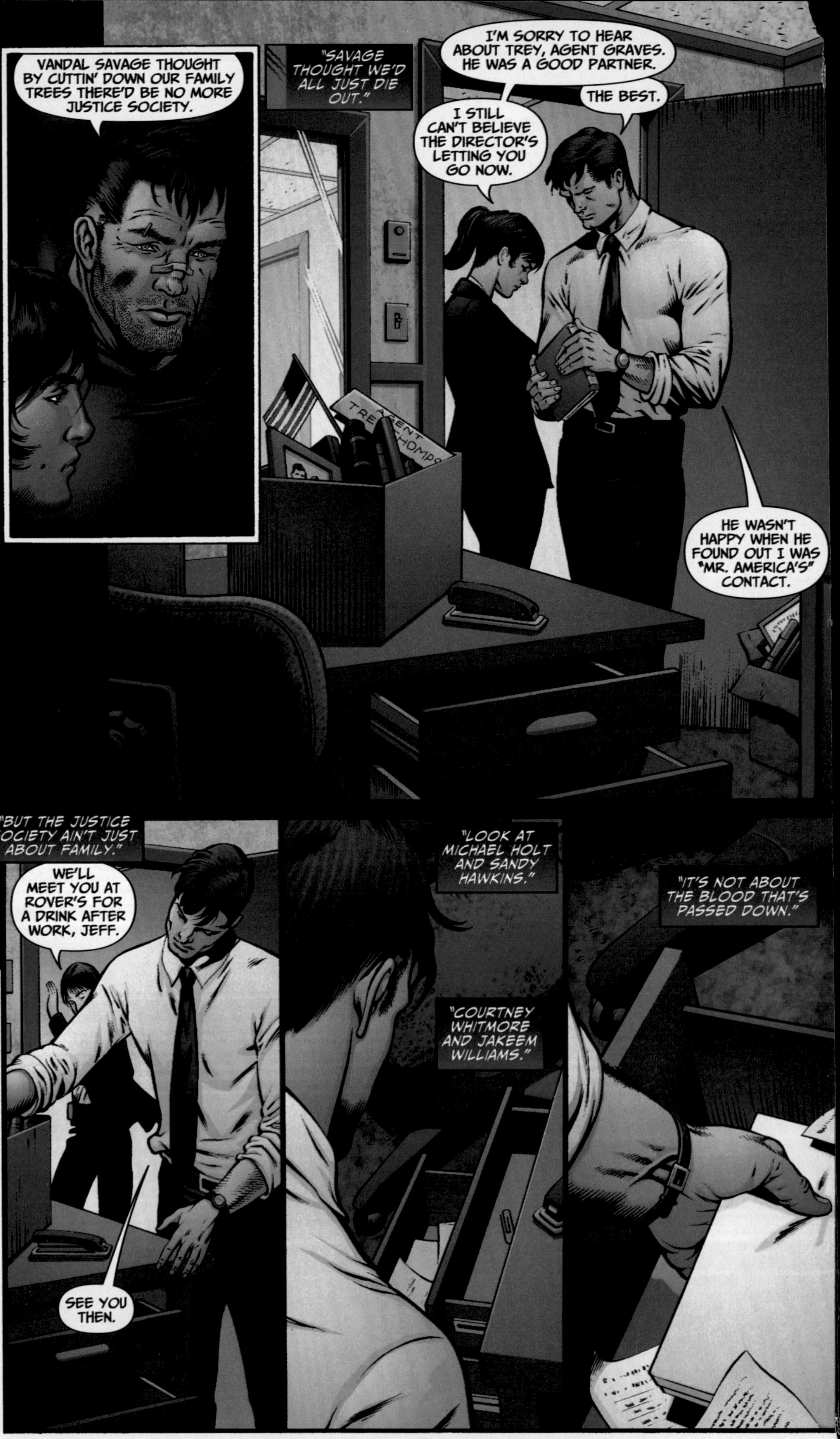
VANDAL SAVAGE THOUGHT BY CUTTIN' DOWN OUR FAMILY TREES THERE'D BE NO MORE JUSTICE SOCIETY.
"SAVAGE THOUGHT WE'D ALL JUST DIE OUT."
I'M SORRY TO HEAR ABOUT TREY, AGENT GRAVES. HE WAS A GOOD PARTNER.
THE BEST.
I STILL CAN'T BELIEVE THE DIRECTOR'S LETTING YOU GO NOW.
HE WASN'T HAPPY WHEN HE FOUND OUT I WAS "MR. AMERICA'S" CONTACT.
"BUT THE JUSTICE SOCIETY AIN'T JUST ABOUT FAMILY."
WE'LL MEET YOU AT ROVER'S FOR A DRINK AFTER WORK, JEFF.
SEE YOU THEN.
"LOOK AT MICHAEL HOLT AND SANDY HAWKINS."
"COURTNEY WHITMORE AND JAKEEM WILLIAMS."
"IT'S NOT ABOUT THE BLOOD THAT'S PASSED DOWN."

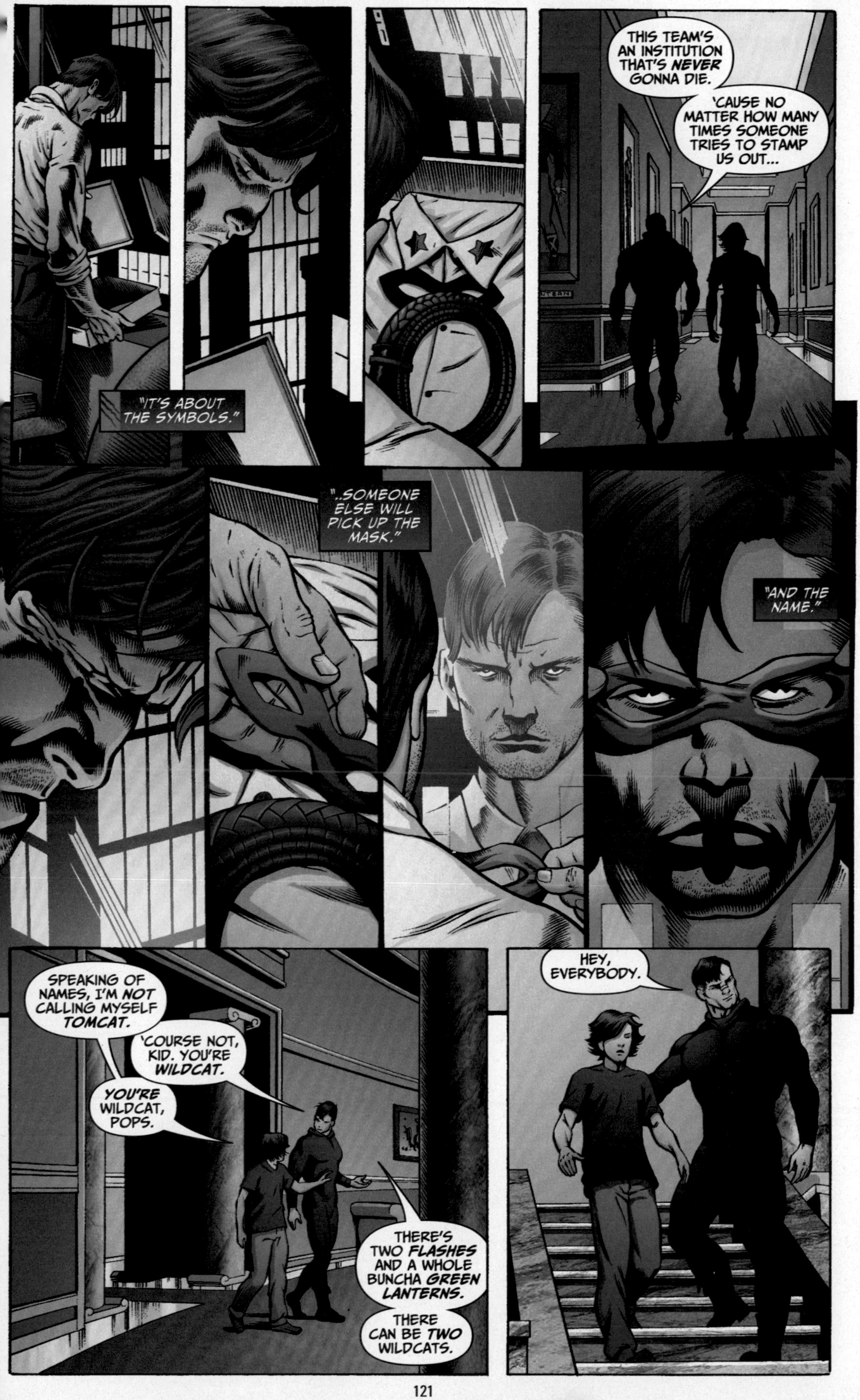
"IT'S ABOUT THE SYMBOLS."
THIS TEAM'S AN INSTITUTION THAT'S NEVER GONNA DIE.
'CAUSE NO MATTER HOW MANY TIMES SOMEONE TRIES TO STAMP US OUT...
"..SOMEONE ELSE WILL PICK UP THE MASK."
"AND THE NAME."
SPEAKING OF NAMES, I'M NOT CALLING MYSELF TOMCAT.
'COURSE NOT, KID. YOU'RE WILDCAT.
YOU'RE WILDCAT, POPS.
THERE'S TWO FLASHES AND A WHOLE BUNCHA GREEN LANTERNS.
THERE CAN BE TWO WILDCATS.
HEY, EVERYBODY.

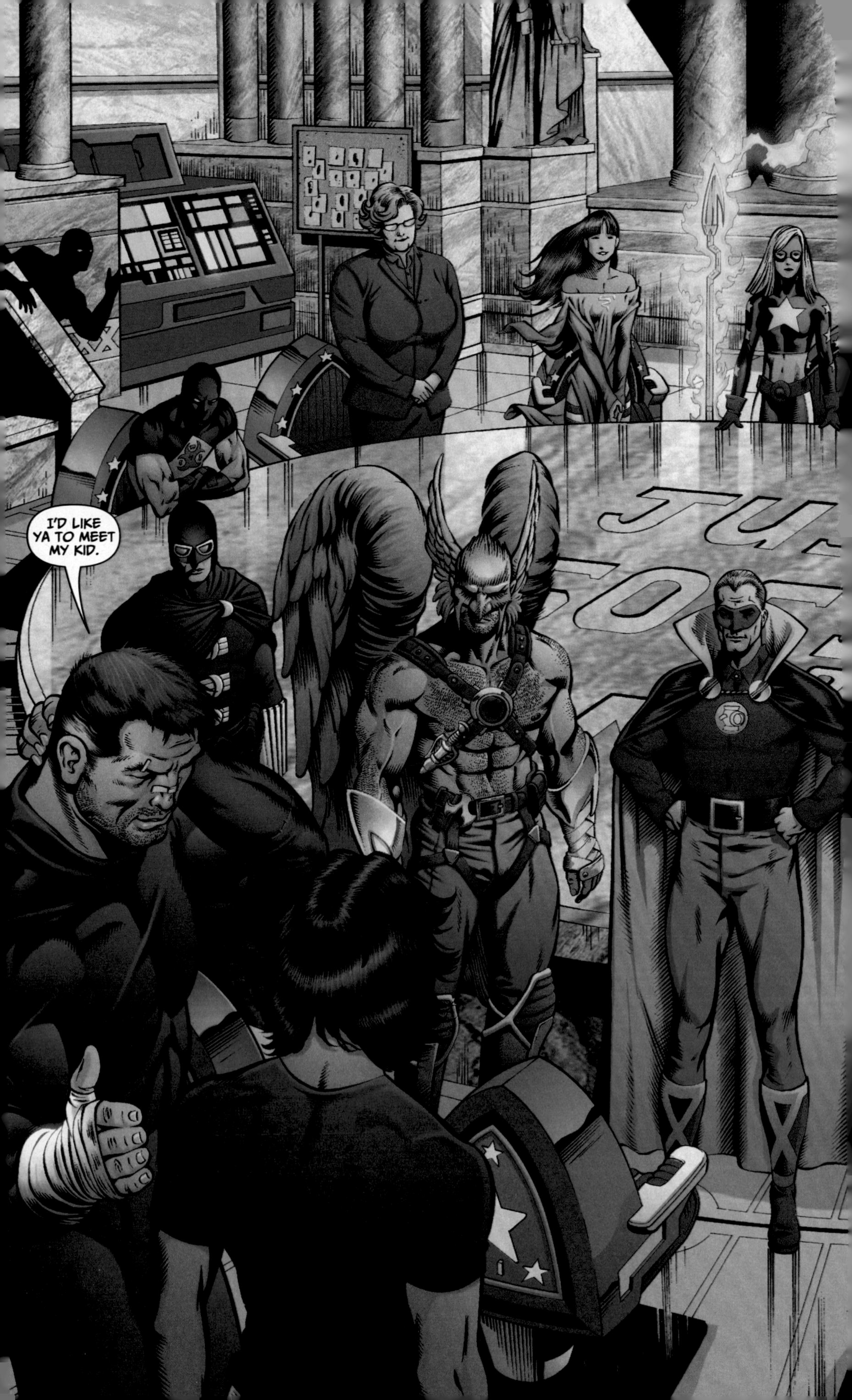
I'D LIKE YA TO MEET MY KID.

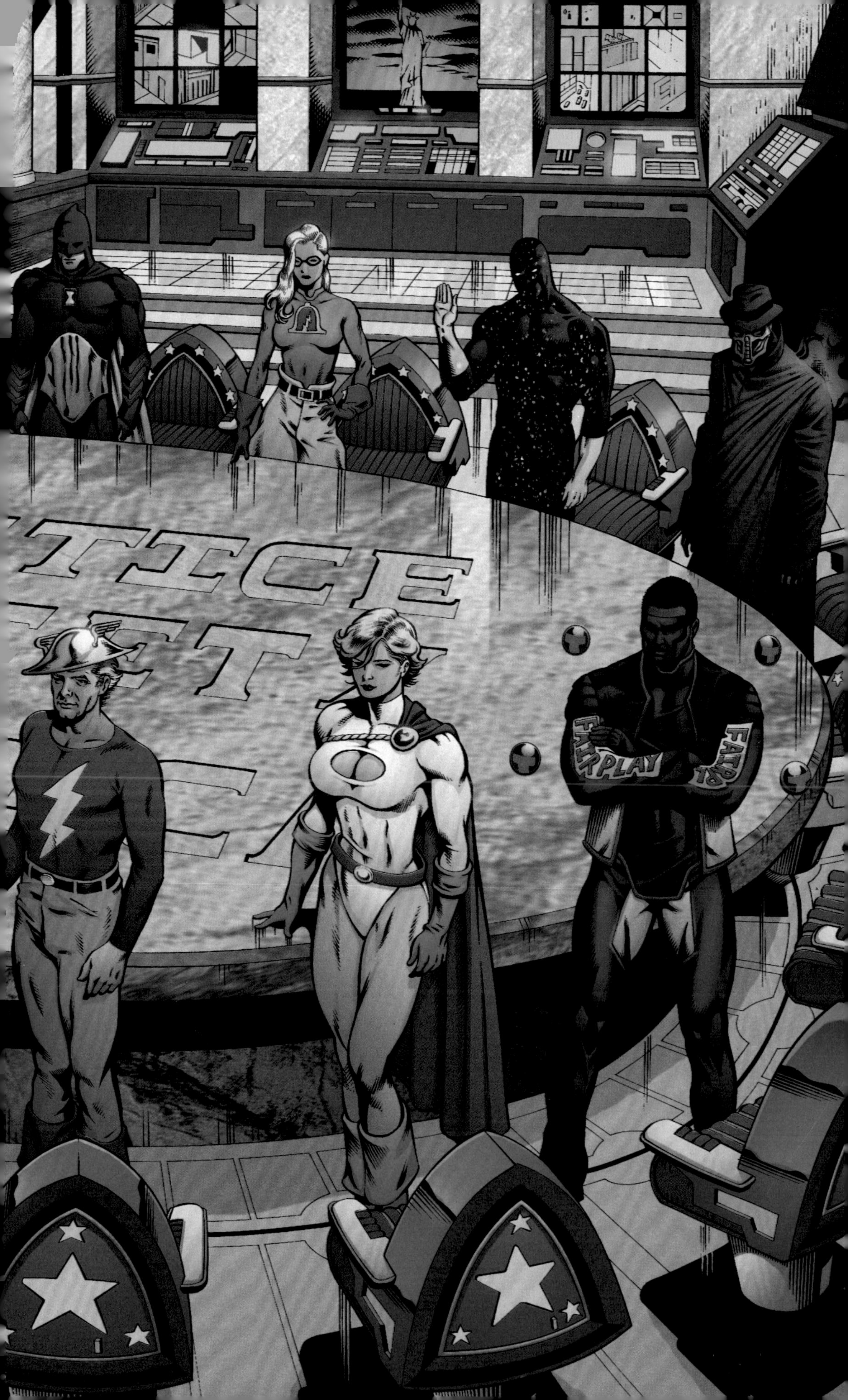
FAIR PLAY

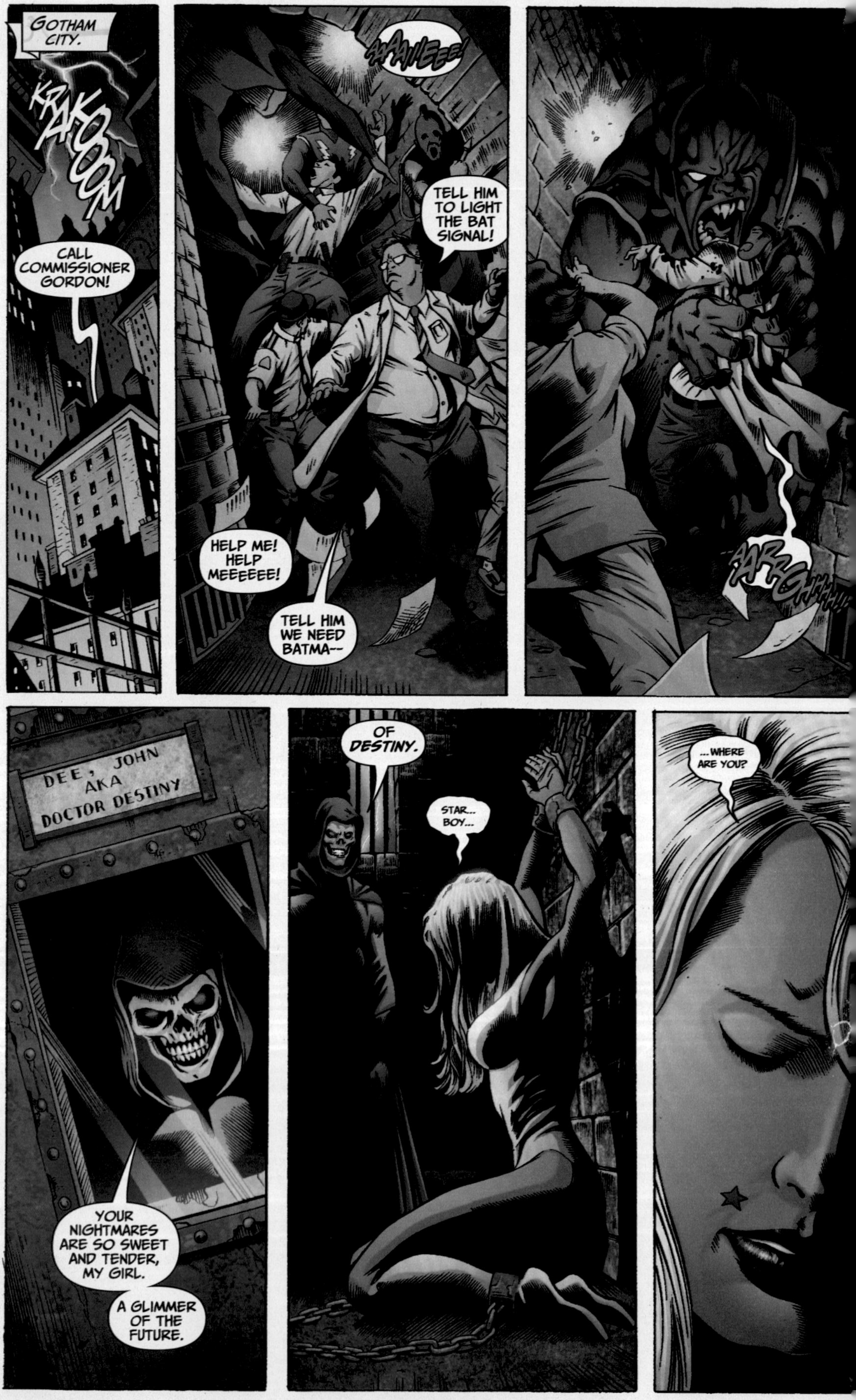
GOTHAM CITY.
KRAKOOOM
CALL COMMISSIONER GORDON!
AAAAIIEEE!
TELL HIM TO LIGHT THE BAT SIGNAL!
HELP ME! HELP MEEEEEE!
TELL HIM WE NEED BATMA--
AARGHHH!!
DEE, JOHN AKA DOCTOR DESTINY
YOUR NIGHTMARES ARE SO SWEET AND TENDER, MY GIRL.
A GLIMMER OF THE FUTURE.
OF DESTINY.
STAR... BOY...
...WHERE ARE YOU?

original covers **by ALEX ROSS**

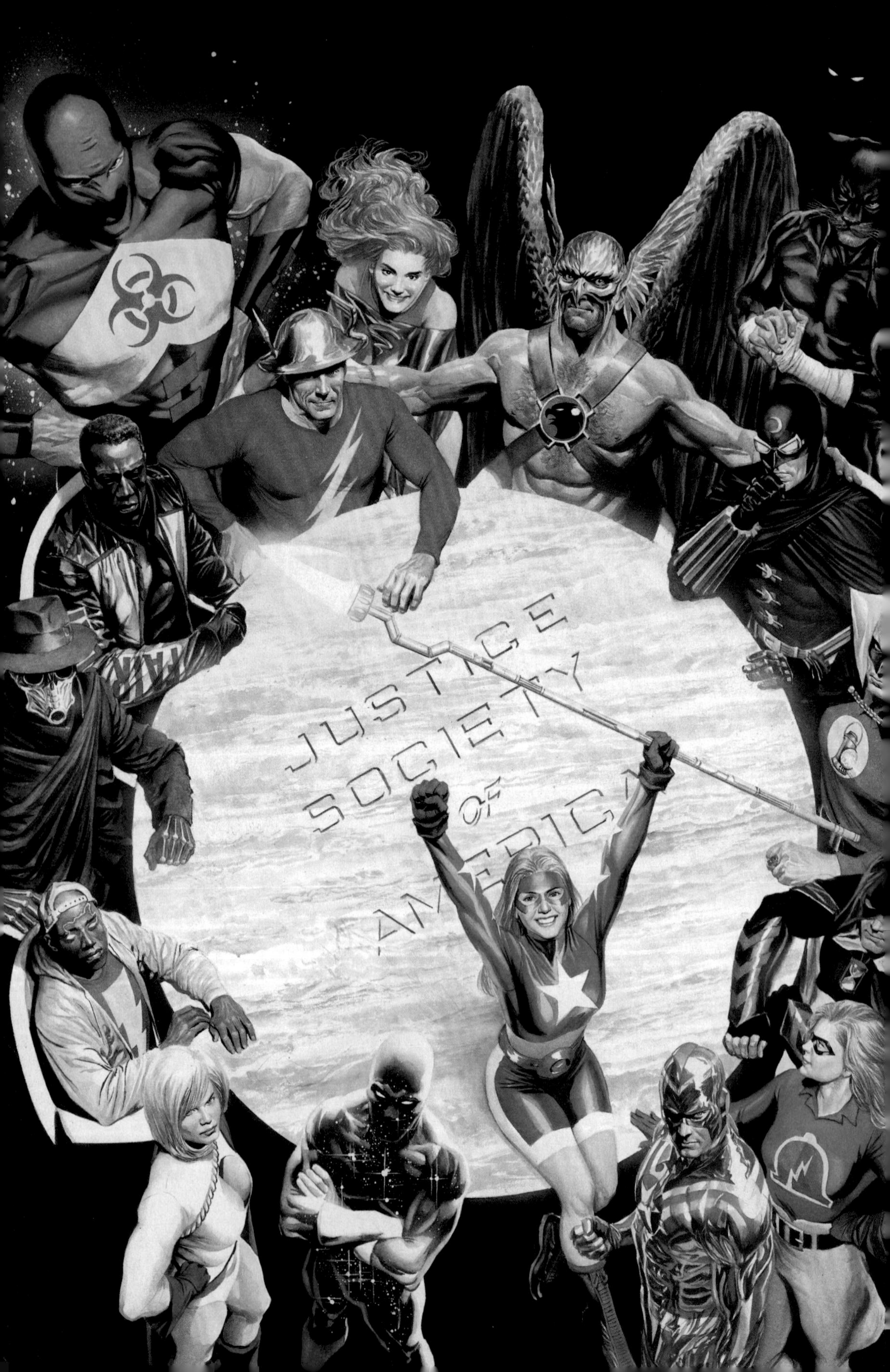

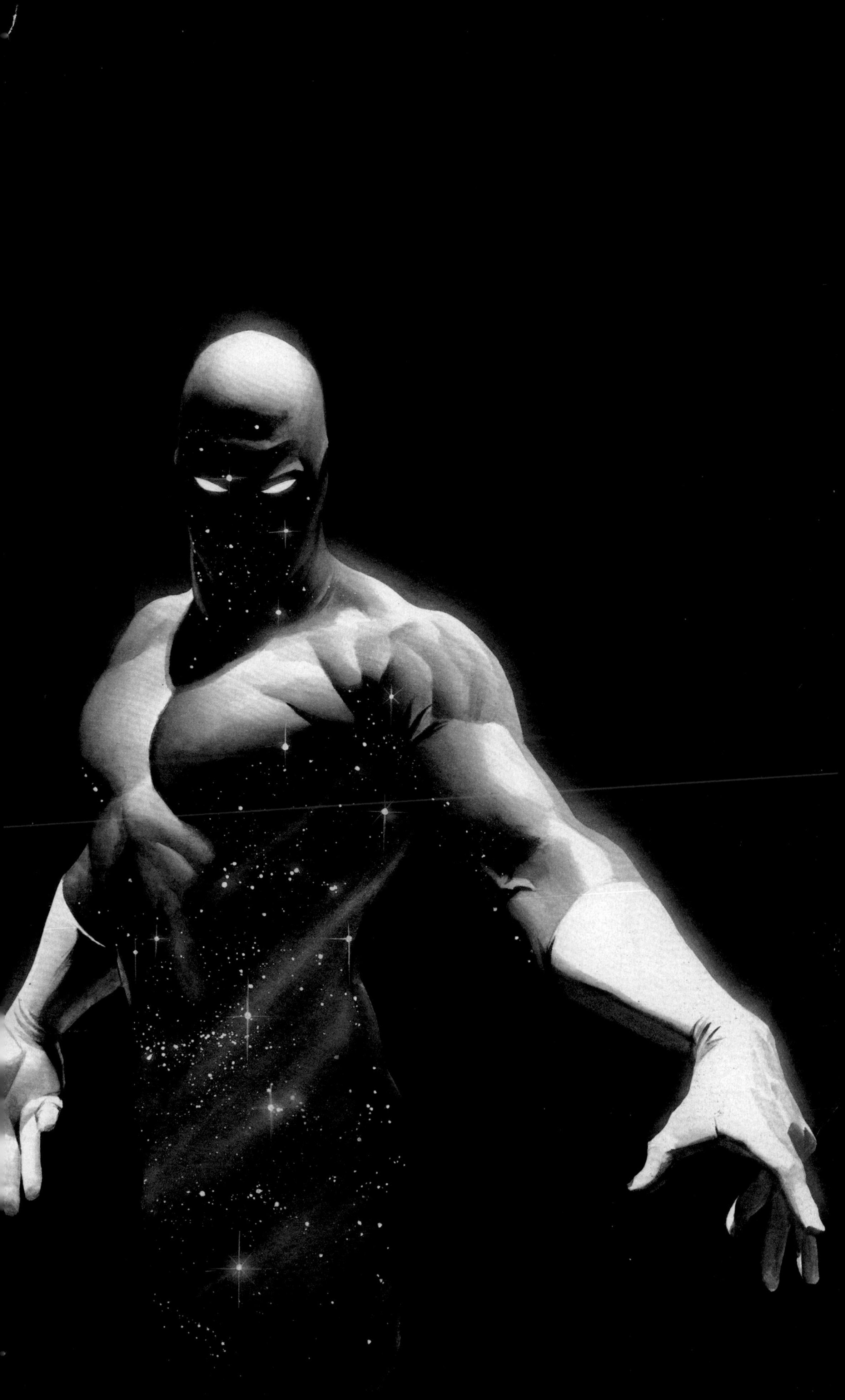

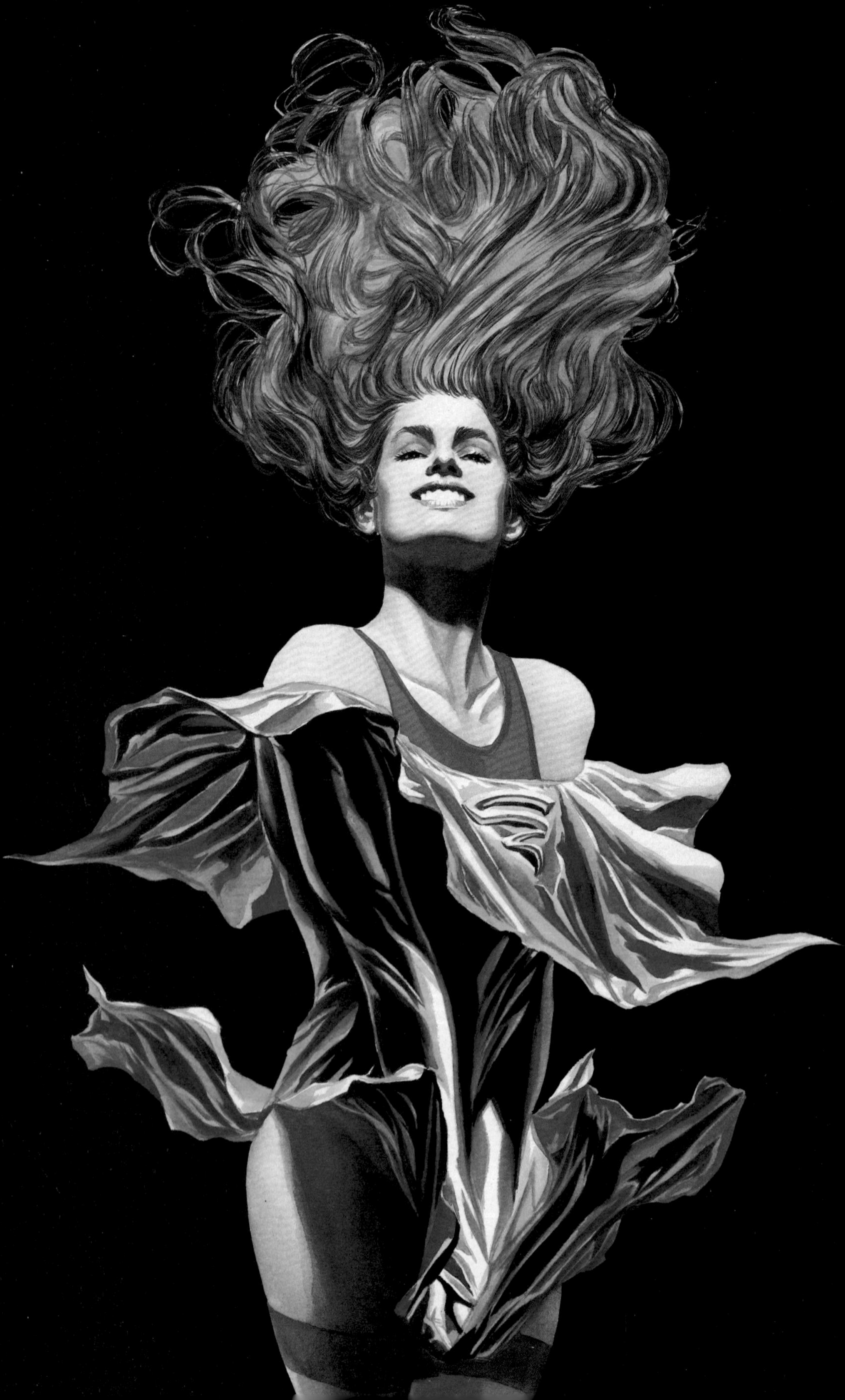

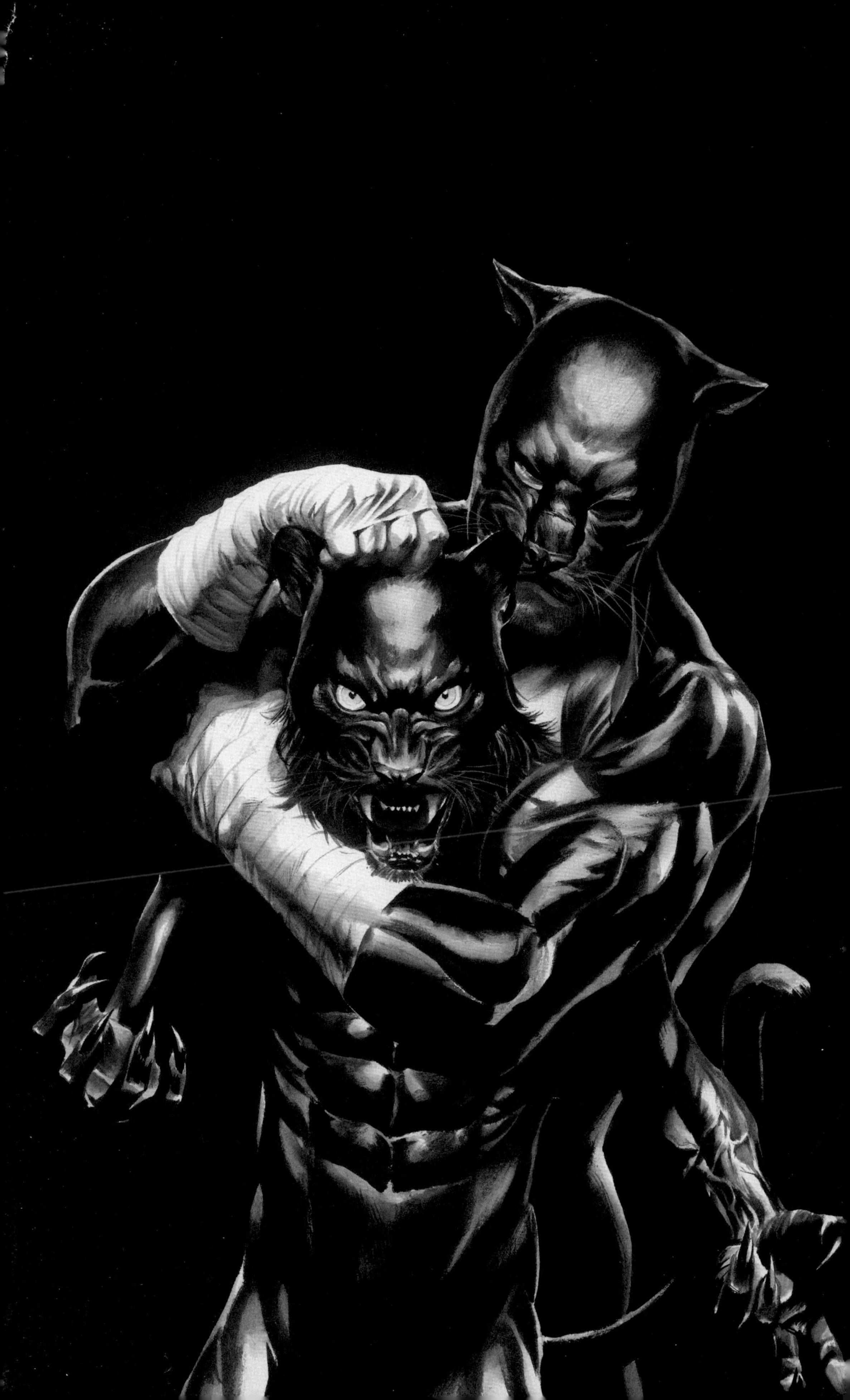

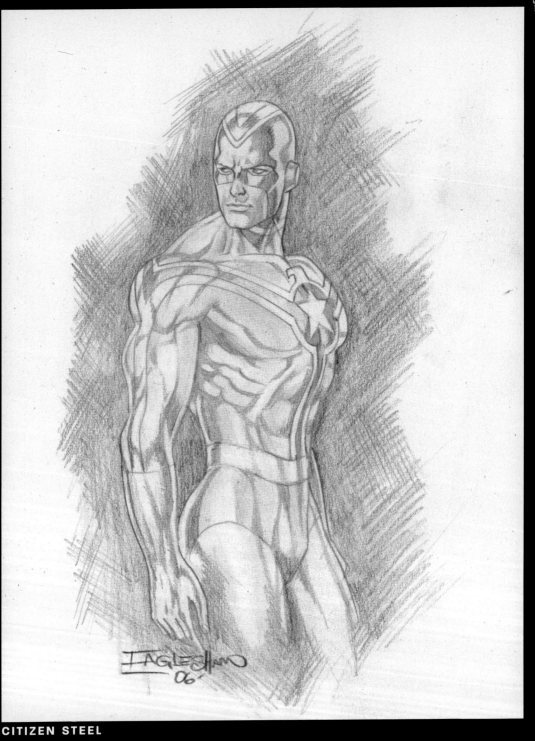

CITIZEN STEEL

SKETCH GALLERY
BY DALE EAGLESHAM

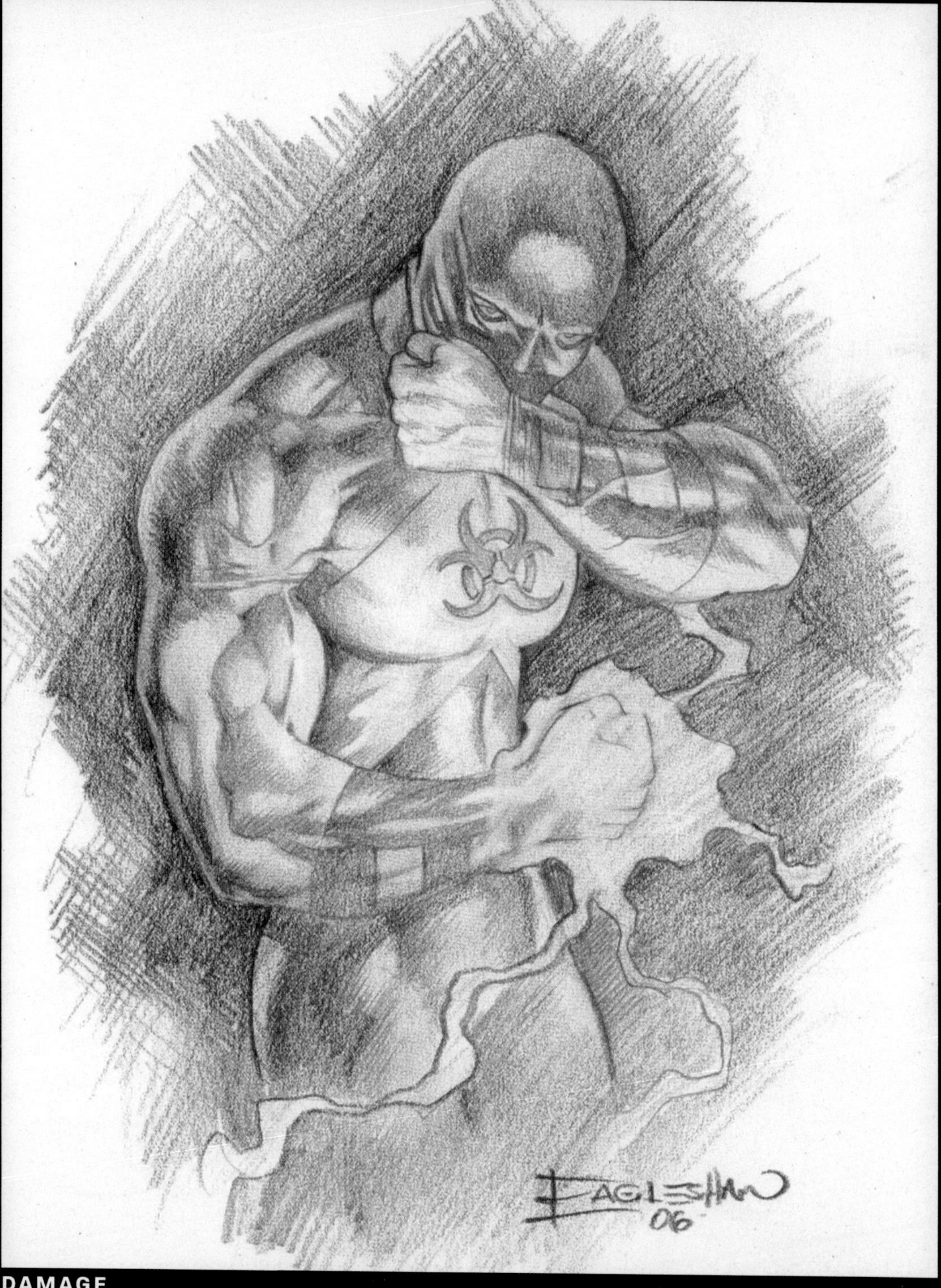
EAGLESHAM
06
DAMAGE

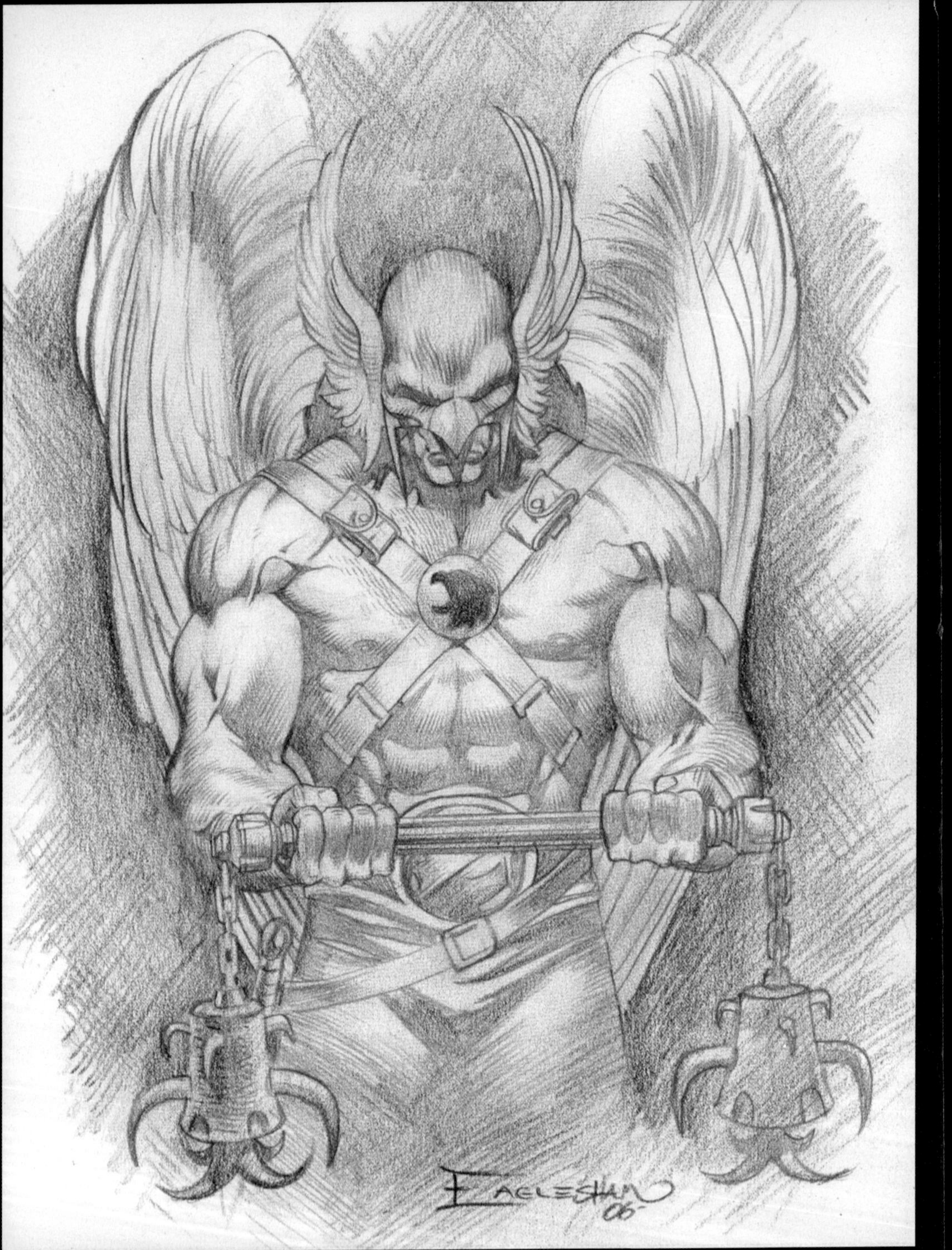
EAGLESHAM
06

HAWKMAN

EAGLESHAM
06

HOURMAN

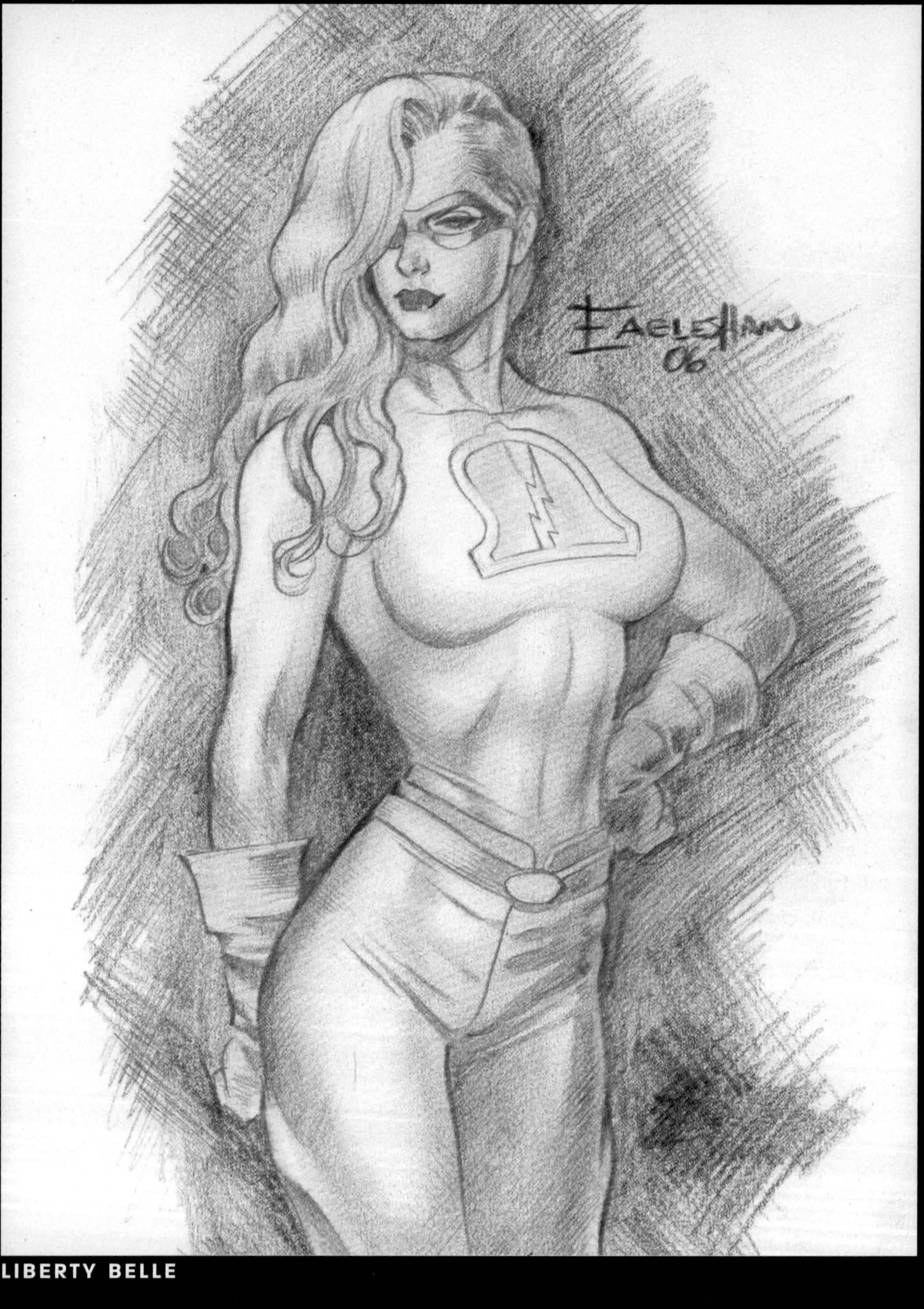

LIBERTY BELLE

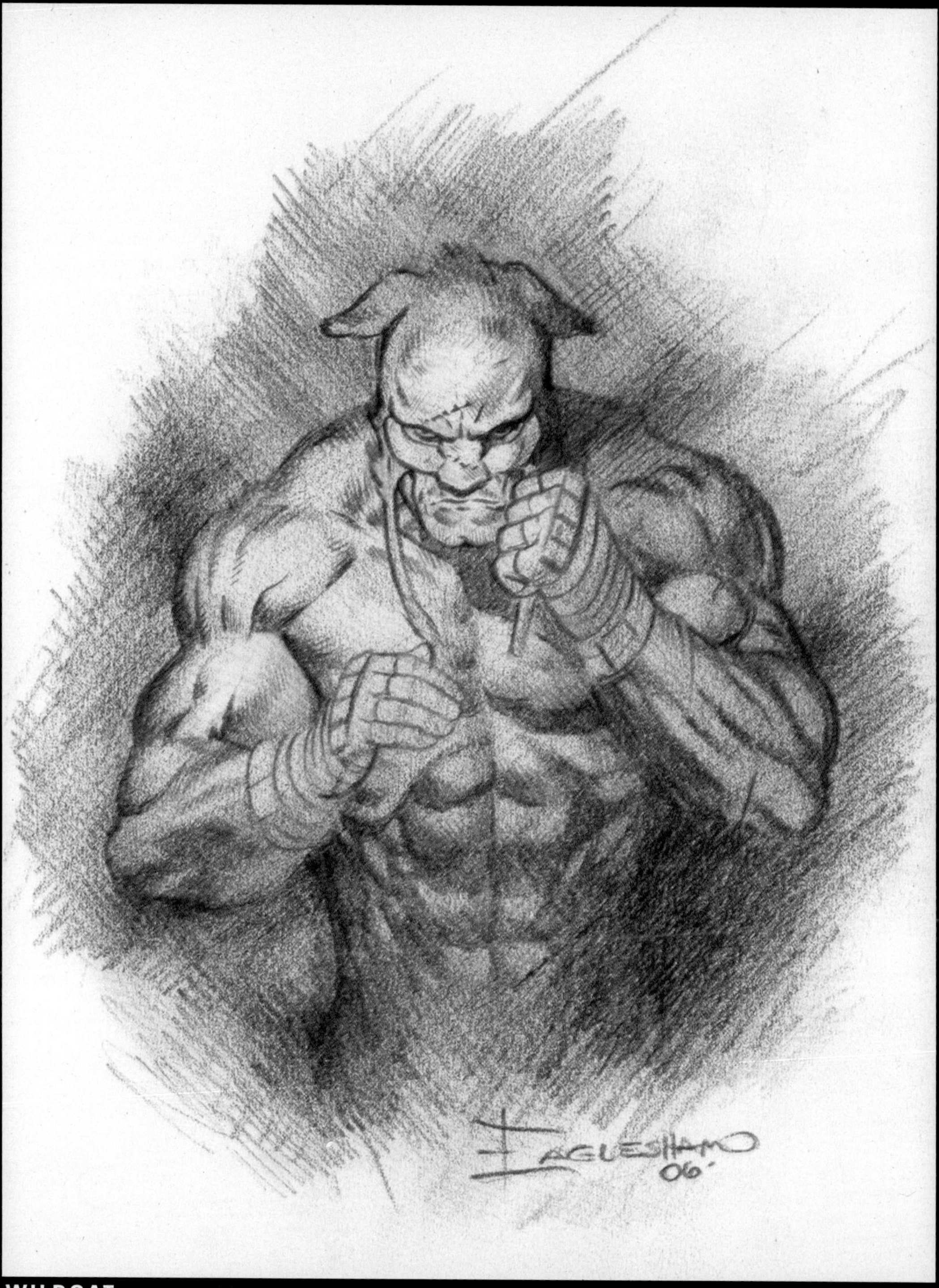
EAGLESHAM
06

WILDCAT

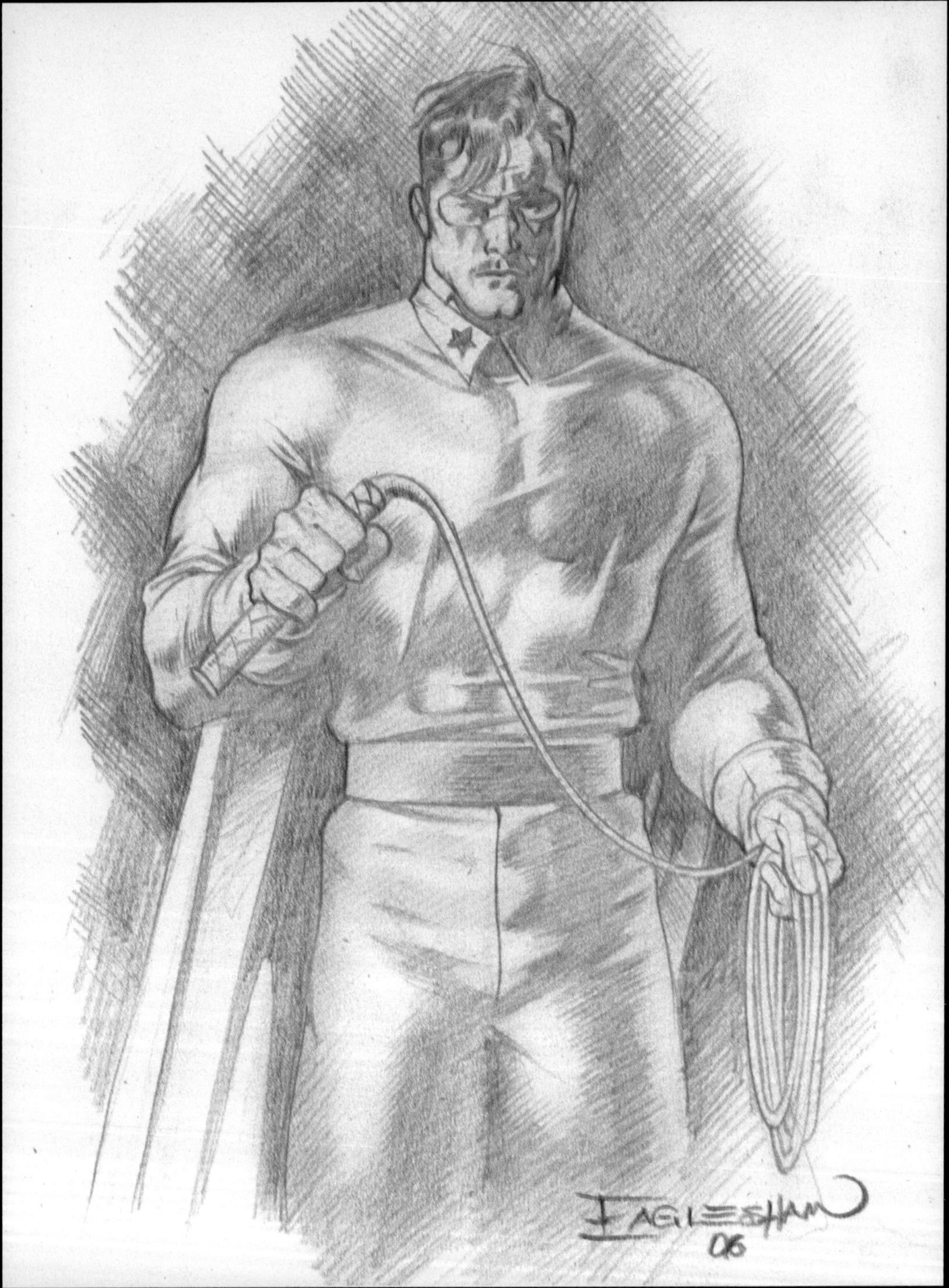
EAGLESHAM
06

MR. AMERICA

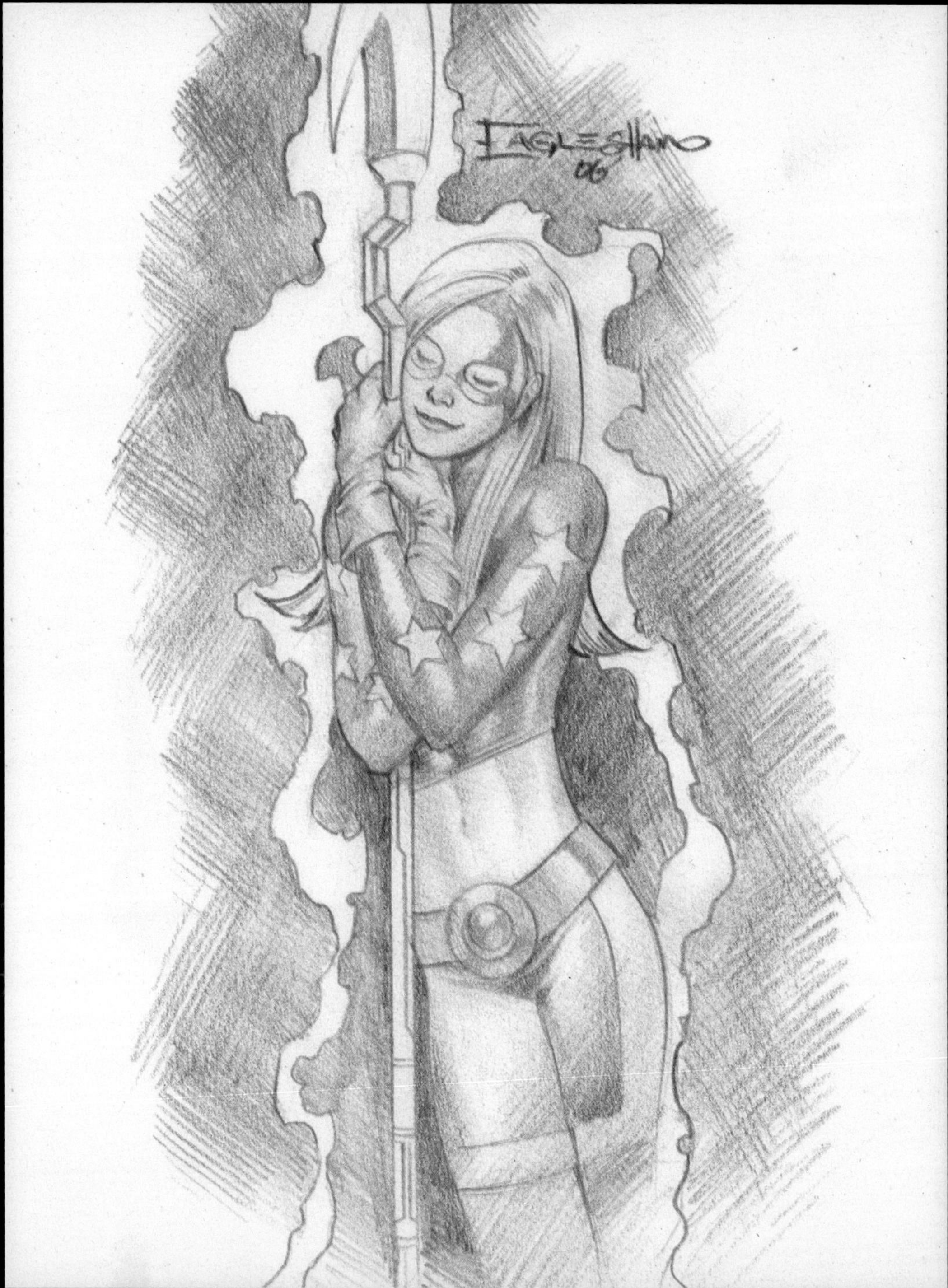
EAGLESHAM
06

STARGIRL

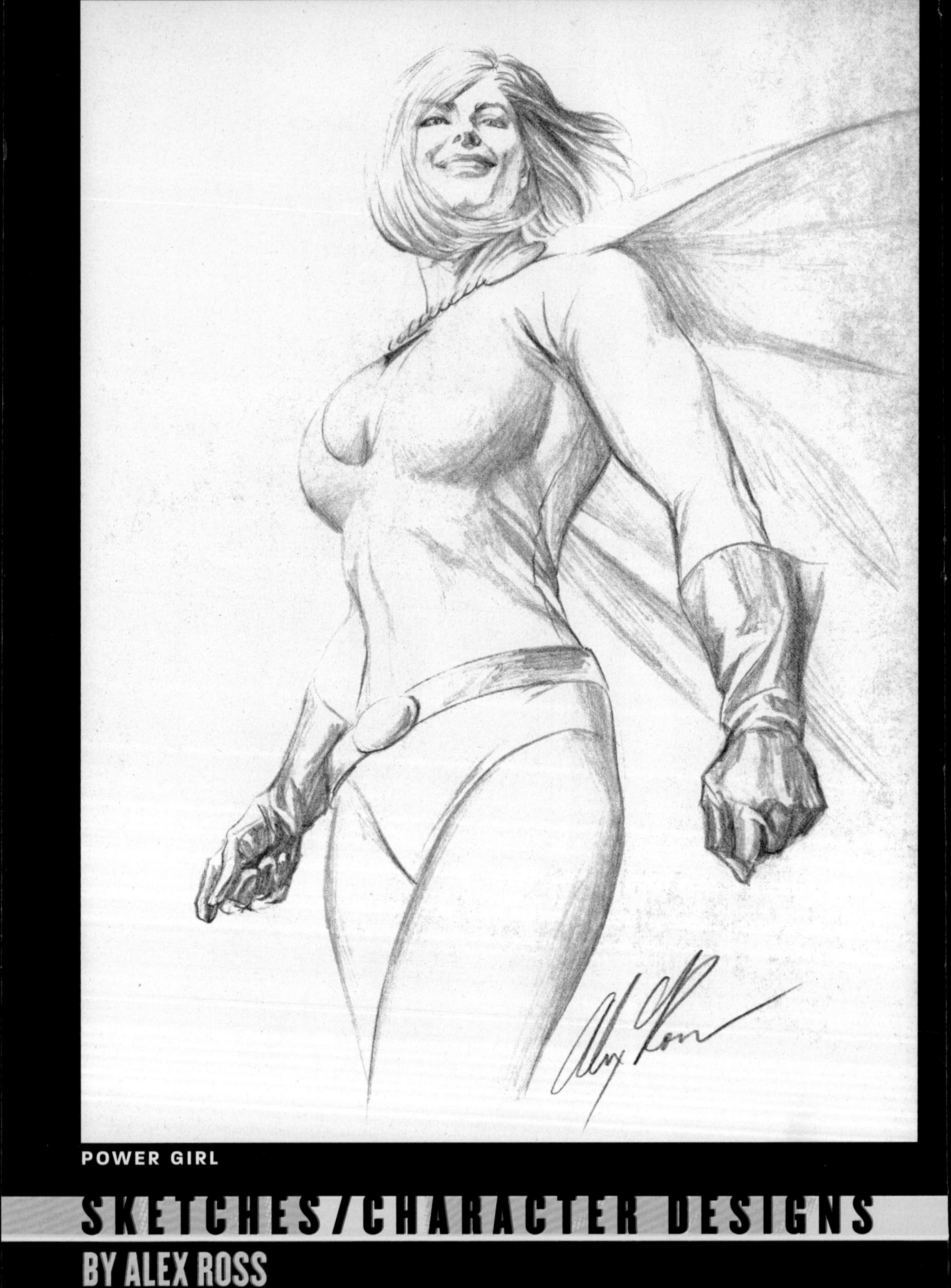
Alex Ross

POWER GIRL

SKETCHES/CHARACTER DESIGNS
BY ALEX ROSS

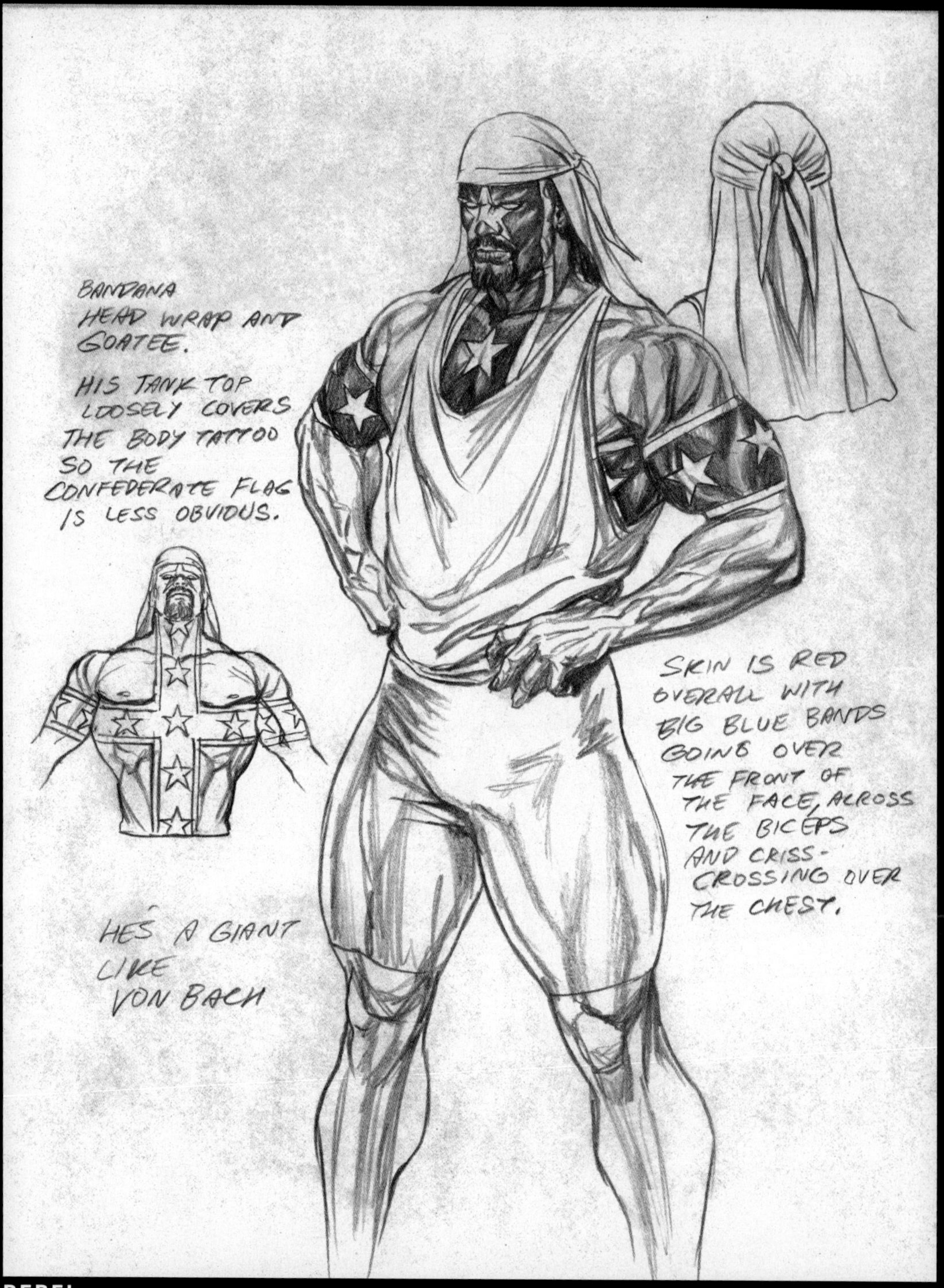
BANDANA
HEAD WRAP AND
GOATEE.
HIS TANK TOP
LOOSELY COVERS
THE BODY TATTOO
SO THE
CONFEDERATE FLAG
IS LESS OBVIOUS.
SKIN IS RED
OVERALL WITH
BIG BLUE BANDS
GOING OVER
THE FRONT OF
THE FACE, ACROSS
THE BICEPS
AND CRISS-
CROSSING OVER
THE CHEST.
HE'S A GIANT
LIKE
VON BACH

REBEL

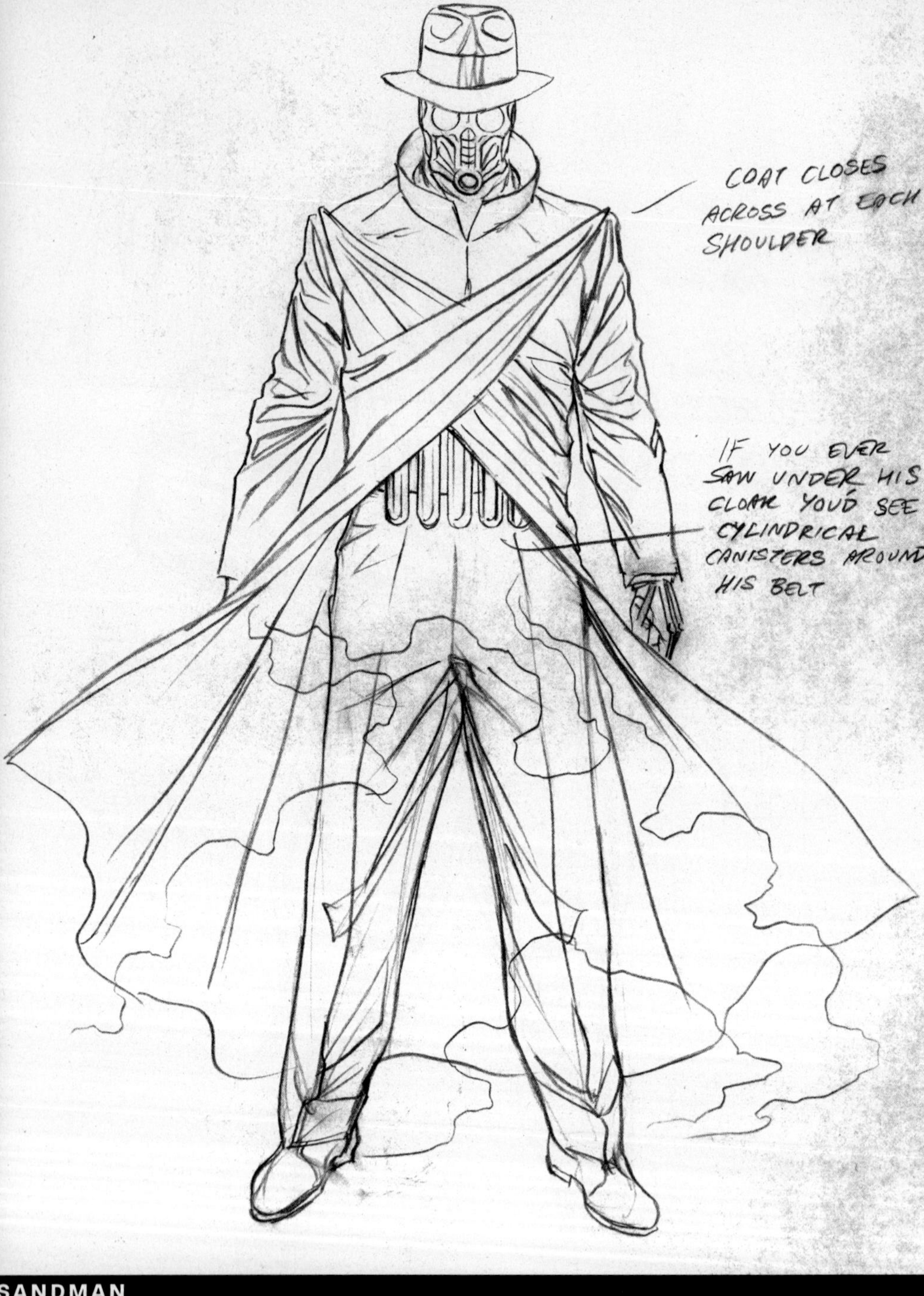
COAT CLOSES
ACROSS AT EACH
SHOULDER
IF YOU EVER
SAW UNDER HIS
CLOAK YOU'D SEE
CYLINDRICAL
CANISTERS AROUND
HIS BELT

SANDMAN

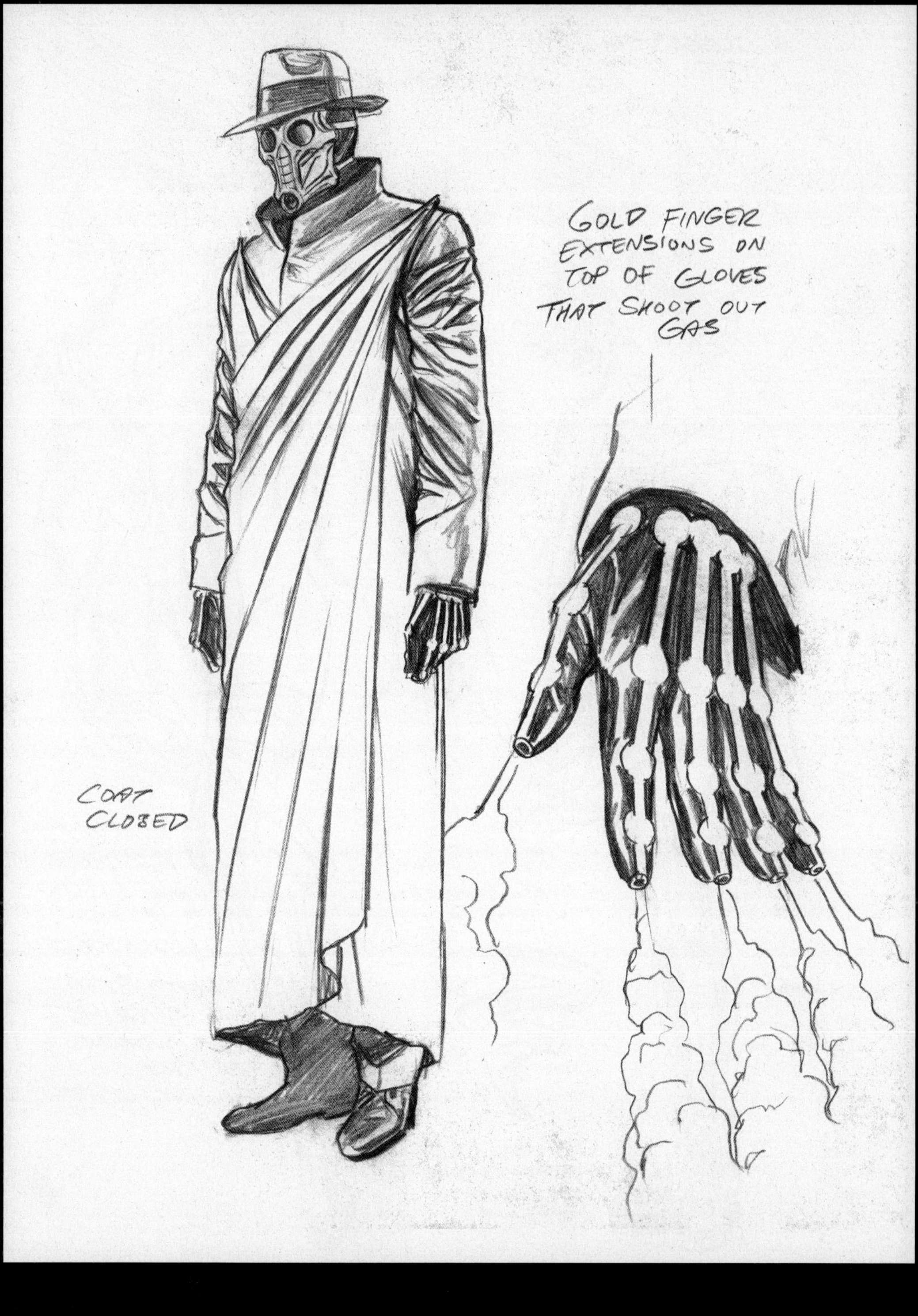
GOLD FINGER EXTENSIONS ON TOP OF GLOVES THAT SHOOT OUT GAS
COAT CLOSED

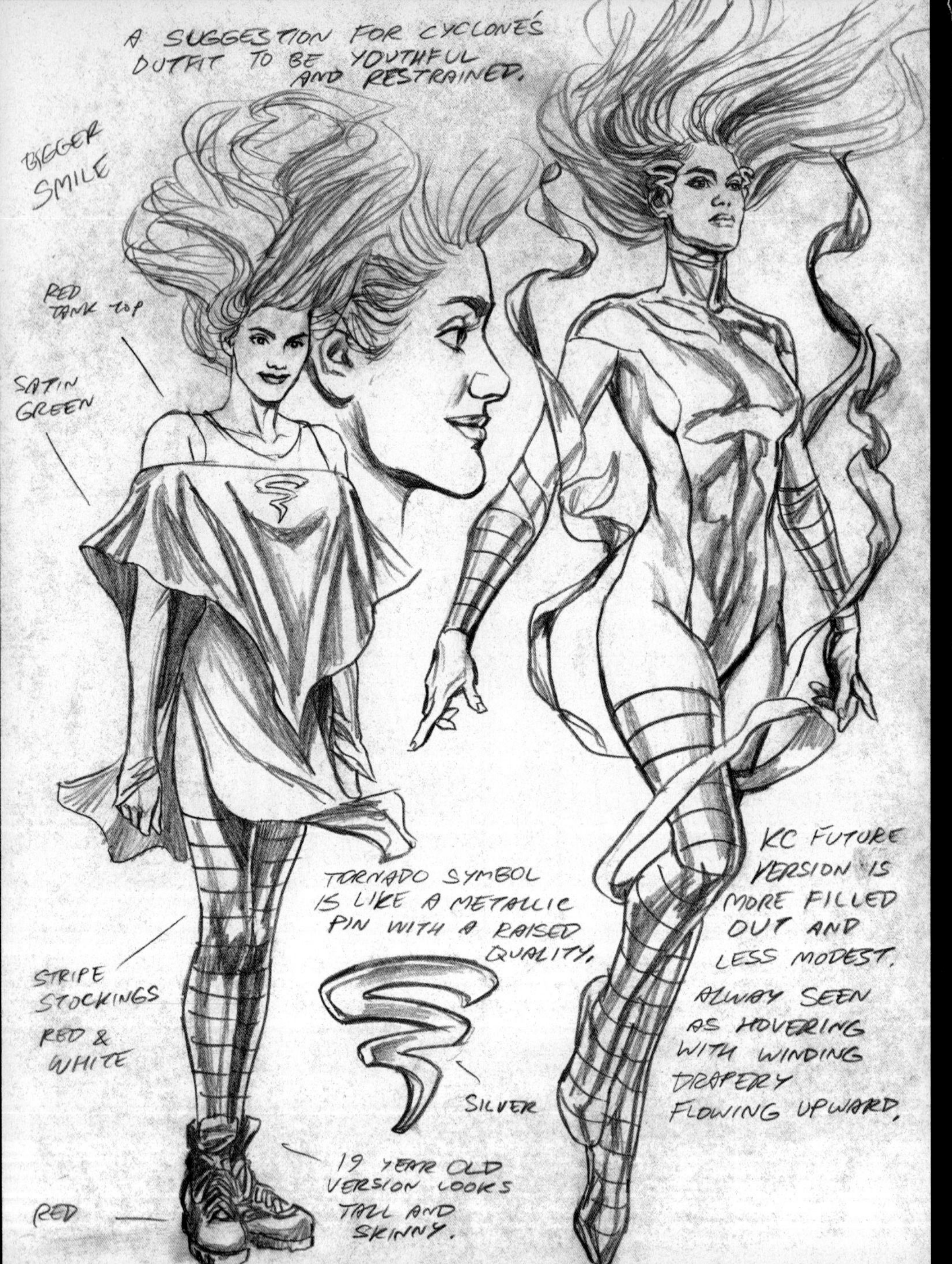
A SUGGESTION FOR CYCLONE'S OUTFIT TO BE YOUTHFUL AND RESTRAINED.
BIGGER SMILE
RED TANK TOP
SATIN GREEN
STRIPE STOCKINGS
RED & WHITE
RED
TORNADO SYMBOL IS LIKE A METALLIC PIN WITH A RAISED QUALITY.
SILVER
19 YEAR OLD VERSION LOOKS TALL AND SKINNY.
KC FUTURE VERSION IS MORE FILLED OUT AND LESS MODEST.
ALWAY SEEN AS HOVERING WITH WINDING DRAPERY FLOWING UPWARD.

CYCLONE

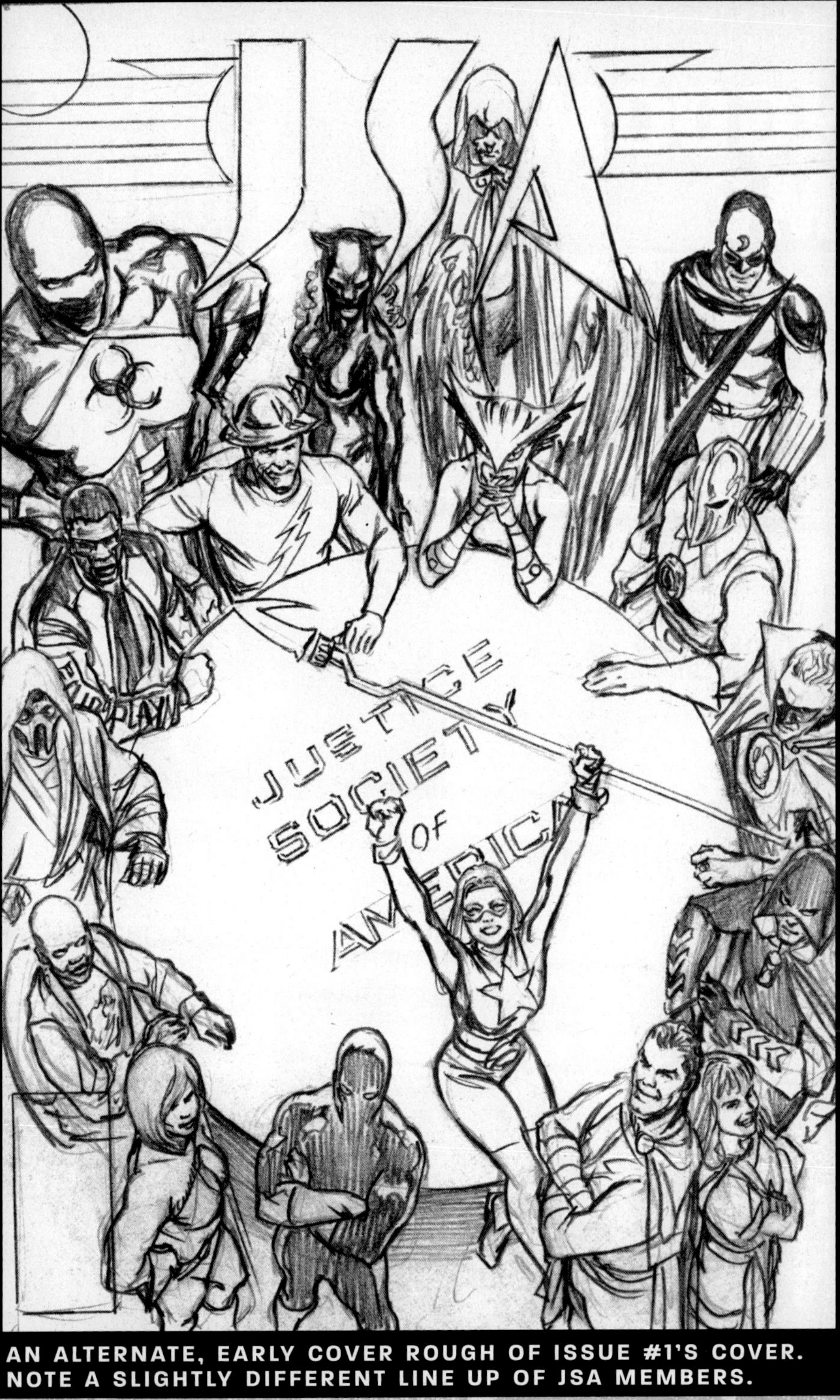
JSA
JUSTICE SOCIETY OF AMERICA
FAIR PLAY

AN ALTERNATE, EARLY COVER ROUGH OF ISSUE #1'S COVER. NOTE A SLIGHTLY DIFFERENT LINE UP OF JSA MEMBERS.

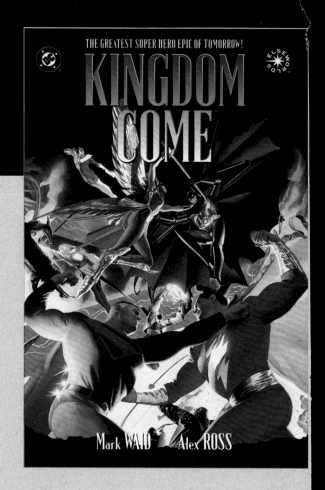
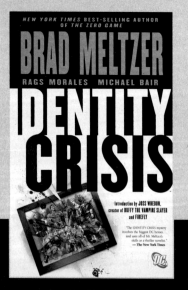